Divergent Writers

Divergent Writers

Disability, Illness, Neurodivergence, and Ableism in Creative Writing

Edited by
Christie Collins and Saul Lemerond

BLOOMSBURY ACADEMIC
LONDON • NEW YORK • OXFORD • NEW DELHI • SYDNEY

BLOOMSBURY ACADEMIC

Bloomsbury Publishing Plc, 50 Bedford Square, London, WC1B 3DP, UK
Bloomsbury Publishing Inc, 1359 Broadway, New York, NY 10018, USA
Bloomsbury Publishing Ireland, 29 Earlsfort Terrace, Dublin 2, D02 AY28, Ireland

BLOOMSBURY, BLOOMSBURY ACADEMIC and the Diana logo are trademarks of
Bloomsbury Publishing Plc

First published in Great Britain 2026

Copyright © Christie Collins, Saul Lemerond and Contributors, 2026

Saul Lemerond, Christie Collins and Contributors have asserted their right under the
Copyright, Designs and Patents Act, 1988, to be identified as Authors of this work.

For legal purposes the Acknowledgments on p. xv constitute an extension of this
copyright page.

Cover design: Jade Barnett
Cover image © Kelsey Howard

All rights reserved. No part of this publication may be: i) reproduced or transmitted in any
form, electronic or mechanical, including photocopying, recording or by means of any
information storage or retrieval system without prior permission in writing from the
publishers; or ii) used or reproduced in any way for the training, development or operation
of artificial intelligence (AI) technologies, including generative AI technologies. The rights
holders expressly reserve this publication from the text and data mining exception as per
Article 4(3) of the Digital Single Market Directive (EU) 2019/790.

Bloomsbury Publishing Plc does not have any control over, or responsibility for, any
third-party websites referred to or in this book. All internet addresses given in this book
were correct at the time of going to press. The author and publisher regret any
inconvenience caused if addresses have changed or sites have ceased to exist, but can
accept no responsibility for any such changes.

A catalogue record for this book is available from the British Library.

A catalog record for this book is available from the Library of Congress.

ISBN: HB: 978-1-3505-0187-4
PB: 978-1-3505-0186-7
ePDF: 978-1-3505-0188-1
eBook: 978-1-3505-0189-8

Typeset by RefineCatch Limited, Bungay, Suffolk
Printed and bound in Great Britain

For product safety related questions contact productsafety@bloomsbury.com.

To find out more about our authors and books visit www.bloomsbury.com
and sign up for our newsletters.

We dedicate this anthology
to all neurodivergent, chronically ill, and/or disabled writers
who have ever been made to feel problematic,
been made to feel they didn't belong,
or been made to feel they weren't writing/publishing quickly enough.

You do belong.
Your pace is the right one.
Please keep writing.

We also dedicate this anthology to our fathers
who passed away during the course of this project:

Charles Francis Collins
1947–2024

Thomas Edward Lemerond
1952–2025

Contents

List of Illustrations ix
List of Contributors x
Acknowledgments xv
Foreword *Stephanie Vanderslice* xvi

Introduction *Christie Collins* 1

Part 1 The Writer's Journey: Late Diagnosis, Recovery, and Post-Diagnosis/Post-Recovery Observations on Writing and Teaching

1   Aphasia as Form and Discontent: Adaptations of a Post-Stroke Poet and Teacher *Aidan Coleman* 13

2   A Martian Poetic Tendency: What I Learned About Writing and Teaching After My Autism Diagnosis *Cath Nichols* 28

3   Why Write?: Reframing Personal Creative Writing Practice in the Light of Changing Diagnoses *Oz Hardwick* 40

4   "Me Here—You There": Writing Contrast without a Self *K. Iver* ... 51

5   Theory of Whose Mind?: A Very Late-Diagnosed Autistic Writer Claps Back *Julia Lee Barclay-Morton* 61

Part 2 Views from the Inside: Writers Confronting Stigma, Exploitation, and Ableism

6   There Is a Charge for the Eyeing of My Scars: Writing the Neurodivergent, Disabled Body for a Dominant Audience *Grace Quantock* 77

7   When Methods Fail: A View from the Perspective of a Dyslexic Writer *Saul Lemerond* 87

8   The Breath of the Bird: My Writing Life with Bipolar Disorder
    Celeste Maria Schueler   94

9   The Gallery Effect: The Visibly Disabled Writer in the Real World
    Tyler Darnell   98

10 What Do You Really Want to Say? A Creative Writing MA Student's
    Experience with Rejection Sensitive Dysphoria (RSD) *Beth Rees*   104

Part 3 Dismantling the Traditional Writing Workshop: Interventions, Reckonings, and Inclusive Alternatives

11 Do Away with Writing Workshops: An Anti-Ableist Treatise *Said Shaiye*   113

12 Perfection of the (Care) Work: A Traditional MFA Workshop
    Experience vs. A Disability-Centric Workshop Experience *Shane Neilson*   121

13 Poem Brut: What the Writing Workshop Can Learn from the Outside
    World *Julia Rose Lewis*   129

14 Spinning Words: Poetry Creation by Autistic People from Brazil
    Gustavo Henrique Rückert   136

Part 4 Ableism in Higher Education, Writing Programs, and Academia: Insights, Pedagogy, and Visibility

15 "Reduced to Depraved Animals": The Need for Faculty and Administrators
    to Consider Disabled, Neurodivergent, and Chronically Ill Students in
    Graduate Creative Writing Programs *Christie Collins*   155

16 Teaching Creative Writing to Neurodivergent Students: A Fairly
    Friendly FAQ *Leigh Camacho Rourks*   170

17 The Power of Words: Neurodiversity, Authenticity, and Inclusion
    in the Creative Writing Classroom *Rachel Carney*   178

18 Embodiment and the Body in Pain: Observations from a Poet in
    Academia *Miranda L. Barnes*   191

19 Barriers to Inclusion in Creative Writing: Questioning Practice in and
    Beyond the Writing Classroom *Audrey T. Heffers*   199

Index   210

Illustrations

14.1 "Self-Portrait" by Ana Cândida Carvalho 147
14.2 Frame from "Echolalia" by Joseane Correa 149

Contributors

Julia Lee Barclay-Morton is an award-winning writer/director, whose work has been produced and published internationally. Her first book, THE MORTALITY SHOT, is out now. She has also recently been published in Autism in Adulthood, Oldster, Prairie Schooner, and [PANK]. She founded Apocryphal Theatre in London, which was the basis of her PhD from the University of Northampton, and her experimental stage texts were streamed in 2022, commissioned by Radio Art Zone in Europe. She lives with her husband and cat in New York City, where she is writing a memoir about being diagnosed Autistic at 57.

Miranda L. Barnes is a poet, academic, and interdisciplinary researcher. While her chapter in this anthology focuses on her chronic pain conditions, Miranda is also neurodivergent. She taught creative writing for five years at Bath Spa University, UK, while undertaking her PhD, and she is now an academic researcher at Loughborough University as part of the Open Book Futures Project. Her personal research interests include the intersection of poetry and science, which influenced both of her poetry titles, including Blue Dot Aubade (2020). She is also an editor at Consilience Journal, a peer-reviewed journal of poetry and science.

Leigh Camacho Rourks is a Cuban-American author living and working in Central Florida, where she is an Associate Professor at Beacon College, a small liberal arts college dedicated to educating students with learning disabilities/differences and ADHD. Like her students, she is neurodivergent (ADHD and dyslexia); she also has chronic migraine and fibromyalgia. Leigh won the St. Lawrence Book Award for her 2019 short story collection, Moon Trees and Other Orphans, and she is the recipient of the Glenna Luschei Prairie Schooner Award and the Robert Watson Literary Review Prize. She is also the co-author of Digital Voices, a creative writing pedagogy book on podcasting (Bloomsbury Academic, 2023).

Rachel Carney is an award-winning poet, visual artist, researcher, and creative writing teacher. Her PhD research focused on the use of ekphrastic writing in museums, and was funded by the South, West, and Wales Doctoral Training Partnership. Her debut poetry collection, Octopus Mind, was selected as one of The Guardian's Best Poetry Books of 2023. Her poems explore the intricacies of neurodiversity, dyspraxia, perception, and the human mind, and have been published in numerous magazines, including *Poetry Wales*, *The Mackinaw*, and *The Ekphrastic Review*. She currently teaches at Cardiff University, UK.

Christie Collins teaches creative writing and literature at Mississippi State University in Starkville, Mississippi, USA. She has also taught at Louisiana State University and Cardiff University, where she completed a PhD in 2020. Her work has been published in *Stirring*, *Phantom Drift*, *Kenyon Review Online*, *Entropy*, *Cold Mountain Review*, *Appalachian Heritage*, *So to Speak*, and elsewhere. She is the author of the chapbook *Along the Diminishing Stretch of Memory* (2014) and the collection of poems *The Art of Coming Undone* (2023). Christie is neurodivergent (dyslexia, ADHD, BAP) and chronically ill (rheumatoid arthritis, fibromyalgia, and migraine).

Aidan Coleman is a Senior Lecturer at Southern Cross University in Australia, where he is the Coordinator for Creative Writing. Aidan's collections of poetry have been shortlisted for national awards. His collection *Asymmetry* (2012) concerns a near fatal stroke he suffered. He has post-stroke aphasia and limited movement in his right hand, but his essay in this collection concentrates on the former. His research has appeared in *New Writing*, *Westerly*, *Journal of the Association for the Study of Australian Literature*, *Australian Dictionary of Biography*, *Text: A Journal of Writing and Writing Courses*, and *The Cambridge Companion to Australian Poetry*.

Tyler Darnell is a teacher and writer in Houston, Texas. He was born with cerebral palsy, and more recently, he was diagnosed with ADHD. He writes novels for children when he isn't in the classroom, and he lives with his husband and cat in the city.

Oz Hardwick, a Professor of Creative Writing at Leeds Trinity University in the UK, has published "a dozen or so" full collections and chapbooks of poetry, including *Learning to Have Lost* (2019), which won the 2019 Rubery International Book Award, and *Retrofuturism for the Dispossessed* (2023). His manuscript *Orion Highway* won the 2024 Dolors Alberola International Poetry Prize. In 2022, he was awarded the ARC Poetry Prize for "a lifetime devotion and service to the cause of prose poetry." Oz received his autism diagnosis at the age of sixty-one.

Audrey T. Heffers, or Audrey T. Carroll, is the author of *What Blooms in the Dark* (2024), *The Gaia Hypothesis* (2024), *In My Next Queer Life, I Want to Be* (2023), and *Parts of Speech: A Disabled Dictionary* (2023). She holds an MFA in Creative Writing from the University of Central Arkansas, USA and an MA in English from the University of Rhode Island, USA. Heffers serves as Chair of the Creative Writing Studies Organization. Her scholarly interests include creative writing studies, queer studies, disability studies, and inclusive pedagogy. She is a bi, queer, and genderqueer writer and chronically ill and disabled.

K. Iver was born in Mississippi. Their diagnoses include PD-NOS, PTSD, and ADHD. Their debut poetry collection *Short Film Starring My Beloved's Red Bronco* won the 2022 Ballard Spahr Prize for Poetry from Milkweed Editions, the Wisconsin Literary Award, and was named a Best Book of 2023 by the New York Public Library. Iver's poems have appeared in *Boston Review*, *Kenyon Review*, *LA Review of Books*, and elsewhere. Iver has received fellowships from the Wisconsin Institute for Creative Writing, the Sewanee Writers Conference, and the Helene Wurlitzer Foundation. They have a PhD in Poetry from Florida State University, USA.

Saul Lemerond lives with his family in Madison, Indiana, and teaches creative writing and literature at Hanover College. His book *Kayfabe and Other Stories* was published in 2013, and his co-authored book *Digital Voices* was published by Bloomsbury Academic in 2023. His stories and essays have been published in *Bourbon Penn*, *Flash Fiction Magazine*, *Flash Fiction Online*, *The Drabblecast*, *JMWW*, *X-R-A-Y*, *The Journal of Creative Writing Studies*, and elsewhere, and he's a member of Science Fiction and Fantasy Writers of America (SFWA). Saul was diagnosed with dyslexia during his PhD program.

Julia Rose Lewis received her MFA in Creative Writing from Kingston University and her PhD in Creative and Critical Writing from Cardiff University, UK. She has taught at Kingston University, Cardiff University, and Indiana University Northwest. Julia has been diagnosed with CPTSD, dyslexia, and repeated mild traumatic brain injuries. Her research explores collaboration, applied neurobiology, and contemporary experimental British poetry. She is the author of *Phenomenology of the Feral* (2017), *High Erratic Ecology* (2020), *The Hen Wife* (2020), *Misuse* (2024), as well as nine poetry pamphlets and two co-authored collections.

Shane Neilson is a MAD and Autistic poet, physician, and critic from New Brunswick, Canada. He is the co-author of *Poetry in the Clinic* and the co-editor for *The Routledge Handbook of Medicine and Poetry*. He is also the author of *Carelanding: Canadian Literature and Medicine* (2024). His poetry has been published in *Poetry Magazine* and *Prairie Schooner*, and his book titled *Saving: A Doctor's Struggle to Help His Children* (2023) is a memoir about intergenerational neurodivergence and the failures of the healthcare system. He teaches Health Humanities at the Waterloo Regional Campus of McMaster University.

Cath Nichols is a queer, disabled writer who was diagnosed with autism at age fifty-two. She also has chronic fatigue syndrome and uses a wheelchair outside of the house. She is a former creative writing lecturer at the University of Leeds, and she is the author of the poetry collection titled *This is Not a Stunt* (2017) and a forthcoming collection titled *I Sing the Body Autistic*. She has published various research papers exploring connections between disabled and trans identities as well as representations of disabled characters in children's fiction. She has also written two picture books.

Grace Quantock is an anti-oppressive psychotherapeutic counselor, writer, and advocate, helping the marginalized to live well with pain, illness, and trauma without disembodiment, burnout, or blame. Grace became seriously ill at eighteen when her underlying autoimmune condition relapsed. She navigates multiple neurodivergences, chronic pain, and invisible disabilities. Her writing has been featured in *The Times*, *The Guardian*, *The Huffington Post*, and *New York Magazine*. Grace's approach, which she calls Somatic Complexity Compassion Therapy (SCCT), integrates psychotherapeutic counseling and activism to recognize our whole selves as we navigate unjust systems. She is committed to inclusion, access, and community in her work.

Beth Rees is a late-diagnosed Autistic/ADHD writer and speaker from Wales, UK. She recently completed her MA in Creative Writing and is currently writing her memoir-in-essays about being misdiagnosed and medicated for a mental health condition she never had. She also has a degree in Media Studies as well as a Public Relations diploma. After her misdiagnosis and becoming a neurodiversity and mental health advocate, she changed careers and now works in health and wellbeing, supporting employees, including those needing neurodiversity and mental health guidance. She hopes that by sharing her experiences she can help others through theirs.

Gustavo Henrique Rückert is a Brazilian poet, researcher, and professor of literature. His poetry books, translated into English, are *Plastic Poems* (2015) and *Are Roses Red in the Dark?* (2021). He also edited the anthology *The Revolt of the Birds* (2016). He teaches at the Federal University of Pelotas, and his research interests include postcolonial approaches to contemporary literature in Portuguese. He coordinates "Spinning Words: Autistic Poetry in Motion," which highlights contemporary autistic poets in Brazil and promotes poetic writing workshops for autistic people. Gustavo was diagnosed Autistic in later life.

Celeste Maria Schueler is a poet and mother originally from Mississippi. She received a BA in English and an MFA in Creative Writing, both from Mississippi University for Women in Columbus, Mississippi, USA. She has been published in *Feral*, *Rooted Magazine*, *Libre*, and elsewhere, and she has taught creative writing workshops in Oklahoma and Washington. Celeste has lived with bipolar disorder for over twenty years. Her first collection of poetry, titled *Peonies of Resurrection* (2027), explores her journey with mental illness.

Said Shaiye is an Autistic and ADHD Somali writer, photographer, and filmmaker, living in Minneapolis. He was a 2024 MacDowell Fellow and was awarded a Minneapolis State Arts Education Grant to lead a BIPOC/Autistic writing workshop in which members publish their own books. His debut book, *Are You Borg Now?*, was a 2022 Minnesota Book Award Finalist in Creative Nonfiction and Memoir. His writing has appeared in *Indiana Review*, *Texas Review*, *Pithead Chapel*, *580 Split*, *Entropy*,

Diagram, and elsewhere. He teaches writing at several community colleges; he also teaches with Unrestricted Interest, an organization dedicated to neurodivergent ways of being.

Stephanie Vanderslice, PhD, is a professor, writer, and seminal scholar in the field of creative writing pedagogy. She teaches creative writing at the University of Central Arkansas, USA, and her publications include *Teaching Creative Writing: The Essential Guide* (Bloomsbury, 2024), *The Lost Son* (2022), *The Geek's Guide to the Writing Life* (Bloomsbury, 2017), *Can Creative Writing Really Be Taught? 10th Anniversary Edition* (Bloomsbury, 2017), and *Rethinking Creative Writing* (2012).

Acknowledgments

We would like to thank those who helped us bring this anthology to fruition. Thank you to our editors at Bloomsbury Academic, Lucy Strong and Aanchal Vij, for their support, patience, and enthusiasm. We owe a tremendous debt of gratitude to our contributors. Without their willingness to share their experiences, this anthology would simply not exist. We would also like to thank our colleagues who presented alongside us on the AWP panels that discussed this anthology and the conference attendees who joined us. Thank you to Stephanie Vanderslice for writing the foreword to this anthology; we were honored by your support. Thanks to Craig Gentry, who served as an editorial assistant. Many thanks to Wilmington-based artist Kelsey Howard for granting us permission to use her painting as the cover image for this book. We must also thank our respective families for their unwavering patience and support while we were hard at work on this project, especially Jennifer Schmidt, Della Lemerond-Schmidt, and Martyn White. Finally, we are grateful to Stephen Kuusisto and his 1998 memoir, *Planet of the Blind*, which paved the way for calling out and combatting the longstanding ableism of this field and its academic institutions.

Foreword Stephanie Vanderslice

As someone in the extremely fortunate position of reading a number of the most current books in the field of creative writing, either to provide a review for a publisher, a blurb, or to prepare for an interview (note to my ten-year-old, book-obsessed self, you have a lot to look forward to), I feel like I have spent a significant amount of my career hailing my latest read in this genre as a "game changer" or one that has been "long overdue." Still, just because I have been in the unique position to preview some of the most important, cutting-edge research of the last two decades, since the early days of creative writing studies and creative writing pedagogy, doesn't make each of my appraisals any less true. There simply aren't that many ways to invoke something as a "paradigm-shifter" without repeating yourself. Trust me, I have tried to find them.

And so, I find myself in this position again with Christie Collins and Saul Lemerond's *Divergent Writers: Disability, Illness, Neurodivergence, and Ableism in Creative Writing*. Colleagues, this is a groundbreaking and necessary work, both capacious and critical; one that will either change the way you teach or, if you have already made moves toward a more disability-inclusive approach, will confirm your best instincts and help you to expand upon them. I wish I'd had this book when I was writing about neurodivergence and disability in *Teaching Creative Writing: The Essential Guide*. In that book, I directed readers repeatedly to the books of Felicia Rose Chavez and Matthew Salesses for a deeper understanding of creating a more inclusive writing classroom. Now, I would urge this book to all readers, as well. Similar to the works of Chavez and Salesses, *Divergent Writers* does the immensely important work of centering creative writers and creative writing students who have long been marginalized in our field; in this work, that focus is on writers who are disabled, the chronically ill, and the neurodivergent. At the time of publication, this was the first anthology of its kind to consider these writers and their experiences within the field.

Full disclosure: my teaching is always evolving but perhaps nowhere more than in the last ten years and in the direction of inclusivity, especially in this post-pandemic era. In trying to move away from the *this is just the way things have always been done* mentality, I have most often gravitated toward the questions: *Why do we have to make the writing classroom such a gauntlet? Why does everything always have to be so hard?* After all, writing is hard enough. Publishing is hard enough. I have tried to err on the side of grace, to do for my students what I wish had been done for me.

The truth is, I am one of those undisclosed neurodivergent writers, who moved through academia at a time when accommodations were virtually nonexistent. Late in high school, I was diagnosed with binocular vision disorder, which means that my eyes are always working hard to bring objects into focus. The default mode is seeing two of everything. The smaller the object, like letters on a page, the more challenging to bring and keep into focus. A lifelong, inveterate reader who was nonetheless exhausted by reading and never understood why, I still remember those first few days after getting glasses. *Was reading this easy for everyone else?*, I thought. Letters no longer swam on the page but lined up in orderly fashion into crisp, clear words. No more splitting headaches when I read or painstakingly dividing long reading assignments into bite-sized pieces in order to finish them. The developmental ophthalmologist who diagnosed me after several hours of tests marveled that I was one of the worst cases he'd ever seen, something that was later confirmed when I was retested by another developmental ophthalmologist thirty years later while getting my kids tested (there was no way I wanted them to go through such a late diagnosis like I had). *They're fine*, the doctor told me afterwards. *But whew, your vision is a whole other story.*

There are a host of comorbid disabilities with binocular vision disorder: dyscalculia (math and numeric learning disabilities), spatial reasoning disabilities, and proprioception disabilities (low awareness of the body moving through space or clumsiness). But once I got my glasses and about six months of physical therapy designed to teach me how to compensate, I "graduated" back into the real world, which, unfortunately, meant masking. There were no accommodations on the SAT back then, something I demonstrated by achieving the highest score in my grade in the verbal section and the lowest in the math, even after six months of intensive SAT math tutoring. Fortunately, I wasn't aiming for a STEM field.

I share these facts about myself not because I'm trying to prove anything, so much as to explain why it is so important that inclusivity in our field and inclusive pedagogy are getting their due. If there are, as Professor Collins describes in her essay in this anthology, only 21 percent of undergraduate students who disclose their disabilities, then we must question: How many don't disclose or haven't even been diagnosed yet? Ultimately, I teach toward grace because I know I need it myself as much as anyone. Any student who has had my class knows I have trouble with transposing dates and numbers in my syllabus no matter how much I proofread. Like Professor Collins describes in her Introduction to this book, I was fifteen minutes late to give my first panel at a national conference—because I, too, misread the schedule. Fortunately, my fellow panel members allowed me to go at the end. Still, I was mortified and have painstakingly "re-translated" conference schedules into a straightforward format I could better read ever since.

Over the course of my career, I have come to believe that the best way to understand what someone is going through and what they need to succeed is to ask them, to listen to them, and to believe them. In fact, in the written survey I now give to students on the first day of class, the last question is always the same: *Is there anything I should know that might interfere with your success in this class?* More often than not, the students' answers are pleas for understanding, ranging from *I am anemic and sometimes need infusions that might affect my attendance* to *I am schizophrenic and struggle with paranoia sometimes, just letting you know*. I wish someone had asked me this question, had asked me what might interfere with my success in a class. As a professor, I am glad to know these circumstances if I can help my students.

What you hold in your hands is a twenty-chapter guidebook to disability, neurodivergence, chronic illness, and ableism in our field written by writers with first-hand experience, many of whom also provide current, relevant research in their essays in addition to their personal accounts. They were asked to answer such questions as: What has it been like to navigate the field of creative writing, including your educational programs and publishing efforts? What has interfered with your learning and your writing? What do you wish was different? What do you wish others knew? How can we shift the paradigm? If we let them, these writers will teach us how we can make creative writing better for everyone: more inclusive, more equitable, more worthy of the diverse voices that inhabit this field.

Introduction Christie Collins

Like the characters in our stories, I began this project after a crisis moment, a personal and very public reckoning with my otherness. For decades, I carried the invisible weight and shame of my undisclosed dyslexia to every class, to every job, to every writing workshop. In time, I would add attention deficit hyperactivity disorder (ADHD) and broader autism phenotype (BAP) to my list of secret burdens, after my long and taxing PhD journey led me to seek further diagnostic evaluations.

Nearing forty, my body began speaking in ways it had not before: debilitating pain in my feet and legs, rendering walking and standing nearly impossible some days. The pain in my inflamed joints combined with brain fog and fatigue would eventually result in a diagnosis of rheumatoid arthritis (RA), another acronym to add to my growing collection. We like to pretend that mental and physical conditions exist within our bodies like separate planets, unaffected by each other and the rest of our biology, our burdens, and our idiosyncrasies. I could not have foreseen the ways in which my new realities of chronic fatigue and brain fog would worsen my pre-existing ADHD, dyslexia, and light sensitivity, though the doctors just looked at me and shrugged. Untreated, isolated, and locked in crippling cycles of pain, stress, shame, and exhaustion, I barely kept myself and my teaching career afloat. My poetry writing? Sending work out to journals and magazines? Both were literal impossibilities when it took all the mental and physical strength I could muster just to walk to my classes, let alone teach them, and meet my basic human needs. On most teaching days during this period, I had to stop and rest just walking from one campus building to the next, even when the distance was only a few hundred feet. The pain was too heavy. As my condition worsened and the pain and stiffness moved to my hands, I became unable to twist doorknobs, and on some days, I had to call my husband to come let me in our home. I am thankful beyond words for his kindness, for his long hugs and cups of tea on bad days, the many glimmers he inspires.

But even now as I share some of my hardest, most isolating moments, I imagine some readers rolling their eyes at my candor, at my "excuses," thinking to themselves the same phrases I've heard before: *You just don't want it bad enough* or *Everyone has problems; you're not special*. Such are the ableist beliefs that have been passed down to so many of us.

This was the state of my existence when I arrived at the 2023 AWP Conference in Seattle: silently juggling pain and fatigue with my career goals, which seemed to be moving further and further out of reach. I had been invited to speak on a panel, titled

"Not Lazy or Stupid: Ableism and Neurodivergence in Creative Writing." I arrived at the conference center for the panel on that cool morning, feeling deceptively calm. Soon, however, a phone call would alert me to a waking nightmare: I was late. I had gotten the time of the panel wrong, and I had left my handouts miles away at my hotel. Because I had thought I was early and had planned to leisurely find my way to the event, I also had no idea as to the location of the assigned room in a massive venue of seemingly endless corridors. My heart dropped onto the low pile carpet, and I began sprinting in the vague direction of the panel, my heavy backpack awkwardly bouncing up and down against my panicked stride.

Despite how the above anecdote makes me sound, I had never in my fifteen-year career been late like this to such an important event in which colleagues were relying on me. I was a responsible do-gooder, annoyingly so. I could have called the panel moderator back, profusely apologized, and bowed out. Who would have blamed me? But I knew in my bones that I had to show up. I walked in, ten minutes late and empty-handed. And when it was my turn to speak, I did something I once couldn't have imagined: I took off the heavy mask in front of the audience.

For the first time in my life, I said the whole truth aloud and into a podium microphone, starting with the events of the morning: being late, running to get there, the handouts I'd spent days creating that had been left in my hotel miles away, the brain fog and fatigue and neurodivergence that had caused this whole situation, the pain in my feet as I spoke. I confessed to everyone, once and for all, that I was *different*, that I had three forms of neurodivergence and a chronic illness, that I was unwell, and that I wasn't coping effectively or receiving proper treatment. I told the conference room full of then-strangers that I can't see language like my peers, that everything takes me longer, that I need clear and specific explanations before I can work effectively in a world where needing further clarifications is often read as problematic and/or a lack of intelligence, that many of these realities had always been true but that I masked, coped, and hid for fear of ridicule and ostracization. I expressed my anger that creative writing, a field I once loved, constantly made me feel like a failure for just being myself in the body and mind I was born with. I expressed my resentment that barometers for writerly "success" are often exclusionary and frankly uninspired: speed, productivity, name recognition, lines on one's CV, and conforming seamlessly to outdated writing beliefs and modes of working.

The fact is—as long as this field, and others like it, are viewed as a meritocratic race to the top, an immense number of gifted and worthy writers will be excluded, merely because they must work differently. What if we dropped the pretenses that are unhelpful and untrue? What if we instead re-envisioned and expanded the concept of "success" for future generations of writers? What if we believed that creative writing could not only be taught but be taught effectively and inclusively to a diverse range of learners? What if we believed that being a "real" writer was not merely defined by writing every single day or by regularly publishing but by continuing to write, and to hone one's craft, at any pace, despite setbacks and hardships?

As I spoke that day, I saw knowing grins on the faces of audience members and nodding heads appear across the room. They laughed with me, embraced me, and after the panel concluded, several writers came up to tell me about their similar experiences with ableism, about their disabled bodies, their autism, their autoimmune disorders. So many thanked me for my story, saying they felt seen for the first time in a largely unkind, unforgiving field. In their words, I, too, found much needed community, visibility, and acceptance.

The truth can feel unbearable because shame leads us to believe that we're alone. Yet this is rarely the case. Much of what we experience is shared by millions of others, and we're made stronger, more confident, and better equipped to face challenges and hardships when we find our community, when we see versions of ourselves in the lived experiences of others. After speaking out at the conference, I didn't just feel less alone, I felt brighter, more hopeful for the future. I felt energized to find caring, competent physicians and begin the treatments that would eventually bring me back to life. In short, every facet of my life improved when I stopped hiding, when I stopped trying to conform, and instead shared my whole, truthful story.

In the weeks after the conference, I reasoned that if so many people at one event were impacted by ableism, then this reality inevitably applied to a significant portion of the writing field. However, there were few resources available on this topic in 2023. More needed to be said; more voices needed to be heard and centered, and more avenues for these conversations and for relevant research were necessary. We'd all waited long enough, hid long enough. Thus, the idea for an anthology on disability and ableism in creative writing was born.

• • •

We began this project knowing that the field of creative writing, which includes academic-based higher education programs as well as publishing entities, is narrowly geared toward neurotypical, non-disabled standards. However, despite existing within a field that marginalizes them, writers with neurodivergence, chronic illnesses, and/or physical disabilities publish world-class poetry, prose, and drama that moves readers, wins awards, and is released from top publishers around the world. But these writers often face stigmas and particular difficulties getting to these achievements, difficulties that often go undisclosed, unnoticed, unmentioned, and underappreciated. We aimed to share these realities with the field.

Yet the ableism inherent in creative writing is a microcosm of the rampant ableism in the world at large, a world that honestly believes our problems would vanish if we just *stopped being weird* or just *took some ibuprofen*. In both this field, as in the wider world, some ableist actions are intentionally cruel. However, ableism is often accidental, resulting from a lack of perspective, experience, and/or information, which is why I want to take the opportunity, here and now, to provide context and insight and address common misbeliefs. For instance, too many people believe that disability is a niche interest, a fixed condition, that one is either disabled or not. But nothing could be further from the truth. While genetic and congenital conditions are often set in motion before birth, this is not true of disability overall. Dan Goodley emphasizes "that disability touches everyone . . . if you are not already a disabled person then consider yourself instead as someone who is Temporarily Able Bodied (TAB). It's likely that you will experience disability or impairment at some point in your life. As a non-disabled person, you are on borrowed time."[1] He further explains that those born with "congenital impairments" are the minority compared with the percentage of people who "will acquire an impairment (with 97% of impairments attributed to injury, illness or diagnosis)."[2] In no uncertain terms, if you are not presently disabled, you almost certainly will be at some point, whether from an injury or an illness or as a result of the aging process. As such, if you currently feel like an "outsider" reading this anthology, this may not always be the case; the essays in *Divergent Writers* may well become more personal to you in the future.

Another misconception is that disability only impacts an insignificantly small portion of the population. To address this erroneous notion, I turn to current data. In their 2023 American Community Survey (ACS), the U.S. Census Bureau found that 13.6 percent of the population is disabled: that is, out of the almost 330 million U.S. citizens in 2023, almost 45 million people faced some form of disability—roughly 1 in 7.[3] Looking beyond the United States, the World Health Organization (WHO) estimates that "1.3 billion people experience significant disability. This represents 16% of the world's population, or 1 in 6 of us."[4] When focusing in on neurominorities[5] in particular, the estimated number goes up. Although more research is needed to fully assess the numbers of people impacted, a 2020 review by Nancy Doyle for the *British Medical Bulletin* found that in the UK, "a reasonable estimate of all neurominorities within the population is around 15–20%, i.e. a significant minority."[6] In my essay within this anthology (Chapter 15), I highlight the substantial number of

---

[1] Dan Goodley, *Disability Studies: An Interdisciplinary Introduction*, 3rd ed. (Sage, 2025), 4.
[2] Ibid.
[3] "2023 American Community Survey: Disabled Population," *United States Census Bureau*. Accessed January 25, 2025. https://data.census.gov/all?q=disability
[4] "Disability," *World Health Organization*. Accessed January 25, 2025. https://www.who.int/health-topics/disability#nstab=tab_1
[5] "Neurominority" is a term that has gained popularity in recent years. Doyle proposes this "umbrella term" because it is "neutral and statistically accurate." In her review, Doyle includes the following conditions within the wider term of "neurominorities": dyslexia, developmental coordination disorder (DCD), dyscalculia, dysgraphia, Tourette syndrome, autism, ADHD, mental illnesses, neurological illnesses, and brain injuries. Related terms include "neurodivergence" and "neurodiversity," both of which appear throughout this anthology. I encourage readers to explore the individual histories and uses of these terms, as traditionally they are not interchangeable. However, new ways of interpreting, approaching, and defining these terms are constantly evolving. Future research may eventually standardize these terms; however, it is worth noting that some individuals prefer/identify with one term over another.
[6] Nancy Doyle, "Neurodiversity at Work: A Biopsychosocial Model and the Impact on Working Adults," *British Medical Bulletin* 135, no. 1 (September 2020): 112, https://doi.org/10.1093/bmb/ldaa021

disabled students in academic programs. Thankfully, as neurodivergence continues to finally get its due, future research will unlock new and crucial findings.

Despite the high number of people impacted, harmful stigmas surrounding disability persist. Laurie Block points out, in her rationale for founding the Disability History Museum, that "traditional stereotypes [of people with disabilities] continue to have currency, as do the limited expectations that go with them. Such attitudes affect the nature of the work that people with disabilities are able to secure, the places where they can live, their social experiences, and their identities."[7] Additionally, the World Health Organization (WHO) reports that "health inequities arise from unfair conditions faced by persons with disabilities, including stigma, discrimination, poverty, exclusion from education and employment, and barriers faced in the health system itself,"[8] highlighting that those impacted can face innumerable inequities in almost every aspect of their lives.

Based on the available statistics, the United Nations names people with disabilities as "the world's largest minority group,"[9] which likely means that "writers with disabilities" are the largest minority group within this field, impacting millions of writers worldwide. It also calls attention to the importance of including writers with both visible and invisible forms of disability within diversity, equity, and inclusion efforts. In fact, disability can be seen as perhaps the one form of diversity that can intersect with all other identities, as disability affects people of all races, ethnic groups, ages, religious groups, socioeconomic backgrounds, sexual orientations, and genders. If we don't work to center writers with disabilities, impacted individuals will continue to face discrimination, and disabled writers belonging to additional diversity groups will continue to be marginalized on multiple fronts, compounding the detrimental effects of otherness and exclusion.

Unfortunately, many interpret disability as a failing, as uninteresting, and/or as a state of perpetual victimhood. But, as Goodley shares, living with a disability "can be a proud identity . . . can be very cool . . . can wonderfully disrupt the ways in which being in the world is typically understood, accounted for and culturally denoted."[10] Similarly, Doyle questions that "if neurodivergence is essentially disablement, why do we keep replicating the gene pool?" In fact, Doyle argues that there's evidence to support "the hypothesis that the evolutionary purpose of divergence is 'specialist thinking skills' to balance 'generalist' thinking skills."[11] In other words, evolution continues to purposefully create different brains to diversify the population, ensuring

---

[7] Laurie Block, "'An Invented Archive': The Disability History Museum." *RBM: A Journal of Rare Books, Manuscripts, & Cultural Heritage* 8, no. 2 (2007): 141–154, 142, https://doi.org/10.5860/rbm.8.2.288

[8] "Disability," *World Health Organization*. Accessed January 25, 2025, https://www.who.int/health-topics/disability#nstab=tab_1

[9] "International Day of Persons with Disabilities, 3 December," *United Nations*. Accessed January 25, 2025, https://www.un.org/en/observances/day-of-persons-with-disabilities/background

[10] Goodley, *Disability Studies*, 7.

[11] Doyle, "Neurodiversity at Work," 112.

that creativity and innovation, and the human race, continue. The field of creative writing supposedly values originality and singular voices; it claims to prize outsiders and complex characters. So, why does it neglect many of the talented writers that innately possess and embody these concepts, merely because they need considerations, accommodations, or because they work differently or at different speeds? It's time for the paradigm to shift, for the field to truly embrace all writers.

This anthology aims to highlight writers who are disabled, neurodivergent, and/or chronically ill and their lived experiences, their writing processes, and their learning needs, to humanize them as more than their condition(s), to raise awareness about forms of disability and about forms of ableism in creative writing spaces, to work to dismantle stigmas, stereotypes, and ableism in the field, and to provide narratives and research by writers with lived experiences of disability. We hope that, after finishing this anthology, readers will carry the insights they glean from these essays into their writing programs, writing communities, and publishing factions. We hope that this anthology will enact real change.

• • •

In conceptualizing this anthology, my co-editor, Saul Lemerond, and I set out to be intentionally broad in scope. We look forward to future publications that will focus on the needs/experiences of writers with specific disabilities within particular contexts,[12] as work of this kind is desperately needed. But with so few resources on disability and/or ableism in the field currently available, we knew, from our own lived experiences and teaching careers, that it was imperative that this anthology readily provide support to as many impacted writers as possible as well as their colleagues, peers, teachers, and publishers. As such, we were adamant about including work from writers who could speak to a wide range of disabilities, including physical disabilities, chronic illnesses, forms of neurodivergence, and forms of mental illness. Additionally, we felt it was important to include essays that cover a wide range of topics within the field, including teaching, learning, workshopping, crafting, and publishing, and to show different perspectives and experiences by including work from contributors at various stages in their careers, from young, emerging writers to those with extensive careers as published writers and/or academics. We also aimed to include a mix of first-person narrative essays, research essays, and hybrid essays as well as pedagogy essays, craft essays, lyric essays, critical and creative essays, and unconventional essays—for example, styling the essay in an FAQ (frequently asked questions) or Q&A (question-and-answer) format, as two of our contributors chose to do. We believe that encouraging a wide range of possible writing styles and approaches to the essay genre allowed contributors to lean into, and to showcase, their individual writing strengths.

---

[12]For instance, entire works could focus solely on such topics as "teaching undergraduate creative writing to students with hearing loss" or "literary marketing and book signing events for writers with physical disabilities."

In total, we are honored to have included nineteen contributors in this anthology from across five countries. Each contributor currently lives with a disability, chronic illness, and/or form(s) of neurodivergence and has personally experienced the impacts of ableism, both inside and outside the field of creative writing. Finally, our methodology for organizing this book was descriptive rather than prescriptive; we devised and titled the four parts only after the final essay drafts were submitted and carefully read, finding that each of the nineteen essays could be placed into one of four categories.

The essays in Part 1 of this anthology, titled "The Writer's Journey," discuss the contributors' experiences of late diagnosis and/or recovery and/or their related observations on writing and teaching from post-diagnosis/post-recovery vantage points. In his essay, Aidan Coleman narrates his post-stroke recovery, including his journey back into teaching and writing with post-stroke aphasia (Chapter 1); Coleman also highlights the rich possibilities of aphasia poetry written by stroke survivors. Julia Lee Barclay-Morton (Chapter 5) examines her late autism diagnosis in connection with her theater background and experimental stage writing. Cath Nichols (Chapter 2), Oz Hardwick (Chapter 3), and K. Iver (Chapter 4) discuss poetry writing and neurodivergence; however, they address these topics in different ways. For instance, Cath Nichols focuses on how her poetry writing and teaching practices transformed after her late autism diagnosis, while Oz Hardwick discusses his own late autism diagnosis alongside his writing and publishing of prose poetry. Finally, K. Iver's essay focuses on late diagnoses of ADHD, post-traumatic stress disorder (PTSD), and personality disorder not otherwise specified (PD-NOS), and they explore the concept of "contrasts" in poetry writing and what it means for a poet to grapple with their identity.

Part 2 of this anthology is titled "Views from the Inside." The contributors in this part of the anthology confront stigma, exploitation, and/or ableism. Through highly personal and vivid narrative essays, each of these writers transports readers into their lives, allowing them to glimpse what they've experienced. For instance, Grace Quantock (Chapter 6) provides readers with insight into her daily life as a disabled individual who uses a wheelchair; she also discusses how mainstream media are not interested in authentic stories of disability, preferring stories that gawk at or dilute the disabled experience. Saul Lemerond (Chapter 7) takes readers into the realities of being a dyslexic child in an elementary school classroom, unable to reproduce written language in the same way or at the same pace as his peers; he then discusses how his PhD program also inflicted harmful ableist expectations. Celeste Maria Schueler's essay, composed of vignettes (Chapter 8), highlights that forms of mental illness are classed as disabilities by the Americans with Disabilities Act (ADA); she also shows readers how her bipolar disorder manifests in terrifying and debilitating ways and how it has impacted her educational journey and poetry writing. Tyler Darnell (Chapter 9), born with cerebral palsy, describes in his essay what it is like to be a visibly disabled writer. For Darnell, as for many writers in this anthology, the act of writing has been an inclusive practice, in an otherwise alienating world. Finally, Beth Rees (Chapter 10) provides readers with insight into rejection sensitive dysphoria (RSD), a common comorbidity of ADHD. She also shows the ways that RSD can complicate the workshopping experience, and she provides suggestions to current and prospective creative writing students who struggle with RSD.

Part 3, titled "Dismantling the Traditional Writing Workshop," is made up of essays that suggest and detail interventions, reckonings, and inclusive alternatives to the traditional writing workshop; each of the writers in this part takes the Iowa Workshop Model to task, calling out the ways that it can be cruelly ableist and exclusionary, not to mention stale and ineffective. Said Shaiye's essay (Chapter 11) explores how two distinct workshops he took part in were not only exclusionary but also racially and religiously insensitive, othering Said in multiple ways; these experiences impacted his own teaching practices, which he outlines for readers. In a lyric essay, Shane Neilson (Chapter 12) compares his Master of Fine Arts (MFA) experience in Canada with a disability-centric workshop he founded, noting the many ways that traditional MFA programs could be kinder and more inclusive to a wide range of disabled writers. Julia Rose Lewis (Chapter 13) introduces readers to the Poem Brut series created by SJ Fowler, arguing that traditional workshops would benefit from the experimental practices of Poem Brut, as experimental writing can, according to Lewis, encourage neurodivergent student-writers to lean into their strengths rather than focusing on their differences. Finally, Gustavo Henrique Rückert's essay (Chapter 14) details his research project at the Federal University of Pelotas in Brazil, which aims to discover and highlight autistic poets in Brazil and to provide inclusive, specialized workshops for autistic writers.

In Part 4, titled "Ableism in Higher Education, Writing Programs, and Academia," the contributors discuss ways that academic programs and faculty can better serve their diverse students and their colleagues. In my own essay (Chapter 15), I focus on graduate writing programs at the MA, MFA, and PhD levels; I also provide hands-on tips and strategies for making writing classrooms, workshops, and programs more inclusive. In an essay using the FAQ format, Leigh Camacho Rourks (Chapter 16) provides readers with best practices to consider when teaching neurodivergent students; she also provides crucial insights into the neurodivergent mind more broadly. Rachel Carney's essay (Chapter 17) suggests ways that creative writing classrooms and workshops can be more inclusive to students, and she stresses the power of language to both harm but also to heal. In her essay, Miranda L. Barnes (Chapter 18) shares her experience as a poet and educator in academia with chronic pain conditions and the hardships and ableist expectations she has faced. Finally, Audrey T. Heffer's essay (Chapter 19), which uses a Q&A format, considers not only creative writing classrooms but also commonly held ableist writing beliefs; she also addresses ways that publishing entities can be more accommodating and accessible.

Ultimately, this book cannot offer one magic, easy-to-implement piece of advice for being more inclusive to all impacted writers. This is because the needs of disabled writers are nuanced and diverse; even writers with the same condition will each have completely different strengths and challenges. However, I offer here a few impactful ways to begin: confront your biases, be curious, be knowledgeable/informed, be mindful, be kind. Ask writers what they need or what would help. Embrace and champion writers with divergent minds and bodies.

Finally, I caution readers against interpreting this anthology as one written *by* disabled, chronically ill, and neurodivergent writers *solely for* neurotypical and able-bodied readers. In truth, this anthology is *for* everyone. Unfortunately, ableism and bias are not solely enacted by those who are neurotypical or Temporarily Able Bodied (TAB), to use Goodley's term. I have witnessed extremely narrow viewpoints, exclusionary language and practices, and forms of ableism perpetrated by individuals who themselves identify as disabled and/or neurodivergent, which can feel particularly insidious. But it goes to show that no one is totally immune to unintentional biases. We all have much to learn and to unlearn. In that vein, I encourage everyone to not only read and consider each of the essays in this anthology but to also spend time with each contributor's bibliography and consider reading the works they reference and recommend as well as other resources on forms of disability, illness, and neurodivergence.

Christie Collins, PhD
Mississippi State University

Bibliography

"2023 American Community Survey: Disabled Population." United States Census Bureau. Accessed January 25, 2025. https://data.census.gov/all?q=disability

Block, Laurie. "'An Invented Archive': The Disability History Museum." *RBM: A Journal of Rare Books, Manuscripts, & Cultural Heritage* 8, no. 2 (2007): 141–154. https://doi.org/10.5860/rbm.8.2.288

"Disability." *World Health Organization*. Accessed January 25, 2025. https://www.who.int/healthtopics/disability#tab=tab_1

Doyle, Nancy. "Neurodiversity at Work: A Biopsychosocial Model and the Impact on Working Adults." *British Medical Bulletin* 135, no. 1 (September 2020): 108–125. https://doi.org/10.1093/bmb/ldaa021

Goodley, Dan. *Disability Studies: An Interdisciplinary Introduction*, 3rd ed. (Sage, 2025).

United Nations. "International Day of Persons with Disabilities, 3 December." *United Nations*. Accessed January 25, 2025. https://www.un.org/en/observances/day-of-persons-with-disabilities/background

Part 1 The Writer's Journey: Late Diagnosis, Recovery, and Post-Diagnosis/Post-Recovery Observations on Writing and Teaching

1   Aphasia as Form and Discontent:¹ Adaptations of a Post-Stroke Poet and Teacher

AIDAN COLEMAN

I. Identity Theft

When, at age thirty-one, I had a stroke, my identity had been firmly fixed as a teacher and writer.

On that first morning, I awoke to the click and dull bounce of machines. My wife, mother, brother, and a few close friends were crowded round me, like one of those nineteenth-century death bed scenes.

I asked a question, but no words arrived. I spoke only air—an empty comic bubble.

For the first few weeks, my thoughts were focused on mere survival. I was afraid of dying for lack of sleep but at the same time afraid, once asleep, that I would never wake.

Soon, my attention shifted to the body: of re-learning to walk and to move my right arm in basic ways.

Those first couple of months, when I wasn't pondering death, I thought about my new identity. Broken words returned in an on/off whisper, shuffling out one corner of my mouth. I wondered if I was still a writer, or a teacher. My memory was intact, but I was less sure of my brain's other compartments.

When writer friends visited (leaving books I could no longer read), I asked myself if I was just my conversation, that ability to make quick connections and quote lines of poetry. My ability—crucial for a poet—to make metaphor was gone.

• • •

In the early weeks, I thought I could point to words in the dictionary but found there an impassably dense thicket of syllables. The paragraphs in a tabloid newspaper

---

¹As a stroke-survivor with aphasia and ongoing physical deficits, I consider the challenges in negotiating the creative writing classroom and academia more generally throughout this essay. After outlining how my aphasia has shaped my teaching practice, I explore—through the work of poets and theorists as well as my own creative practice—how aphasia might suggest a form or style and new possibilities for writers. The essay closes with some creative activities for aphasia poetry.

looked familiar, but the words came off the page at different speeds, switching and dissolving as they entered the static in my head.

When I started to write again (typing with only my left hand), I found my sentences were full of holes and the words were out of order. My pronouns and participles were wrong: "I" became "you"; "ours" became "mine"; "walking" became "walked"; "rested" became "resting." Each "but" became an "and" and each "and" a "but." I'd invariably miss particular words, such as the verb "be." Neglecting the word "not"—a common mistake in both my writing and reading—wreaked havoc.

My spelling too was shot to bits. I could not break down words into syllables or sound them out phonetically, and I spelled, roughly, by sight. Often, I couldn't remember how a word began, or couldn't get near enough for the spellchecker to guess. But I did learn some tricks. Searching with a synonym, scouring my mind for a rhyme or similar-sounding word, often proved helpful, but could take minutes.

Numbers hid behind their figuration. What was in my mind's eye was often ill-matched to the words I spoke aloud. Post-Freud, such arbitrary slips seem embarrassingly revealing.

These kinks in speech. These dropped, added, and mangled syllables continue to blur the edges of my articulacy. I don't trust the first sound to come out of my mouth. I feel my way into speech or sit it out on the sidelines.

• • •

In the months following the stroke, I thought of my brain as a bombed-out city: its bridges and roads damaged beyond repair, its great storehouses reduced to piles of smouldering ash.

My publisher sent me a book, *The Brain that Changes Itself*, by Norman Doidge. Though frustratingly beyond my reading level and powers of attention, this book—which my wife, a science educator, read and relayed to me—reconceptualized the brain in sanguine terms. Through some extraordinary cases, Doidge wrote about the brain's weird capacity to reorganize itself: if the main highways are obliterated, secondary roads will open.[2] Through eighteen months of intensive rehab, I slowly improved. The problems with speech and writing remain, but they are less pronounced. I didn't get a full recovery in my right hand, but it was the loss of language that continued to bother me the most.

II. *The Velcro Under My Tongue*: Tertiary Teaching

My inability to initiate speech, to trust my voice, my slow reactions, and the countless extra hours it took to draft and mark student work were among my reasons for leaving secondary teaching. But my memory was intact; I could think as well as I did before and—with looser time pressures—I could write, as well. I didn't want to give

---

[2]Norman Doidge, *The Brain that Changes Itself: Stories of Personal Triumph from the Frontiers of Brain Science* (Penguin Books, 2007).

up teaching, so, when I enrolled in a PhD, I set my sights on adult education in a tertiary context. There, I reasoned, my deficits would show up far less as liabilities. Still, I knew that—in the eyes of many—I wouldn't present well enough to attain a permanent faculty position.

I felt that my disability, for the most part hidden, would be hard for an institution that prides itself on the qualities of rationality and intellectual rigor to accommodate. In Margaret Price's eloquent challenge to mental ableism, titled *Mad at School*, she argues that "rationality" and "criticality" are among the "most important common topoi of academe" and that these "intersect problematically with mental disability."[3] As Price explains, "For thousands of years academe has been understood as a bastion of reason, the place in which one's rational mind is one's instrument. But what does that mean for those of us with atypical (some would say 'impaired' or 'ill') minds who work, learn, and teach in this location?"[4] Ultimately, to answer the question that Price poses, it means that many with cognitive deficits will not measure up to the institution's neurotypical biases; many more, who have the capacity for the required level of rational rigor, will not be able to adequately "perform" this rationality. While the idea of a shared rational standpoint has been increasingly challenged, Price notes that the neurodiverse are "still required to pantomime our way through our work, embodying—or enminding—as best we can the 'good man speaking well.'"[5] Price conceives the academy as a collection of "kairotic spaces," each of which is characterized by "the real-time unfolding of events; impromptu communication that is required or encouraged; in-person contact; a strong social element; and high stakes."[6] It is a physical space and time that incorporates all the formal and informal exchanges, and all the "unnoticed areas of academe where knowledge is produced and power is exchanged."[7] It is in these kairotic spaces that the neurodiverse will continue to fall short. Prospective job candidates are expected to be at ease in the world, charming, confident, and eloquent. But the successful will also be machines for research "production" and "creative outputs."

After years of casual employment, I was getting shortlisted for interviews for continuing positions, but my deficits manifested themselves in these high-pressure situations.[8] My speech lacked color and crispness, and the cognitive effort of articulation left little room to search for the necessary content or tone. I felt my speech cast a pall over my writing, research, and teaching record. The expectations were

---

[3]Margaret Price, *Mad at School: Rhetorics of Mental Disability and Academic Life* (University of Michigan Press, 2011), 6.
[4]Ibid.
[5]Price, *Mad at School*, 40–41.
[6]Ibid., 61.
[7]Ibid.
[8]I find Price's description of a student at lunch with their supervisor (pp. 61–62) as analogous to the cognitive load I experience when negotiating factors like tone and eye contact while achieving recall and eloquence; her description embodies many of the complications I experience in negotiating job interviews and even during networking and social interactions at academic events.

high. Various professors remarked: "We loved your CV but . . ."; "You were the most qualified but . . ."; "We don't want a Ted Talk but . . .".

After one particularly shambolic conference presentation, I decided to begin disclosing before I delivered a paper. "I have post-stroke aphasia," I said, "so I may garble a few words." Although it was always more than a few—and the cognitive complications were more complex than mere articulation—this statement put me at ease. I wondered if I could say something similar at the beginning of a job interview. People's responses when I put this question to them were mixed. But the first interview in which I disclosed my disability was successful. The disclosure settled my nerves, and though my delivery wasn't perfect, it was the best interview I had yet done. This experience aligns with a central focus of *The Power of Neurodiversity* by Thomas Armstrong regarding the idea of "niche construction": the neurodiverse carving out a space for themselves in which they can thrive.[9] The concept of niche construction extends from a sensible choice of career to the way a person structures every aspect of their lives. My "niche construction"[10] encompasses the way I perform my job, including my avoiding giving too many formal presentations to peers because of the time-devouring preparation and rehearsal they require and employing more dialogic methods. At home, it entails pacing myself socially, reading via audiobooks and various playback devices, and writing almost everything through voice recognition. It also requires specializing in the domestic tasks I do most efficiently—or at least not too inefficiently.

While aphasia makes my job more challenging, I feel there have been some hard-won benefits to my teaching. Out of necessity, I disclose my condition from the beginning. My lectures are more dialogic, and the responses from my students have been overwhelmingly positive. I don't set myself up for a fall by being captious or high-handed. I apologize for my errors immediately, in the context that they are to be expected, and find this attitude fosters a similar goodwill and candour in my students. I ask for their help to read aloud in class and to keep me abreast of the incoming written chat in online teaching. Students know that I rely on them as much as they rely on me, and I feel this sets the tenor for my classes.

In ancient skepticism, aphasia is "the silence enjoined on us after we have suspended judgement on things."[11] Indeed, I am less judgmental because of my aphasia. It has made me a humbler and more empathetic teacher. The personal, interpersonal, and societal benefits of "owning one's limitations" are being increasingly reported in the literature.[12] Furthermore, teachers who model such "intellectual

---

[9]Thomas Armstrong, *The Power of Neurodiversity: Unleashing the Advantages of Your Differently Wired Brain* (Da Capo Press, 2011), 25.
[10]Armstrong introduces the concept of "niche construction" in his introduction, noting that the first to use the term was biologist Richard Lewontin. However, Armstrong returns to this term in each chapter as he considers a variety of neurodiverse conditions.
[11]Simon Blackburn, "Aphasia," *The Oxford Dictionary of Philosophy*, 2nd rev. ed. (Oxford University Press, 2008).
[12]Dennis Whitcomb et al., "Intellectual Humility: Owning Our Limitations," *Philosophy and Phenomenological Research* 94, no. 3 (2017): 509–539, https://doi.org/10.1111/phpr.12228

humility" also support vulnerability and a willingness to take risks, which are essential conditions for a creative writing classroom.[13] Importantly, I have found that acknowledging my difficulties seems to help students deal with theirs because my frankness about my condition builds trust and allows students to declare their struggles more openly.

III. *First Words and Second Thoughts*: Writing the Stroke

It is worth asking, for all the obvious difficulties it presents, whether aphasia could in any way benefit the writer. Could there be a poetry of aphasia, and what would it look like? Aphasia, itself, is generative, but its poetry often goes unrecognized. Heidi Andrea Restrepo Rhodes seems to focus on anomia when she states that "a poetics born of aphasia, opens onto infinite possibilities as the brain finds anything but the proper name for the thing."[14]

When I wrote "sleep depraved" instead of "sleep deprived,"[15] in an early draft of one of the poems in my collection *Asymmetry*, I let it stand as a happy accident, far richer in its connotations than the cliché of my original intention. When Michael Obel-Omia's spoke his first post-stroke words—"Can I please have tomorrow?"[16]—he was then unaware that he was setting down a line for his future book. In her writing, Chris Ireland, who works collaboratively with her "poetry editor," Carole Pound, looks to preserve those features of aphasia that are invariably read as errors, including variant spellings.[17] She shares that she often must explain her work to editors in her correspondence: "Before published in the journal, I discussed with the editor. She was correcting. I explained that there are *not* spelling errors but 'creative errors' to show aphasia. Allowed them! Readers were GP/nurses, educating and sharing regarding about the creativity and depth to more understanding of aphasia voice."[18] Ireland explains that the distinctiveness of her work is often toned down by such a process, noting that in her second submission she "was more careful with 'errors'—because for a wider audience who probably do not know about aphasia."[19] Many avant-garde poets have written about the generative possibilities of mistranslation and the "errors" arising through mishearing.[20] Aphasia itself can be similarly generative in its "errors."[21]

---

[13] Jason Baehr, *Deep in Thought: A Practical Guide to Teaching for the Intellectual Virtues* (Harvard Education Press, 2021), 161–162.
[14] Heidi Andrea Restrepo Rhodes, "Impossible Word: Toward a Poetics of Aphasia: On the Words We Lack," *Poetry Magazine*, October 1, 2020, https://www.poetryfoundation.org/poetrymagazine/articles/154200/impossible-word-toward-a-poetics-of-aphasia
[15] Aidan Coleman, "First I Step," *Asymmetry* (Brandl & Schlesinger, 2006), 23–24.
[16] Michael Obel-Omia, "Sign Language," *Finding My Words* (Still Water, 2021): 52.
[17] Chris Ireland and Carole Pound, "Celebrating Aphasia Poetry Power," *Aphasia Inside Out*, eds. Susie Parr et al. (McGraw-Hill, 2003): 145.
[18] Ibid., 148.
[19] Ibid.
[20] See the work of David Musgrave, Toby Fitch, and Charles Bernstein.
[21] David Musgrave, "Mishearing and the Voice in Poetry," *TEXT* Special Issue 64 (2021), https://textjournal.scholasticahq.com/article/30991-mishearing-and-the-voice-in-poetry.pdf

Halvard Johnson's poem "Ambulance" is one example of this: "ambience" becomes "ambulance"; "patients" becomes "patents"; "another" morphs into "udder."[22]

As Carole Ireland shows, aphasia is also avant-gardist in its disruptions to syntax. The neurologist Katharina Fuerholzer praises the "aphasic-like disruption of prevalent patterns of saying and seeing the world," and she gives particular emphasis to "the creative potentials within the poetic destructions of the familiar."[23] Additionally, Heidi Andrea Restrepo Rhodes recognizes a peculiar poetry in a patient of Carl Wernicke, recorded in Freud's *On Aphasia* (1891), noting the similarities between the text of Wernicke's patient and the poetics of E. E. Cummings's modernism. In doing so, she laments that our concern for literary intention and preference for wellness over illness often obscure our appreciation of the poetry for what it is.[24]

It is possible that certain types of aphasia could also suggest a style.[25] A stroke in 1990 left the Swedish Nobel laureate Tomas Tranströmer half-paralyzed and unable to speak. Despite the severity of the event, Tranströmer wrote some new poems, most of them in the form of the haiku.[26] He had always been austere, but the late poetry is even more concentrated.[27] In his study of aphasia, the linguist Roman Jakobson states that those with motor aphasia, who present with a "contiguity disorder," lose the ability "to propositionize," as the context for their speech "disintegrates."[28] The result, Jakobson explains, is the agrammatism of the "so-called telegraphic style," in which "relational words are omitted" and speech predominantly consists of nouns and verbs, which are not modified according to their functions in sentences.[29] Likewise, Tranströmer's late works are essentially agrammatical and telegraphic in style. In these poems, the nouns are foregrounded, and articles and prepositions are fairly rare.

---

[22] Halvard Johnson, "Ambulance," *The Bellevue Review* 6, https://blreview.org/poetry/ambulance/
[23] Katharina Fuerholzer, "Aphasic Poetry: Making Sense of It with Katharina Fuerholzer." Interview by Emma Telaro, SPOKENWEBLOG, December 4, 2020, https://spectrum.library.concordia.ca/id/eprint/990892/1/Telaro_Fuerholzer_4Dec2020_Aphasic%20Poetry_%20Making%20sense%20of%20it%20with%20Katharina%20Fuerholzer%20-%20SpokenWeb.pdf
[24] Restrepo Rhodes, "Impossible Word."
[25] For example, brevity has been noted as distinctive in the work of other poets with aphasia. For example, Christina Scheuer writes of the poetry of Karen Fiser: "As she begins to experience aphasia, Fiser's form of expression moves from the academic essay to the short lyric poem, and this shift shows us how poetry can accommodate, even embrace, the changes that the body experiences, allowing the artist radically to recreate the way in which she communicates." See Christina Scheuer, "Bodily Compositions: The Disability Poetics of Karen Fiser and Laurie Clements Lambeth," *Journal of Literary & Cultural Disability Studies* 5, no. 2 (2011): 172, https://doi.org/10.3828/jlcds.2011.13
[26] Ivan Iniesta, "Tomas Tranströmer's Stroke of Genius: Language but No Words," *Progress in Brain Research* 206 (2013): 157–167, https://doi.org/10.1016/B978-0-444-63364-4.00026-0
[27] Schiöler, Niklas, "Tolkningar/redaktör," *Bonnier, Stockholm* (1999), quoted in Iván Iniesta, "Tomas Tranströmer's Stroke of Genius: Language but No Words." *Progress in Brain Research* 206 (2013): 157–167, https://doi.org/10.1016/B978-0-444-63364-4.00026-0
[28] Roman Jakobson, *Studies on Child Language and Aphasia* (Mouton, 1971), 46.
[29] Ibid. See also p. 64 and pp. 99–100 for Jakobson's discussion of the telegraphic style.

Aphasia has influenced the process of my writing in similar ways, though the changes are not linear or easy to map. For almost a year I wrote nothing, and then began writing love poems to my wife, Leana, who was also my carer. It took longer still to write about the stroke. But when I began the work, the poems came quickly. My collection of poems, *Asymmetry* (2012), opens on my wordlessness, fear of death, and alienation from my body: of showering in a chair with assistance; of being fed through a PEG tube; of being always in the company of machines. Half of the stroke poems concern my long journey toward greater independence, and many consider my social isolation. After Leana returned to work, I found the days too full of hours. I had a sense of being left behind, while the lives of everyone around me had moved on. When I went to the shops, I reflected upon the parallel lives of others and my separateness from them:

I make a point of coffee lately

to slip the house or break

the day.

At the counter my first word

is the wrong foot.

But I make myself understood

and pocket change,

straightforwardly, natural.

A thank-you comes from distance.

I have my book and my strategies

and time.[30]

In these lyrics, I looked to break the fluency of the parsing line. The music is deliberately awkward, the typography irregular and untidy.

One of the things that kept my spirits up during the darker days of my recovery was treating everything, and especially rehab, like a game. I expressed the frustrations of forcing and cajoling my new-old body into unlikely action through the metaphor of "The Chocolate Game," a staple of Scout Halls and school camps in the 1980s.[31] The

---

[30] Aidan Coleman, "Coffee," *Asymmetry* (Brandl & Schlesinger, 2006), 40.

[31] If you can't recognize the game from its epithet, it works as follows: a block of chocolate, together with a knife and fork, are placed in the center of a circle of children, along with some items of oversized clothing. A die is passed from child to child, and to eat the chocolate a child must roll a six and put on the clothes. Then, they may keep eating until someone else rolls a six. A participant will often wriggle into the ill-fitting clothes in a panicked hurry, cut loose a square of chocolate with the knife and fork, only for a competitor to roll a six. And then they are forced to wriggle out of the clothes, without having so much as a taste of the chocolate.

poem blurs the petty vagaries of post-stroke living and rehab, on the one hand, and that game on the other:

> Catch a face before it slides
>
> from the plate. Screw in
>
> an unblinking eye. Into one
>
> corner hammer a tent peg
>
> so a smile flaps but
> holds good. Now shrug on
>
> an amorphous coat. Hurry.
>
> No. Panic won't make for fast—
>
> buttoning; think reattaching
>
> lead to dog, lock-picking,
>
> wire-cutting. The fork-hand
>
> easy but the truculent right:
>
> a fist, a nest of magnets from
>
> which you pry the index out
>
> and fit it the length of that
>
> silver spine, while those
>
> around you spill the loaded die.[32]

Asymmetry charts two years of recovery and rehab, ending with my return to work and the accommodation of my continuing deficits:

> Pockets are so
> the hand doesn't hang
>
> when I step up to the high stage of conversation.
>
> The one-two pass of the
> 'Hi. How are you?'
> leaves me clutching the wrapping

---

[32] Aidan Coleman, "To Play," *Asymmetry* (Brandl & Schlesinger, 2006), 38.

of a tattered word.[33]

[. . .]

I stand near the desk and the handrail of my notes,

my sour smile answered
by a twinkle of whispers.

I open my mouth and wait

for the lesson to begin.[34]

The poems in *Asymmetry* insisted on a form: spare, direct, and imagistic. But this aesthetic was similar in many ways to the writing of my first book, *Avenues and Runways* (2005), if perhaps a little sparer. I feel now that I was not as open as I could have been to the generative possibilities of aphasia.

It was in the years following *Asymmetry* that I started to reflect more on literary style, as I began to write disjunctively. The reasons for writing as we do are legion and largely inscrutable.[35] A poet-friend, who is also a doctor, suggested that the new disjunctive work was my mind forging new connections and that these poems were part of the brain's rewiring. I didn't take him very seriously at the time. After all, this poetry that characterizes my third book, *Mount Sumptuous* (2020), was more outward focused—more political than personal. Although the effects of the stroke were ongoing, I thought I had left that part of my life behind when I finished *Asymmetry*. On reflection, I'm not so sure.

If not caused by the stroke, I at least believe that disjunction is a form better fitted to aphasia. In these (still-short) opaquer lyrics, difficulty is a kind of defense. For the poet-critic James Longenbach, difficulty is one of poetry's main attractions.[36] In *The Resistance to Poetry*, Longenbach invokes the psychoanalyst D. W. Winnicott, when he reflects upon the poet's urgent need to "communicate" without being "found."[37] Difficulty can be a defense against society's demands for immediacy and clear communication. Where *Asymmetry* is near naked in its confessionalism, this newer work eschews communicative directness. Like aphasia, the poetry resists the modern world's demand for speed and instant accessibility.

---

[33]Aidan Coleman, "Return to Work," *Asymmetry* (Brandl & Schlesinger, 2006), 47.
[34]Ibid., 48.
[35]My conscious purpose in writing disjunctively was to include more non-experiential knowledge in my poetry. See: Aidan Coleman, "Closure and the Omnivorous Lyric." *New Writing* 18, no. 1 (2021): 98–108.
[36]James Longenbach, *The Resistance to Poetry* (University of Chicago Press, 2004), xii.
[37]Ibid., 11.

While my recent work is not written in the telegraphic style as such, smaller fragments of language—what I call "units of sense"[38]—become more important in these poems. The nouns, and to a lesser extent the verbs, are foregrounded in the process and final composition, while the connectors become less important, in some cases even arbitrary. This mode of writing is mimetic of aphasia's cognitive disruptions, while the lyrics are multi-tonal and dialogic qualities are in keeping with a less stable sense of self.

IV. Aphasia in the Creative Writing Classroom

Where poets have survived a stroke, aphasia has often killed their art—think Charles Baudelaire[39] and Ralph Waldo Emerson,[40] or, more recently, Tobias Hill.[41] But aphasia has made poets, as well. Creative endeavors such as music, painting, and poetry have proved effective therapies to support those living with a range of neurological conditions from dementia to addiction.[42] The writing of poetry, as Shafi and Carozza note, functions as a "medium to express [the writer's] poststroke life experiences and feelings," when they may be unable to vocalize such things in conversation.[43] In such groups, the primary focus is on content, but the poems and activities below focus on form.

Christina Scheuer remarks that the short lyric poem is a fitting form for aphasia because it allows the poet "radically to recreate the way in which she communicates."[44] This opinion is supported by Jessica Lewis Luck. Professor Luck teaches a unit at

---

[38]In an interview, the poet John Forbes discussed the effect he aimed for in moving "blocks of meaning" around, explaining how these blocks "work off each other" to "create tension." See "John Forbes Interview, 1980," Interview by John Jenkins. *Journal of Poetics Research*. http://poeticsresearch.com/article/john-forbes-interview-1980. I label these blocks of text, that can be whole sentences or lines or noun phrases "units of sense," and they have proved productive in my own disjunctive writing. See: Aidan Coleman, "Does Function Follow Form: Openness and Formal Association in the Early Poetry of John Forbes," *Text: A Journal of Writing and Writing Courses* 23, no. 2 (2019), https://doi.org/10.52086/001c.18603

[39]A severe stroke at fifty robbed the nineteenth-century symbolist of his whole vocabulary but for a single expletive. For a scientific discussion of his condition, see: Bruno Kusznir Vitturi and Rubens José Gagliardi, "Post-Stroke Aphasia in Famous Writers: When Neurology Left Geniuses Speechless," *Arquivos de Neuro-Psiquiatria* 79, no. 3 (2021): 251–253, https://doi.org/10.1590/0004-282X-ANP-2020-0282

[40]Ralph Waldo Emerson experienced non-fluent aphasia after a stroke at sixty-four. Despite his best endeavors, he did not write anything of substance through his long decline. See: Vitturi and Gagliardi.

[41]Kamila Shamsie, "Tobias Hill Obituary," *The Guardian*, September 14, 2023, https://www.theguardian.com/books/2023/sep/13/tobias-hill-obituary

[42]Noel Shafi and Linda Carozza, "Poetry and Aphasia: A Clinical Outlook," *Journal of Poetry Therapy* 24, no. 4 (2011): 255–259, https://doi.org/10.1080/08893675.2011.625208

[43]Ibid.

[44]Christina Scheuer, "Bodily Compositions: The Disability Poetics of Karen Fiser and Laurie Clements Lambeth," *Journal of Literary & Cultural Disability Studies* 5, no. 2 (2011): 172, https://doi.org/10.3828/jlcds.2011.13

California State University, San Bernardino titled "Neurodiversity and the Poetic Imagination" that includes aphasia poetry. "One of the most interesting conversations that came out of this unit," she recalls, "centered around poetry and its flexible forms of language as a boon to writers with diverse forms of consciousness."[45] In teaching a poetics of aphasia, and of neurodiversity more broadly, educators need to expose their students to as many poetic forms as possible, encouraging them to think about form disruptively and experimentally. They need, likewise, to encourage students to embrace—even amplify—atypical differences in thought processes.

Through the darker days of my recovery, I coped by treating the privations of the stroke and rehabilitation as a game. In the creative writing classroom—and especially in poetry—I encourage a similar spirit of play. We can be serious about aphasia and our vocation as writers, without being solemn in our approach to language, embracing what Tim Beasley-Murray recommends as "the risky and transgressive activity of serious play."[46] Such a stance, productive in most creative writing contexts, is even more efficacious for aphasics. Additionally, Hiram Maxim recommends a playful approach to reading and writing poetry for students of English in a foreign language curriculum. He suggests that these students should approach the language as "an object of play rather than as some monolithic entity that they are fated to never master."[47] Aphasics should do likewise. Many with aphasia relearn language from a very basic level and suffer an estrangement from their first language that is comparable to the foreign speaker's.[48] Seeing the language as an object of play, while embracing accidental transgressions, could potentially have both therapeutic and creative benefits. When it comes to language, we have deviancy forced upon us and we should embrace our rule-breaking! It is in this spirit of play that I recommend the following activities.

Exercise 1: (Re)Aphase Your Poem

For this activity, take a poem that you have written in the past. Alternatively, you can use a poem by someone else. To (re)aphase the chosen poem, you should consider

---

[45] Luck, Jessica Lewis. "Disability, Poetry, Pedagogy," *Wordgathering: A Journal of Disability Poetry and Literature* 4, no. 2 (2010), https://wordgathering.com/past_issues/issue14/

[46] Tim Beasley-Murray, "Back to Life, Back to Reality: From the Game of Academia to the Risk of Creative-Critical Writing," *Thinking through Relation: Encounters in Creative Critical Writing*, edited by Iorian Mussgnug et al. (Peter Lang, 2021), 67.

[47] Hiram Maxim, "Giving Beginning Adult Language Learners a Voice: A Case for Poetry in the Foreign Language Classroom," *Poetry & Pedagogy*, edited by J. Retallack and J. Spahr (Palgrave Macmillan, 2006). Krusche and Krechel (1992), whom Maxim cites, write of the benefits of playing with language. They suggest that in these language classes students are open to such playfulness because of the novelty the language presents for them.

[48] It should be acknowledged too that many stroke survivors lose a number of languages. I note the case of the Arizona-based poet and translator of Afghan poetry, Felisa Hervey, who suffered a severe stroke when she was thirty-one, by which she lost the five additional languages she spoke other than English. See: Alden Woods, "A Stroke Stole This Poet's Words. Now She's Trying to Get Them Back," *AZ-Central*, May 9, 2019, https://www.azcentral.com/story/news/local/arizona-best-reads/2019/05/09/felisa-hervey-poet-no-words-her-language-stolen-aphasia-stroke/3656755002/

those areas in which aphasia most affects your speech or writing. Brooke Lang provides the following useful taxonomy of aphasia's effects:

1. Phonology: the individual sound system.
2. Semantics: the meaning of words.
3. Syntax and grammar.[49]

(Re)aphase the poem, focusing on any, or all, of these areas:

- Erase words or replace existing words with a different word.
- Replace one word with another that sounds similar, or that is almost visually identical, or a word that rhymes with it.
- Disrupt the syntax of your sentences, as you move words and phrases around.

You will find that some effects will be more interesting, meaningful, or strange than others and you will discern between these effects in the editing process, seeking to make the poem eloquently strange.

Exercise 2: Aphasia the Game

For this activity, write your aphasia, loosely or metaphorically, using the rules of an existing or make-believe game.

- For best effect, this poem should be written in the imperative mood.
- My stroke poem "To Play" might be employed as a model, though it is concerned more with the stroke's physical effects than aphasia. For some other examples by non-aphasia poets, see Vasko Popa's "Game" poems[50] and Peter Goldsworthy's "Games."[51] This activity, and the one below, might give scope for inventive use of typography.

Exercise 3: Location Poem

As aphasics, many of us struggle to locate the right word for a particular thing, but we can be highly creative in the way we bridge the gap between our available words and the precise word we are looking for. Consider the Denver-based poet, Eric Baus,

---

[49] Brooke Lang, *After Aphasia: A Guide to Rebuilding Your Communication Skills after a Stroke* (IRAphasia Books, 2020).
[50] Vasko Popa, *Selected Poems*, trans. Anne Pennington (Penguin, 1969), 34–46.
[51] Peter Goldsworthy, *This Goes with That: Selected Poems 1970-1990* (Angus & Robertson, 1991), 49–50.

who—after suffering a stroke—noted his propensity to "create neologisms to try to speak around absent nouns," such as calling his phone a "contact remote."[52]

- For this exercise, you should dwell on the ways in which your condition makes you linguistically inventive, as you recreate elements of the process of word location, through metaphor, word association, and neologisms.
- Involve all the senses, as you attempt to see, listen, smell, touch, and taste the word.
- You might begin with a phrase such as "I spy in my mind's eye a word that begins with the letter B" or "I spy in my mind's eye a word that rhymes with artichoke."
- The poem could be a list poem, but you should embrace digressions where they occur. The title of the poem could be the word the speaker is looking for or the poem might function closer to an Anglo-Saxon (or a Martian) riddle.[53]

Exercise 4: Working Within Constraints and The MakeWrite App

As aphasics, we have various constraints imposed upon us in life that can spill over into our art. In my poetry, for example, I often write to the constraints of my own speaking/performance voice. But poetry has a long history of constraints being drivers for creativity.

The MakeWrite App, which "supports the constrained creation of digital texts through automated redaction" was designed for people with aphasia by a team at the University of London.[54] As with other poetry generators, the app can be used profitably by those new to poetry, as it can be by experienced poets. Much of the poetry created tends toward the concise telegraphic style discussed above.

Bibliography

Armstrong, Thomas. *The Power of Neurodiversity: Unleashing the Advantages of Your Differently Wired Brain*. Da Capo Press, 2011.
Baehr, Jason. *Deep in Thought: A Practical Guide to Teaching for the Intellectual Virtues*. Harvard Education Press, 2021.

---

[52]Eric Baus, "Communicasick: Poetry Inside Aphasia." *Poetry Foundation*, December 9, 2019, https://www.poetryfoundation.org/harriet-books/2019/12/communicasick-poetry-inside-aphasia
[53]The Martians were a school of English poets, whose work was highly metaphorical. These poets focused on de-familiarizing or making the known world strange, writing things as they would be seen, perhaps, by an alien life form. Often, as in the poem "A Martian Sends a Postcard Home" by Craig Raine, the reader is left to guess the event or object being described.
[54]Timothy Neate et al., "Empowering Expression for Users with Aphasia through Constrained Creativity," *Proceedings of the 2019 CHI Conference on Human Factors in Computing Systems*, New York, USA, May 2, 2019, https://doi.org/10.1145/3290605.3300615. This paper includes a detailed explanation of the app, its trialing, and some of the results. For more on the app, visit https://blogs.city.ac.uk/inca/makewrite/

Baus, Eric. "Communicasick: Poetry Inside Aphasia." *The Poetry Foundation*. December 9, 2019. https://www.poetryfoundation.org/harriet-books/2019/12/communicasick-poetry-inside-aphasia

Beasley-Murray, Tim. "Back to Life, Back to Reality: From the Game of Academia to the Risk of Creative-Critical Writing." *Thinking through Relation: Encounters in Creative Critical Writing*. Edited by Iorian Mussgnug, Mathelinda Nabugodi, and Thea Petrou. Peter Lang, 2021.

Blackburn, Simon. "Aphasia." *The Oxford Dictionary of Philosophy*, 2nd rev. ed. Oxford University Press, 2008.

Coleman, Aidan. *Asymmetry*. Brandl & Schlesinger, 2012.

Coleman, Aidan. *Avenues & Runways*. Brandl & Schlesinger, 2005.

Coleman, Aidan. "Does Function Follow Form? Openness and Formal Association in the Early Poetry of John Forbes." *Text: A Journal of Writing and Writing Courses* 23, no. 2 (2019). https://doi.org/10.52086/001c.18603

Coleman, Aidan. "Closure and the Omnivorous Lyric." *New Writing* 18, no. 1 (2021): 98–108.

Coleman, Aidan. *Mount Sumptuous*. Wakefield Press, 2020.

Doidge, Norman. *The Brain That Changes Itself: Stories of Personal Triumph from the Frontiers of Brain Science*. Penguin Books, 2007.

Forbes, John. "John Forbes Interview, 1980." Interview by John Jenkins. *Journal of Poetics Research*. http://poeticsresearch.com/article/john-forbes-interview-1980

Fuerholzer, Katharina. "Aphasic Poetry: Making Sense of It with Katharina Fuerholzer." Interview by Emma Telaro. *SPOKENWEBLOG*, December 4, 2020. https://spectrum.library.concordia.ca/id/eprint/990892/1/Telaro_Fuerholzer_4Dec2020_Aphasic%20Poetry_%20Making%20sense%20of%20it%20with%20Katharina%20Fuerholzer%20%E2%80%93%20SpokenWeb.pdf

Fulton, Robin. "Tomas Tranströmer Obituary." *The Guardian*, March 31, 2015. https://www.theguardian.com/books/2015/mar/31/tomas-transtromer

Goldsworthy, Peter. *This Goes with That: Selected Poems 1970-1990*. Angus & Robertson, 1991.

Iniesta, Iván. "Tomas Tranströmer's Stroke of Genius: Language but No Words." *Progress in Brain Research* 206 (2013): 157–167. https://doi.org/10.1016/B978-0-444-63364-4.00026-0

Ireland, Chris, and Carole Pound. "Celebrating Aphasia Poetry Power." *Aphasia Inside Out*. Edited by Susie Parr, Judith Ducan and Carole Pound. McGraw-Hill, 2003.

Jakobson, Roman. *Studies on Child Language and Aphasia*. Mouton, 1971.

Johnson, Halvard. "Ambulance." *The Bellevue Review* 6. https://blreview.org/poetry/ambulance

Lang, Brooke. *After Aphasia: A Guide to Rebuilding Your Communication Skills after a Stroke*. IRAphasia Books, 2020.

Longenbach, James. *The Resistance to Poetry*. University of Chicago Press, 2004.

Luck, Jessica Lewis. ""Disability, Poetry, Pedagogy." *Wordgathering: A Journal of Disability Poetry and Literature* 4, no. 2 (2010). https://wordgathering.com/past_issues/issue14/

Musgrave, David. "Mishearing and the Voice in Poetry." *TEXT* Special Issue 64 (2021). https://textjournal.scholasticahq.com/article/30991-mishearing-and-the-voice-in-poetry.pdf

Neate, Timothy, Abi Roper, Stephanie Wilson, and Jane Marshall. "Empowering Expression for Users with Aphasia through Constrained Creativity." *Proceedings of the 2019 CHI Conference on Human Factors in Computing Systems,* New York, USA. May 2, 2019. https://doi.org/10.1145/3290605.3300615

Obel-Omia, Michael. *Finding My Words*. Still Water, 2021.

Popa, Vasko. *Selected Poems*. Translated by Anne Pennington. Penguin, 1969.

Price, Margaret. *Mad at School: Rhetorics of Mental Disability and Academic Life*. University of Michigan Press, 2011.

Raine, Craig. *A Martian Sends a Postcard Home*. Oxford University Press, 1979.

Restrepo Rhodes, Heidi Andrea. "Impossible Word: Toward a Poetics of Aphasia: On the Words We Lack." *Poetry Magazine*, October 1, 2020. https://www.poetryfoundation.org/poetrymagazine/articles/154200/impossible-word-toward-a-poetics-of-aphasia

Scheuer, Christina. "Bodily Compositions: The Disability Poetics of Karen Fiser and Laurie Clements Lambeth." *Journal of Literary & Cultural Disability Studies* 5, no. 2 (2011): 155–172. https://doi.org/10.3828/jlcds.2011.13

Shafi, Noel, and Linda Carozza. "Poetry and Aphasia: A Clinical Outlook." *Journal of Poetry Therapy* 24, no. 4 (2011): 255–259. https://doi.org/10.1080/08893675.2011.625208

Shamsie, Kamila. "Tobias Hill Obituary." *The Guardian*, September 14, 2023. https://www.theguardian.com/books/2023/sep/13/tobias-hill-obituary

Skloot, Floyd. *In the Shadow of Memory*, University of Nebraska Press, 2003.

Vitturi, Bruno Kusznir, and Rubens José Gagliardi. "Post-Stroke Aphasia in Famous Writers: When Neurology Left Geniuses Speechless." *Arquivos de Neuro-Psiquiatria* 79, no. 3 (2021): 251–253. https://doi.org/10.1590/0004-282X-ANP-2020-0282

Whitcomb, Dennis, Heather Battaly, Jason Baehr, and Daniel Howard-Snyder. "Intellectual Humility: Owning Our Limitations." *Philosophy and Phenomenological Research* 94, no. 3 (2017): 509–539. https://doi.org/10.1111/phpr.12228

Woods, Alden, "A Stroke Stole This Poet's Words. Now She's Trying to Get Them Back." *AZ-Central*, May 9, 2019. https://www.azcentral.com/story/news/local/arizona-best-reads/2019/05/09/felisa-hervey-poet-no-words-her-language-stolen-aphasia-stroke/3656755002/

2 A Martian Poetic Tendency: What I Learned About Writing and Teaching After My Autism Diagnosis

CATH NICHOLS

Since the late 1950s in the West, poetry has, arguably, been expected to address emotional states such as grief, loss, and love without the trappings of "history" or religious myth, as it once did. As readers, we have become more in tune with *personal* stories. Yet neurodivergent (ND) poets who explore their atypical experience are relatively new, although neurodivergent writers have, arguably, been published within the canon for centuries. The difference now, in the second decade of the twenty-first century, is that we can be explicitly "out" about our atypical brains, and may embrace our unique cognitive styles.

One reason I think ND writers have been present all along is that to be diagnosed as autistic we must have differences from neurotypical people in five areas: communication, special interests/obsessions, anxiety, a tendency to experience meltdowns or withdrawals under pressure, and hypersensitivity to sensory stimuli. Communication differences are most often identified in a person who is non-verbal, or one who speaks in a monotone, *but* autistic communication can include excessive fluency, repeating oneself (in my case this is usually in order to get to the best expression of an idea), and using unusual or long (but highly accurate) words. In the field of creative writing, to be obsessed with reading, to be curious, to be sensitive to sensory stimuli, and to have highly accurate or unusual forms of communication are definite assets.

I wonder if some of the published literature of extreme distress has actually been written by autistic poets. People with autism have a higher suicide risk than the general population: we are 1 percent of the UK population but 11 percent of the suicides.[1] Plus, autistic women are *twice* as likely as autistic men to commit suicide.[2] Gender studies has enabled us to see that many women poets of the past had to struggle to be accepted by the male establishment, and it strikes me that neurodivergent women

---

[1] Sue Willgoss, "Suicide and Autism, a National Crisis," Royal College of Psychiatrists, effective June 30, 2025, https://www.rcpsych.ac.uk/docs/default-source/improving-care/nccmh/suicide-prevention/workshops-(wave-4)/wave-4-workshop-2/suicide-and-autism---slides.pdf?sfvrsn=bf3e0113_2

[2] Hannah Furfaro, "Autistic Women Twice as Likely as Autistic Men To Attempt Suicide," *The Transmitter*, Simmons Foundation, August 7, 2019, https://www.spectrumnews.org/news/autistic-women-twice-as-likely-as-autistic-men-to-attempt-suicide/

will have experienced not only being a poor fit with gender roles, but might have had the stubborn mind-set that enabled them to continue their writing work regardless of others' dismissal. The high suicide rate might be associated with either our struggles to fit into femaleness/domesticity/the literary world, or our struggles to turn those categories and worlds to fit *us*.

Within the sphere of fiction, confident autistic writers are now writing autistic characters who are meant to be seen and accepted as such, for example, the school fiction of Elle McNichol or the *Geek Girl* series by Holly Smale. Such writers have to deal with some common tropes around real and fictional autism. These might be summarized as characters appearing who provoke horror or pity (villains or victims, rarely the protagonist). This othering is similar to that created by mainstream experience in relation to other minorities, such as people of color living in mainly white worlds, or LGBT+ people living in mainly straight worlds. However, whilst race and sexuality have, arguably, broken through to public and academic consciousness as areas where discrimination and hate may occur, disability and neurodivergence are less understood. To provide much needed insight into disability and neurodivergence, particularly within the field of creative writing, this chapter details my autism diagnosis and explores my creative writing practice before and after. I also discuss my experience teaching and mentoring neurodivergent students, my decision to be out to students and colleagues, and my choice to leave module teaching in favor of my health and wellness. At the end, I have provided a reading list of books by autistic writers that address autism in some way.

I. My Autism Diagnosis

I asked a National Health Service (NHS) doctor for an assessment referral in April 2021, but he said that an example I gave from childhood was "bad behaviour" and not an indication of autism. I had savings, so I decided to go to a private assessment center. My diagnosis, in January 2022, at the age of 52, was not a surprise, but I was surprised at how confident the assessors were. At the end they said that at the halfway point, they had both decided I was autistic, and they expected I would fulfill the rest of the criteria in the following session. Curiously, in the second session I was asked to draw objects from a lucky dip bag and tell a story with them, and later to describe what I saw on the pages of a picture book story. Given that imagination, connection, and observing specific detail are tools of my profession as a writer, I expected to "do well" at the exercises, but perhaps the autistic trait here is to do "too well" and offer detail and thought that is not required by the activity. I remain unsure about this but share it as an interesting observation that may touch on stereotypes about autistic people's lack of interest in story versus non-fiction.

In the years prior to my assessment, I had attended three Literary Disability Studies conferences across five years. This meant I had the good fortune of meeting other openly autistic academics and writers. Laura Guthrie had stayed overnight with me to attend a conference in Liverpool. Meeting her in 2016 de-stigmatized autism for me.

She was doing her Creative Writing PhD on autism and depictions of autistic characters in children's books. She also wrote a teen novel with an autistic protagonist, later published as *Anna*.[3] I also met some autistic poets online, including Joanne Limburg. Knowing them made my own autism easier to accept as they were lovely, kind, ordinary people. I realized we did not fill out the traditional autistic stereotypes and learned that old diagnostic criteria had been built around "maleness" and extreme male behaviors, which is why so few of us were diagnosed during our school years in the 1970s and 1980s. I wryly conclude at the end of the poem "Why Didn't You Know?": "no-one was looking at girls, / no-one was looking for problems where none existed." Autistic people can struggle with a diagnosis late in life from having to confront these stereotypes that we grew up with, another example being the belief that autistic people lack empathy or emotional range. I believe many autistic people have a full range of emotions, but we express them differently from neurotypical people, either down-playing or exaggerating what we feel, e.g. we may find our empathetic response so overwhelming we have to hide it, or because it is not immediately seen, we exaggerate.

My autism report remarked that I had empathy for others and could read them well, but others often did not read *me* well. This explained the doctors in 2017 who did not assess my physical pain accurately and sent me to a CFS (chronic fatigue syndrome) clinic when a pain clinic would have been more suitable. I connect this with my exhibiting low *responses* to pain despite high *feelings* of physical pain. Most animals conceal their pain responses: showing pain makes yourself vulnerable to predators. For me, this is instinctive and not a conscious action. My apparent "coolness" can be valuable when, for example, facing others' crises. In the past, I have worked with survivors of sexual abuse in childhood and been able to hear them out and acknowledge the horror while not trying to make things better or change the focus to now. I have also supported people whose loved ones have died. I can be present and quiet or articulate in ways that are supportive. In contrast, I have seen people who identify as neurotypical resorting to cliches or avoidance of those in such emotional extremity.

Autism might also explain the comment my PhD supervisor made once about a certain "coolness" in my writing. Generally, we think "warmth" to be a positive quality so initially I was perturbed. In retrospect, I decided the comment meant I had observational qualities that were surprising because they allowed for a certain distance or multiplicity of viewpoint. I know that I can write with warmth and emotion as, when I have read from my poetry collections, people in an audience sometimes cry or laugh (appropriately).

II. My Autism Diagnosis and My Poetry: Before and After

After my diagnosis of autism in the summer of 2022, I had a clear-out of my cabinet and found printouts of poems that I had not seen in years. I recycled many in the

---

[3]Laura Guthrie, *Anna. Isle of Lewis* (Gob Stopper, 2020).

paper bin, but I also found poems I wanted to keep. I now had a diagnosis, but I must have been autistic all along, so I wondered if this would show up in old poems.

In the 1970s and 1980s, there was a poetry movement in the UK which became known as the Martian movement, after Craig Raine's poem "A Martian Sends a Postcard Home." Within this poem, we are asked to assume an alien has arrived on planet earth and has chosen to describe various ordinary things to their relatives back home. Thus, the Martian writes lines such as these:

> In homes, a haunted apparatus sleeps,
> that snores when you pick it up.
>
> If the ghost cries, they carry it
> to their lips and soothe it to sleep
>
> with sounds. And yet, they wake it up
> deliberately, by tickling with a finger.[4]

The object described in this poem is a mid-century telephone, though it is the Martian's alternative viewpoint that reminds me of autism. Others have also noticed an aesthetic link between an autistic point of view and Martian poetry. Angela Readman, another poet with a late diagnosis of autism, riffs on this notion in her poem, "The Female Alien's Dictionary," that has the epigraph "after Craig Raine." In this poem, Readman's poetic-speaker makes the following observations:

> Mittens are sleeping bags to give rainy roses and railings a rest.
> An umbrella is a manual for turning inside out. Skipping rope
> is a bridle for the invisible horses you ride through traffic.
> A playground is a board without instructions.[5]

Similar to Raine's poem, the human objects in Readman's poem are observed by the alien as peculiar and are afforded surprising descriptions or uses.

When clearing my filing cabinet, I found unwitting "autistic sensibility" poems I had written years before. There are two of particular interest: one from 2004 and one from 2018. The poem from 2004 has a narrator perplexed by the country she finds herself in—rather like Raine's martian and Readman's female alien. It was initially called "Foreign Language," and then "Foreign," for reasons that will become obvious. The full version of the 2004 draft is included below:

> We hear that people in other countries like
> to sit in groups and talk with their breath.
> We like the pulsing space between people.

---

[4] Craig Raine, "A Martian Sends a Postcard Home," *A Martian Sends a Postcard Home* (Oxford University Press, 1979), 9.
[5] Angela Readman, "The Female Alien's Dictionary," *Bunny Girls* (Nine Arches Press, 2022), 21.

I tell you this, for those places where people
talk with mouths and sound, must be so overwhelming. They look with eyes to lipread sounds

that might be missed, for example, when the weather
or music is loud. Our land is bright and colourful,
yet looking another in the eye is rude; most of our

communication is done through our feet. We look
down. For us, it is such a pleasure to see skirts ruffle
as we dance and sway. I have never seen a skirt lie

still except at a funeral.
So long as we keep dancing there will be music.

In this poem, I chose to elevate *physicality and movement* and downgrade verbal language as a form of communication. There is a comfort in dancing and feeling together with others who dance that is not the same as mental connection through sharing talk (verbal knowledge or personal histories). This is very close to my autistic viewpoint and love of dancing, which some might see as stim dancing. I can express this idea in prose, as I have just done, but I wanted to evoke it in a way that was closer to the experience, so I allowed for dance and movement to become a language. I felt when re-reading this poem that the poem knew of my autism before I was able to acknowledge it.

I recall being seen as "mature for her age" as a child, which might be an observation that a child communicates well with adults but not so well with children their own age. Some of my own traits that I value, and now attribute to my autism, are often criticized in girls or women: leadership qualities, being loud, opinionated, having the confidence and ability to interrupt a conversation or debate (assuming a male speaker to be holding forth). We can be persistent when faced with injustices and stubborn in our points of view.

My poem included above, formerly titled "Foreign," is now re-named "Not from Round Here," and has since been tweaked to alter the order of lines, to improve the rhythm, and it now has a different ending, one that challenges the reader with a question rather than remaining comfortably in its own world. This revised ending became possible because of my diagnosis:

My delicious land is colourful, and talking
is done through our feet. We all wear skirts,
and know that so long as we keep dancing
there will be music, and for me, it's such a pleasure
to see skirts ruffle. I've rarely seen a skirt lie

still. Here you do not dance, you sit in groups
and talk with shortened breaths.
When the weather sings its songs, how
do you hear one another? You must strain
so hard to lip-read between sips of rotted grain.

How do you cope?[6]

In both versions, I enjoyed the double-edge of the word "lie" and my feelings towards truth-telling and liars. Thus, it remained at the end of a line on a stanza break.

A further poem written prior to my diagnosis in 2018 had been written to capture the weird sprawling shape of a "late season foxglove" (the original title). A regular foxglove has a pillar-like shape with bell-like purple flowers that are larger at the bottom than the top. As time progresses, these flowers become seeds and then further stems sprout from the base of the plant. Very long stems may tip over, but once touching the ground, they will move against gravity into the sky once more. This creates the "hydra-headed" beast I describe.

In 2023, this poem had barely altered from its original draft, but I now recognized the poem as potentially describing *me*. Although I did not set out to create that, once I saw this, I changed the title to "Late Diagnosis: *superbus digitalis* (arrogant foxglove)," which suggests a metaphor or at least alternative meanings beneath the surface. The Latin and the arrogance came in for fun: the plant over-stretches itself and fancies itself very clever to grow so big. I made two other changes in January 2024: to the opening word, which had originally been "Days" to signify the passage of time; then to the penultimate line, which had held the word "desire." It is now "speech":

Words squeeze up my throats
force bee tongues skyward,

mauve above green stems.
I am King-of-the-Walk,

Jack-and-the-Beanstalk!
Till wind and rain topple

these thinning boom-arms,
and in that horizontal moment

bobbled seed-heads start to flicker,
rampant tips rear up,

---

[6]The poems of mine I discuss in this section will be included in my next collection, titled *I Sing the Body Autistic*.

speech

becomes hydra-headed, lurid and wild.

I prefer the match of "Words" against the flowerheads" "throats," and as the poem now leans into language and communication as subject matter, the word "speech" has more resonance at the end.

In terms of creating totally fresh work in response to knowing I am autistic, I will share a poem that was initially called "O brave new world that has such people in't." The early draft led with the following:

Puzzled by their strangeness, their kiss

chase and shrieking, I sit on a

bench with my best friend Darren

to show the other children I can kiss him

without palaver. I think that'll help them;

they'll see how pointless their running is, their squeals.

Puzzled, they run away from me.

Lightyears in the future, I wonder, what was

this state of observance I held? Certainly,

they all seemed strange to me.

Martian curiosity; I had a vocation

for estranging object and language.

"Kiss chase" is a game of chase whereby the person who is "on" has to kiss someone of the opposite sex on the cheek; the kiss-ee then becomes the chaser. When I describe the game of "kiss chase" to modern youngsters and their parents, they all think it *very* strange and objectionable. Of course, in the 1970s, most children went along with the herd instinct to play such games whilst I did not. I later cut this section from the poem as it too obviously brought the Martian angle into play (line 11). In terms of where the poem then went, the playground scene did not fit. Having ditched the original opening, I focused on atypical speaking and eventually re-named the poem "Glossolalia" (speaking in tongues):

I sometimes feel the need to speak,

then speak again the thing spoken

but a little more slant—Again! Again!

I wish to circle round, approach

leftfield, tweaking nuance as I go until

you scream at me *I understood the first time!*

but I don't think you did or do.

Colleagues talk in a meeting, and I speak
too long, too hard, off-key, offer unforeseen
punnery. Is it any wonder, then, when
wrangling words in conversation,
my concentration skips out, would rather
dance on its own at parties? Isn't this
the stance of so many poets? We circle, slant,
approximate, and it's OK.
Blessed are the differently social,
we are surprising and surprised.
Oh, wonder!
How many goodly creatures are there here!
How beauteous mankind is!
O brave new world, that has such people in't!

Such differences in communication, like the ones described in this poem, can cause a lot of pain for autistic people. It has been a relief for me to realize that some of the irritating things I do with speech are slightly beyond my control. An example can be found in the poem above; the line that reads "*I understood the first time!*" came from my irate partner. I have mostly thought of myself as a linguistically proficient person, who has succeeded at school and university, someone who can make a good argument or speak out in public, but I do know that I can go awry. I vividly recall excruciating embarrassment at committee meetings, where I have said a double entendre without realizing it. In other instances, I am speaking to someone about a brilliant idea, and suddenly I realize I have spoken for too long, lost track, and not made sense. At school, I was regularly called a chatterbox, and once a friend described me (ironically in a writing exercise) as being "verbal Lucozade,[7]" which I liked until it occurred to me that her first thought might have been "verbal diarrhea."

The title of this poem, "Glossolalia," means speaking in tongues and might be viewed as positive or negative depending on your viewpoint. As well as showing my verbal awkwardness, the poem presents the case that our autistic fixation on language and our desire to be accurate and find exactly the right word is also what makes us potentially fabulous poets.

III. My Autism Diagnosis and My Teaching: Before and After

I have taught at universities for fifteen years and in four locations. There are students that I have taught as far back as 2008 whom I now suspect may be neurodivergent.

---

[7]Lucozade is a British brand of soft drinks and energy drinks.

But as they did not disclose a diagnosis at the time, I will not discuss them here. I regret not speaking to them in a way that helped. All teachers "get it wrong" at times, I think.

I will offer two constructive examples of working with students who were cognitively atypical, one previously diagnosed, one not. In 2016–2017, I taught a female student, who had a diagnosis of autism that was sent to me at the start of the semester. She was "super-keen" and always put her hand up first to answer questions. She gave her answers at great length, and her longwinded discussions became an issue in the class, as I needed to hear from other students, who were getting impatient with her. So, I planned an intervention. I interrupted the student during one of her monologues and said, "It's really great to hear what you're saying and that's so interesting, but next time I ask a question I'd like to hear from somebody else. Is that okay?" To which she nodded.

Later, she asked for a meeting, and I was nervous because I thought she might want to take me to task over this intervention. However, she was delightful and wanted to talk about Boy George, Steve Strange, and the 1980s nightclub Blitz, which were integral to her script. She also said how much she was enjoying my approach to the module. We talked a little about her desire to answer questions quickly, and I admitted that I was like this as a student myself. (Note: I did not have a diagnosis in 2016.) In all, it was a very satisfactory encounter, and it shows that we can be direct with our autistic students, though another option is chatting with a student in private about their classroom behavior, if that's preferable.

In the autumn of 2022, I started to co-supervise a PhD student online. This student was experiencing ongoing mental health problems and had six months' leave in their first year of research. On their return, they explained that they were facing some issues with communication and were awaiting the results of an MRI scan. They disclosed that sometimes they couldn't process information and were unable to speak. I suggested via email that it might be helpful in that case to have a visual signal so that the co-supervisor and I knew that a verbal shutdown was happening. I know that if a person experiences something tricky in terms of social interaction, it is only made worse by the feeling that other people don't understand. In our supervision session, we agreed that if the student couldn't speak, they could raise their hand in front of their face, and the co-supervisor and I would back off and give them space. We also heard that the MRI scan had found nothing to indicate a physical cause for the verbal shutdowns, such as a brain tumor.

After careful consideration, I decided to raise the issue of cognitive difference as a possible explanation. I broached this topic by saying that I had found my autism diagnosis useful. I also praised some of the qualities I saw in the student which might relate to autistic qualities ("obsessive" commitment, keen observations, justice-seeking), and observed that I had not seen their mental health break coming. This suggested to me that neither the co-supervisor nor I were reading the student's emotional state well, and that, as this was something that had turned up on my autism report (the "coolness" I mentioned earlier), I wondered if they had considered that they might be autistic. The student was receptive and agreed that they could likely be neurodivergent in some way. My co-supervisor pointed out that if they were to have an assessment and diagnosis, then other forms of support at the university might be triggered. This positive interaction with a possibly autistic student rests upon my own comfort with my diagnosis and my lived experience with and knowledge of autism. Other educators may not feel comfortable broaching such topics with students, but they should be aware of forms of neurodivergence and common symptoms/traits, and they should refer students who could benefit to health and wellness services on campus.

One of the difficulties with teaching creative writing is that we often use pairs work or small group work to review writing, and this might not always be productive or easy for autistic students. However, students with autism are as likely or unlikely as neurotypical students to be talented writers, and like their neurotypical counterparts, they deserve to workshop and discuss their creative work and the work of their peers. It is also worth remembering that they can be very direct and that this might come across as rude, but if you stay calm, an understanding might be achieved. As an educator, don't forget your own directness can also be helpful in these situations.

Lastly, I want to discuss disclosure and the academic workplace. In 2020, I took to creating a short video to introduce myself and the module I was teaching, and from 2021, it became important for me to mention that I am queer, disabled, and autistic. I have done this self-identification during on-campus introductions since 2011, at least as far as queer was concerned, in order to support students who might share such identities. I think declaring oneself makes it easier for students who wish to write under-represented characters into their stories or poems. It also makes the business of identifying themselves easier should they wish to open up to me.

I gave up module teaching in 2023 for several reasons. In 2020, shifting to online teaching was a fast learning curve; however, not having to travel for work helped my chronic conditions stabilize. When the university required me back on campus, returning to the 150-minute train journey was too much. If I were back teaching on campus, I would still make those videos as I think they help allay the nerves of students who are anxious about joining a module with a new group of students and a new professor. Even if I weren't queer, disabled, and autistic, offering a "known" person to replace an "unknown" one is of assistance to many who experience anxiety, so I would recommend this, if your university allows for it. The other reason for my resignation from module teaching was a recognition of the massive stress I felt with certain aspects of university admin that were never going to change: perpetual IT upgrades, new systems often implemented with no thought as to when lecturers were marking, and copious "re-vamps" of policy to no real end. My autism diagnosis finally *gave me permission* to accept that I was unlikely to overcome the repeated stress these caused me. I also realized that I had anxiety made worse by these factors. Atypical of anxiety, I do not especially *feel* anxious in respect to worrying or mentally thinking bad thoughts, but my body exhibits poor health responses: dizziness, weakness, pain, and diarrhea. Therefore, I now take anti-anxiety medications, which are stabilizing in terms of avoiding sudden acute health crises. I highly suggest that other neurodivergent faculty and staff in academia face up to the things they find difficult, or even nearly impossible, and either work out accommodations or acknowledge the need to reduce hours or even leave duties, in order to deal with the fall-out and avoid autistic burn-out.

To conclude, I have found my diagnosis of autism to be useful. It has enabled me to reflect on my life and on my writing in different ways. I can see evidence of a Martian poetic tendency expressed by autistic poets including myself. I have been able to explore aspects of my childhood that I was previously embarrassed by or just took for granted. I believe being open about a diagnosis of autism is likely to encourage atypical students to be open about their viewpoint and needs. In addition, by being enthusiastic, thoughtful, compassionate, and creative, we may challenge some of the myths neurotypical students and academics have about neurodivergent writers, thinkers, or people more generally.

IV. Recommended Reading

The following is a list of additional literary books by autistic writers that address autism in some way, beyond the ones discussed in this essay. I hope these works find their way into the hands of impacted writers and onto creative writing and literature course syllabi, as visibility and representation are needed.

Poetry
- Jane Burns, *Be Feared* (Nine Arches Press, 2021).
- Kate Fox, *The Oscillations* (Nine Arches Press, 2021).
- Oz Hardwick, *My Life as a Time Traveller: a Memoir in 18 Discrete Fragments* (Hedgehog Poetry Press, 2023).
- Joanne Limburg, *The Autistic Alice* (Bloodaxe Books, 2017).

Children's and Teen Fiction
- Laura Guthrie, *Anna* (Gob Stopper, 2020).
- Rachael Lucas, *The State of Grace* (Macmillan, 2018).
- Elle McNichol, *A Kind of Spark* (Knights Of, 2020).
- Holly Smale, *Geek Girl* (HarperCollins, 2013).
- Marieke Nijkamp, ed. *Unbroken: 13 Stories Starring Disabled Teens* (Farrar, Straus, and Giroux, 2018).

Other Genres
- Lizzie Huxley-Jones, ed. *Stim: An Autistic Anthology* (Unbound, 2020).
- Joanne Limburg, *The Woman Who Thought Too Much: A Memoir* (Atlantic Books, 2010).

- Joanne Limburg, *Letters to My Weird Sisters: On Autism and Feminism* (Atlantic Books, 2022).
- Chris Packham, *Fingers in the Sparkle Jar* (Ebury Press, 2016).

Bibliography

Furfaro, Hannah. "Autistic Women Twice as Likely as Autistic Men to Attempt Suicide." *The Transmitter*. Simmons Foundation, August 7, 2019. https://www.spectrumnews.org/news/autistic-women-twice-as-likely-as-autistic-men-to-attempt-suicide/

Raine, Craig, *A Martian Sends a Postcard Home*. Oxford University Press, 1979.

Readman, Angela, *Bunny Girls*. Nine Arches Press, 2022.

Willgoss, Sue. "Suicide and Autism, a National Crisis." Royal College of Psychiatrists. Effective June 30, 2025. https://www.rcpsych.ac.uk/docs/default-source/improvingcare/nccmh/suicide-prevention/workshops-(wave-4)/wave-4-workshop-2/suicide-and-autism---slides.pdf?sfvrsn=bf3e0113_2

3 Why Write?: Reframing Personal Creative Writing Practice in the Light of Changing Diagnoses

OZ HARDWICK

There's an old neurodiverse joke:

Q: So, you're autistic—does that mean you take everything literally?
A: No, that's a kleptomaniac.

Aside from wittily engaging with the interface between the literal and the figurative—something which is at the heart of this essay—I cite the above joke because it introduces the broad undercurrent of uncertainty which will run beneath my discussion: in part, the uncertainty of interpretation; in part, the uncertainty of expression; and, at root, the uncertainty of what one is trying to express, and why. In turn, this discussion is consciously informed by an acknowledged undercurrent of personal uncertainty, as for much of my career as a writer, prior to a late diagnosis of autism, I struggled with the uncertainty of where and how—and, indeed, if—I fit in, in a "normal" world, the unspoken rules of which I found (and continue to find) largely baffling. Robert Chapman's description of undiagnosed autism resonates with my own experience and, I'm sure, that of many: "I did know I was different from those considered 'normal'. But I felt too much shame to explore what this difference might consist in.... At the time, the disposition of my experience was largely one of confusion, anxiety, and hopelessness."[1] While I'm aware that uncertainty may initially sound like rather shaky ground upon which to build a solid argument, it nonetheless may be an important aspect of thinking about the therapeutic value of creative writing.

With that in mind, I'd like to begin with what I expect is a broadly uncontentious assertion: writing is good for you. Along with other art forms, expressive writing has been shown in numerous studies to be effective in the mitigation of numerous health conditions, both psychological and physical.[2] Since the late twentieth century, interest in the therapeutic effects of writing has increased dramatically amongst both health

---

[1] Robert Chapman, *Empire of Normality: Neurodiversity and Capitalism* (Pluto Press, 2023), 2.
[2] Joanne Frattaroli, "Experimental Disclosure and Its Moderators: A Meta-Analysis," *Psychological Bulletin* 132, no. 2 (2006): 823–865, https://doi.org/10.1037/0033-2909.132.6.823. See also: *PTSD and the Arts: A Path to Healing Our Healers*, https://www.artsandmindlab.org/ptsd-and-the-arts-a-path-to-healing-our-healers/

professionals and the public,[3] and can be characterized in the words of Laura A. King, who notes that, "Two strong conclusions can be made with regard to the benefits of writing. First, expressive writing has health benefits. Second, no one really knows why."[4] That the extent of these benefits is variable—and indeed that there are on occasions no benefits at all—is well attested by the research,[5] and for me as a layperson, this makes it all the more fascinating and mysterious.

My interest is further piqued by specific personal reasons: in part because I am someone who habitually—some might say obsessively—writes every day; and in part because I am someone for whom writing has in the past been prescribed by a Mental Health professional, and for whom it was unsuccessful. In my early forties, as part of the treatment for a serious recurrence of what was diagnosed as severe depressive illness, I was recommended to keep a journal[6] and to free write at the same time every day, allowing for a fluid combination of creativity and self-exploration. As Karen K. Baikie and Kay Wilhelm have observed,

> The immediate impact of expressive writing is usually a short-term increase in distress, negative mood and physical symptoms, and a decrease in positive mood. . . . However, at longer-term follow-up, many studies have continued to find evidence of health benefits in terms of objectively observed outcomes, self-reported physical outcomes and self-reported emotional health outcomes.[7]

As it transpired in my case, however, while the short-term negative effects were as described, the longer-term benefits did not manifest themselves, and my situation deteriorated, necessitating a change of therapeutic tack. I subsequently kept writing, as I have done since childhood, fitting it around life's other demands as much as possible; but although as a poet I would sometimes address issues relating to my mental health, this was avowedly not undertaken in a therapeutic context.

In summer 2016, however, I returned to writing in a daily scheduled pattern, but this time as a participant in the Prose Poetry Project centered upon the International Poetry Studies Institute at the University of Canberra, which had been set up in 2014 to provide a network for stimulating cross-fertilization between writers in the form.[8] As

---

[3] A point observed by Stephen J. Lepore and Joshua M. Smyth in the introduction to their edited collection, *The Writing Cure: How Expressive Writing Promotes Health and Emotional Well-Being* (American Psychological Association, 2002), 1–2.
[4] Laura A. King, "Gain Without Pain? Expressive Writing and Self-Regulation," *The Writing Cure: How Expressive Writing Promotes Health and Emotional Well-Being*, eds. Stephen J. Lepore and Joshua M. Smyth (American Psychological Association, 2002), 119.
[5] Frattaroli, "Experimental Disclosure," 823–865.
[6] For a current study on this topic, see Monika Sohal et al.'s "Efficacy of Journaling in the Management of Mental Illness: A Systematic Review and Meta-Analysis," *Family Medicine and Community Health* 10, no. 1 (2022), https://fmch.bmj.com/content/10/1/e001154
[7] Karen K. Baikie and Kay Wilhelm, "Emotional and Physical Health Benefits of Expressive Writing," *Advances in Psychiatric Treatment* 11, no. 5 (2005): 339, https://doi.org/10.1192/apt.11.5.338
[8] On the foundation of the Prose Poetry Project and its aims, see Cassandra Atherton et al., "The Prose Poetry Project," *Axon: Creative Explorations*, Capsule 1 (2016), https://www.axonjournal.com.au/issues/c-1/prose-poetry-project

mentioned earlier, I am quite obsessive about my writing, and participating in the group allowed me free rein to focus upon and indulge this obsession. Since becoming involved with the project, I have written a first draft of at least one prose poem every day—usually first thing in the morning—each stimulated by a combination of drafts shared by other members of the group, along with half-formed daily plans, half-remembered dreams, radio chatter, hopes, concerns, and the countless mundane morning activities that have yet to shape themselves into precise coherence through the magic of coffee.[9] Many of these have been worth developing further, and a few hundred have become published poems, including in a number of chapbooks and a full collection, picking up a few awards and prizes along the way. This, however, is not the place to explore this side of the process, but it's significant here to stress that my daily writing is undertaken from a perspective which is diametrically opposite to the "private, for themselves" approach of therapeutic journaling,[10] and is, rather, the practice of a widely published writer constantly wishing to exercise themselves and become better in their chosen medium.

My chosen medium—or perhaps I should say the medium that chose me, as I recall gravitating toward aspects of the form before I was consciously aware that it was a form—is prose poetry, a mode of writing characterized by openness to multiple meanings and interpretations.[11] It's a form which embraces focus upon closely observed details, while gesturing to an at-best unresolved "big picture," which is very much how I personally perceive the world: I'm someone who is very precisely focused but who can become overwhelmed by too much information. In consequence of this, I have, more specifically, gravitated toward what has been characterized by others—I always feel a bit presumptuous making claims for myself—as neo-surrealist prose poetry.[12] And, again quoting others, these poems are "relentlessly thoughtful about the nature of time," and "play with time . . . with highly compelling, disconcerting results,"[13] to the extent that a recent review somewhat colorfully described me as "an Einstein of prose poetry, reconfiguring our understanding of time and space."[14] I am of course more than happy with these assessments, but what interests me here is how the work is perceived by attentive readers, as this is not at the front of my mind when writing. What I am seeking to do is simply to articulate my perception of a world which, as I'm acutely aware, is for me mostly

---

[9]I discuss my daily writing practice in Amina Alyal and Oz Hardwick, "Summoning Ghosts and Releasing Angels: Challenging the Tyranny of the Blank Page," *Writing in Practice* 6 (2020): 99–105.
[10]Baikie and Wilhelm, "Emotional and Physical Health Benefits," 343.
[11]Paul Hetherington and Cassandra Atherton, *Prose Poetry: An Introduction* (Princeton University Press, 2020), 79–82.
[12]Hetherington and Atherton, *Prose Poetry*, 125.
[13]Paul Munden, "Playing with Time: Prose Poetry and the Elastic Moment," *TEXT* 21, no. Special Issue 46 (2017), https://textjournal.scholasticahq.com/article/25810
[14]Hannah Stone, "Review: Oz Hardwick, *A Census of Preconceptions*," *The Lake* (September 2023), http://www.thelakepoetry.co.uk/reviews/sept23/

constructed from closely observed fragments of experience and oddments of language.

When I first read the interview with Russell Edson in which he described his compositional process as "looking for the shape of thought more than the particulars of the little narrative,"[15] it struck me as the perfect description of my own process. Some of my prose poems may suggest narrative, but that is never part of the impulse. Rather, the guiding compositional principles are rhythmic and metaphoric—this latter aspect in the sense that all language, by its very nature, is metaphoric. As Paul Hetherington and Cassandra Atherton put it, prose poems "are always trying to point to something about their language or their subject that sits outside of any narrative gestures they make (and frequently outside of the work itself)."[16] I shall return to the matter of metaphor (and, indeed, alliteration) shortly, but first I would like to say something about the thought to be shaped.

In a 2006 interview, Eavan Boland made a comment on what poetry does, which I think is worth quoting in full here:

> Where poetry excels is as a method of experience, not expression. It has a unique capacity to render an experience in a fresh, unsettling way. I don't write a poem to express an experience, but to experience it again. In a truly good poem the experience is alive, unfinished, set there by sound and meaning. What's so thrilling about that is that the reader can finish it out of their own experience. That's the real power of poetry.[17]

The thought which I seek to shape in everything I write—and sometimes I think I succeed, sometimes I don't—is the experience of its moment of becoming. It is both a perceptual moment and a linguistic moment which, both paradoxically and inevitably, is beyond the possibility of language to articulate with anything approaching accuracy, because there is way too much going on. My mode of perception can best be described by Murray, Lesser, and Lawson's term, *monotropic*; that is, characterized by intense attention and narrow focus, while simultaneously missing larger contexts or, indeed, the connections between discrete perceptions.[18] My impetus in writing, then, is to articulate this as precisely as I can, given the limitation of words, which thereby gives rise to the sort of imagistic and temporal juxtapositions which have been characterized by others as "surrealist." My prose poems, to paraphrase Boland's remarks above, seek to enact my experience, "alive [and] unfinished."

---

[15]Russell Edson, "Interview: The Art of the Prose Poem," *Truths, Falsehoods, and a Wee Bit of Honesty: A Short Primer on the Prose Poem with Selected Letters from Russell Edson*, ed. Peter Johnson (MadHat Press, 2020), 43.
[16]Hetherington and Atherton, *Prose Poetry*, 14.
[17]Eavan Boland and Pilar Villar, "'The Text of It': A Conversation with Eavan Boland," *New Hibernia Review / Iris Éireannach Nua* 10, no. 2 (2006): 64–65.
[18]Dinah Murray et al. "Attention, Monotropism and the Diagnostic Criteria for Autism," *Autism* 9, no. 2 (2005): 139–156.

I earlier mentioned an intervention for mental ill health in my early forties. It is something for which I had been treated on and off for most of my adult life, before which I had just been considered a very "withdrawn" or "odd" child and teenager who was of occasional concern to those around me. However, in my early sixties, I encountered an unexpected difficulty. As a Professor of Creative Writing, a poet, and a fluent writer and reader in many modes, I was perturbed to find myself struggling more and more with comprehension as my university required more online engagement. I still cannot fully describe the experience, but the words ceased to convey linguistic meaning. This provided the prompt for my GP (general practitioner) to refer me for assessment for autism, something which had occasionally been mentioned over the years, largely on account of my monotropic tendencies, social awkwardness, and environmental sensitivities, but which had previously been dismissed. Contrary to the popular trope of the computer "savant,"[19] my own neuroprocessing struggled with the intangibility of the transient digital environment.

In practical terms, the diagnosis facilitated access to the support necessary for me to undertake all aspects of my job. Beyond this, however, the new perspective it offered on every aspect of my life up to that point reframed decades of mental health issues. That uncertainty born of mismatch with the "normal" world, to which I referred in my opening paragraph was, if not eliminated, at least explained and ameliorated. The relationship between autism and assorted conditions, including bipolar disorder, with which I had been diagnosed at one point, is complex, but many perceptual and cognitive traits associated with autism—missing social cues, feelings of not belonging, mental exhaustion of "masking" practices, perfectionism, and so on—can render individuals more susceptible to depressive disorders and prone to prolonged duration and increased intensity of depression.[20] Recognizing and accepting my autism has begun to relieve the pressure—notably the pressure of masking to myself—at the root of past difficulties, and it has concomitantly afforded me a clearer understanding of my relationship with writing.

To begin to connect the discrete and diverse fragments, which I have this far gathered, I will observe that the daily writing practice which I have described— habitually crafting prose poems from the discrete and diverse fragments which make up my perception of the world—has, in contrast to that which my therapist prescribed twenty years ago, actually proved beneficial for my mental health. In order to explore why I think this may be the case, I would like to nuance my earlier claim about writing, and assert that poetry—both reading and writing thereof—is good for you, as demonstrated by many studies, even if there is still that same air of "we know it works but we don't know why" about it.[21] As Grace Brillantes-Evangelista notes, summarizing

---

[19] For an astute discussion of this association, see James McGrath's *Naming Adult Autism: Culture, Science, Identity* (Rowman and Littlefield, 2019), particularly pages 30–34.
[20] This is discussed in Tony Attwood, *The Complete Guide to Asperger's Syndrome*, rev. ed. (Jessica Kingsley, 2015), 152–155.
[21] For a brief overview of some recent studies, see Richard Sima, "More Than Words: Why Poetry Is Good for Our Health," *International Arts + Mind Lab*, March 11, 2021, https://www.artsandmindlab.org/more-than-words-why-poetry-is-good-for-our-health/

the work of Nicholas Mazza on poetry therapy, one beneficial aspect of engaging with poetry is that:

> metaphors embedded in poetry also serve as symbolic representations of the clients' thoughts, emotions, actions, and beliefs, which are explored by both the clients themselves and the therapist. These metaphors allow the clients to convey their inner realities to the therapist and to understand themselves better.[22]

This is interesting in terms of the therapeutic. However, it seems to me that this rather limits the appreciation of metaphor and, indeed, poetry. And this brings me back to my opening joke.

There is a common assumption that people with autistic spectrum disorder (ASD) have difficulties with figurative language[23] and take things literally. However, a 2014 study by Anat Kasirer and Nira Mashal recorded no difference in the comprehension of metaphors between adults with ASD and those from a typically developing (TD) group. The findings of this study reveal that "adults with ASD outperformed age-matched TD peers in metaphor generation" and that an "inspection of the type of metaphors generated indicated that the ASD group produced more original and creative metaphors than did the TD group."[24] The authors concluded that the study "points to unique verbal creativity in ASD which has not been studied in this way before."[25]

I can only speak for myself, but I have always had a tendency to take language at face value, which brought about a certain amount of teasing in childhood and can still on occasions leave me unexpectedly at sea in conversations to this day. However, over the years, this has evolved from pure inconvenience into a delight in taking misreadings to their logical extremes, beginning with puns and developing into more complex wordplay. This has always been coupled with what, in hindsight, I may characterize as an instinctive structuralist approach to the world, which in equal parts frets over and plays with the divide between language and that which it strives to represent, describe, and articulate. Don Paterson's observation that "Poets' brains have a wiring error that makes them think words are real things" rings almost true to me: *almost* in the sense that words *are* real things.[26] This, in turn, has facilitated enormous freedom in my approach to metaphor, in which language can be said

---

[22] Grace Brillantes-Evangelista, "An Evaluation of Visual Arts and Poetry as Therapeutic Interventions with Abused Adolescents," *The Arts in Psychotherapy* 40, no. 1 (2013): 74, https://doi.org/10.1016/j.aip.2012.11.005

[23] I acknowledge that, though still common, the term is losing currency on account of the problematic connotations of "disorder." However, I use the term in this instance as it is employed in the 2014 study discussed.

[24] Anat Kasirer and Nira Mashal, "Verbal Creativity in Autism: Comprehension and Generation of Metaphoric Language in High-Functioning Autism Spectrum Disorder and Typical Development," *Frontiers in Human Neuroscience* 8 (2014), https://doi.org/10.3389/fnhum.2014.00615

[25] Ibid.

[26] Don Paterson, *Toy Fights: A Boyhood* (Faber and Faber, 2023), 1.

almost to precede understanding; consequently, rather than simply acting as a figurative articulation of a given referent, language for me acts as a stepping-off point for further exploration. By way of illustration, I offer my prose poem "Painting by Numbers" as an example:

> When I close my eyes, everything is that colour between Sunday night and Monday morning, when the sacred has been left behind and the ink and oil of the city are already staining my fingertips. It's the colour of all those thoughts that come and go as I'm brushing my teeth or falling into my usual seat on the early train. It's the colour of all the voices that tell me I'm wrong, that I need to change. When I open my eyes, the day ahead is paint-by-numbers, with a neat 9 in every identical square. I dip the brush into the corner of my eye and paint each square in order, careful not to cross the lines. I consider number 9 in the context of John Lennon's oeuvre, emergency services, and German pronunciation; and I wonder what my grandmother—who could ward off door-to-door evangelists with her perfect recall of biblical minutiae—knows of divine completeness now that she rests in the presence of her Lord. By the time I finish, it is dark, I don't know what day it is, and I can't decide whether my eyes are open or closed.[27]

In this poem, the assertion that "the day ahead is paint-by-numbers" is expanded by the observation that it has "a neat 9 in every identical square." This can be explored in terms of what it might mean about predictability and drab uniformity, but instead, "I dip the brush into the corner of my eye and paint each square in order, careful not to cross the lines," before metaphorically crossing the lines in order to draw in references to pop culture, the emergency services, the play of homophones, and an apparently random recollection of my maternal grandmother—part of the three generations amongst whom I lived in a small terraced house until, when I was fourteen, she became the first person close to me to die. All these associations come rushing in, in search of a pattern of language in which to settle. And it is this aspect of pattern to which I find I gravitate, more than a concern with linear sense. It is, for me, where the sometimes contentious division between prose poetry and flash fiction stands[28]: even an implied narrative dimension—the example given above, for instance, offers a sequence of actions and thoughts—is purely an adjunct of the patterning of language and its associations.

Evidence points to an inherent response to rhythmic patterns, even in newborns,[29] which persists into adulthood and accounts in no small part for poetry's emotional

---

[27]Oz Hardwick, *My Life as a Time Traveller: A Memoir in 18 Discrete Fragments* (Hedgehog Poetry Press, 2023), 21.

[28]See Perazzo and Dal, who make the useful distinction between writing a "story" and writing a "moment": Cathryn Perazzo and Sif Dal, "Flash Fiction, Prose Poetry and Ambiguity: The Distinction Between Flash Fiction and Prose Poetry on Ambiguous Terms," *TEXT* 21, no. Special Issue 46 (2017), http://www.textjournal.com.au/speciss/issue46/Perazzo&Dal.pdf

[29]Emma Suppanen et al., "Rhythmic Structure Facilitates Learning from Auditory Input in Newborn Infants," *Infant Behavior and Development* 57 (2019), https://doi.org/10.1016/j.infbeh.2019.101346

impact.[30] While acknowledging this as a feature of poetry, Hanne De Jaegher's insights into the ways in which autistic individuals perceive the world add a further perspective:

> An often-ignored factor in perception is the aesthetic element. There may be a value to some autistic sense-making which is simply that of enjoying or remarking on patterns—patterns in space, in ideas, in numbers, in size, in time. Rich patterns exist everywhere in the world, and many autistic people value them, care about them, even enjoy them. This makes ignoring the pattern or the detail doubly difficult. People with autism not only do not initially or without prompt or necessity perceive holistic meaning, but they may feel that they will lose something salient if they (are made to) try to capture the gist of something.[31]

This is not to suggest that the subject of a poem is insignificant to me—far from it. Rather, though, I trust patterns and the associative meanings of individual words—many of which carry their own inherent ambiguities and contradictions—to reveal their own relation to the subject in the process of writing. This is, of course, a characteristic of all poetry to some extent, but my own practice over the years has come to focus solely—and, I confess, somewhat obsessively—on this aspect, a significant element of my own personal attempt at "sense-making" in a world which I find consistently overwhelming, in terms of detail and movement, both physical and temporal.

To return to the earlier observation of my work being "relentlessly thoughtful about the nature of time . . . with highly compelling, disconcerting results,"[32] my poetic practice is likewise an attempt to make sense of—or at least to articulate—the irregular and non-linear way in which I experience time. Lorna Wing has noted that in autistic individuals, the "problems with time are not related to telling time by the clock. . . . The difficulties lie in comprehending the passage of time and linking it with ongoing activities."[33] For me, time tends to fall under the broad categories of *now*, *recent*, and *a long time ago*, yet even these distinctions can—and frequently do—break down. What is important here is that my "neo-surreal" prose poetry offers a space in which I can embody, rather than describe, my experience of the world, using that neat, contained box of the form to briefly hold what I can best describe as the *all-too-much*ness of, to borrow a recent film title, *Everything-Everywhere-All-at-Once*[34] before it disperses into the chaos. The making of the poem, then, is a focused, developed manifestation of that aesthetic pleasure which De Jaegher notes in autistic

---

[30]Sima, "More Than Words."
[31]Hanne De Jaegher, "Embodiment and Sense-Making in Autism," *Frontiers in Integrative Neuroscience* 7, no. 15 (2013), https://doi.org/10.3389/fnint.2013.00015
[32]Munden, "Playing with Time."
[33]Lorna Wing, *The Autistic Spectrum: A Guide for Parents and Professionals*, 2nd ed. (Robinson, 2021), 88.
[34]*Everything Everywhere All at Once* is a film released in 2022. It was written and directed by Daniel Kwan and Daniel Scheinert.

individuals can include "patterns in space, in ideas, in numbers, in size, in time."[35] This is, however, something I have only recognized in retrospect, and my daily writing regime began, as I have noted, in a very different mindset from that of my unsuccessful brush with therapeutic writing.

Why this should be is, I think, both simple and complex. The process is, after all, much the same: get up, write about whatever comes to me, and see where it leads. The only difference is that one was called a therapeutic exercise, the other participation in a creative community. This simple matter of naming perhaps wouldn't matter to most people, who would just get on with it, whatever. However, try as I might, I can never shake the literalness of these designations. By simply calling an activity "therapy," I could not get beyond the focus on my health. To riff on the joke with which I began:

Q: So, you're writing for therapy—does that mean you're ill?
A: Yes.

Whereas in poetry therapy, as noted earlier, "metaphors . . . serve as symbolic representations of the clients' thoughts, emotions, actions, and beliefs, which . . . allow the clients to convey their inner realities to the therapist and to understand themselves better,"[36] my own use of metaphor promotes the aesthetic. Yes, my prose poetry expresses, even embodies, my "inner realities," and in doing so, however "surreal" it may appear to others, it expresses, to the best of my ability—and in that imperfect medium of language—"outer reality." And it is not analysis and discussion of "thoughts, emotions, actions, and beliefs"[37] which proves therapeutic. Rather, to return to Brillantes-Evangelista's observations, it is "simply . . . enjoying or remarking on patterns—patterns in space, in ideas, in numbers, in size, in time," and giving myself up to these patterns with no demand to "try to capture the gist of [any]thing."[38]

As an autistic individual, I am often uncertain of my interpretation of events and of language. As a writer, I am acutely aware of the uncertainty which is an inevitable part of all linguistic expression. As an autistic writer—and though I speak solely to my own experience, I doubt that I am unique in this—I simply try to express the moment in what seems to me the most effective manner. And why? Because, in the act of writing, the chaos briefly makes some kind of sense; and just being allowed to make this happen, without further expectations beyond aesthetic satisfaction, can for some of us be the most health-enhancing creative act possible.

Bibliography

Alyal, Amina, and Oz Hardwick. "Summoning Ghosts and Releasing Angels: Challenging the Tyranny of the Blank Page." *Writing in Practice* 6 (2020): 99–105.

---

[35] De Jaegher, "Embodiment and Sense-Making."
[36] Brillantes-Evangelista, "An Evaluation of Visual Arts and Poetry," 74.
[37] Ibid.
[38] De Jaegher, "Embodiment and Sense-Making."

Atherton, Cassandra, Owen Bullock, Jen Crawford, Paul Munden, Shane Strange, and Jen Webb. "The Prose Poetry Project." *Axon: Creative Explorations*, Capsule 1 (2016). https://www.axonjournal.com.au/issues/c-1/prose-poetry-project

Attwood, Tony. *The Complete Guide to Asperger's Syndrome*, rev. ed. Jessica Kingsley, 2015.

Baikie, Karen K., and Kay Wilhelm. "Emotional and Physical Health Benefits of Expressive Writing," *Advances in Psychiatric Treatment* 11, no. 5 (2005): 338–346. https://doi.org/10.1192/apt.11.5.338

Boland, Eavan, and Pilar Villar. "'The Text of It': A Conversation with Eavan Boland." *New Hibernia Review / Iris Éireannach Nua* 10, no. 2 (2006): 52–67.

Brillantes-Evangelista, Grace. "An Evaluation of Visual Arts and Poetry as Therapeutic Interventions with Abused Adolescents." *The Arts in Psychotherapy* 40, no. 1 (2013): 71–84. https://doi.org/10.1016/j.aip.2012.11.005

Chapman, Robert. *Empire of Normality: Neurodiversity and Capitalism*. Pluto Press, 2023.

De Jaegher, Hanne. "Embodiment and Sense-Making in Autism." *Frontiers in Integrative Neuroscience* 7, no 15. (2013). https://doi.org/10.3389/fnint.2013.00015

Edson, Russell. "Interview: The Art of the Prose Poem. Russell Edson." *Truths, Falsehoods, and a Wee Bit of Honesty: A Short Primer on the Prose Poem with Selected Letters from Russell Edson*. Edited by Peter Johnson. MadHat Press, 2020.

Frattaroli, Joanne. "Experimental Disclosure and its Moderators: A Meta-Analysis," *Psychological Bulletin* 132, no. 2 (2006): 823–865, https://doi.org/10.1037/0033-2909.132.6.823

Hardwick, Oz. *My Life as a Time Traveller: A Memoir in 18 Discrete Fragments*. Hedgehog Poetry Press, 2023.

Hetherington, Paul, and Cassandra Atherton. *Prose Poetry: An Introduction*. Princeton University Press, 2020.

Kasirer, Anat, and Nira Mashal. "Verbal Creativity in Autism: Comprehension and Generation of Metaphoric Language in High-Functioning Autism Spectrum Disorder and Typical Development." *Frontiers in Human Neuroscience* 8 (2014). https://doi.org/10.3389/fnhum.2014.00615

King, Laura A. "Gain Without Pain? Expressive Writing and Self-Regulation." *The Writing Cure: How Expressive Writing Promotes Health and Emotional Well-Being*. Edited by Stephen J. Lepore and Joshua M. Smyth. American Psychological Association, 2002.

Lepore, Stephen J., and Joshua M. Smyth, eds. *The Writing Cure: How Expressive Writing Promotes Health and Emotional Well-Being*. American Psychological Association, 2002.

McGrath, James. *Naming Adult Autism: Culture, Science, Identity*. Rowman and Littlefield, 2019.

Munden, Paul. "Playing with Time: Prose Poetry and the Elastic Moment." *TEXT* 21, no. Special Issue 46 (2017). https://textjournal.scholasticahq.com/article/25810

Murray, Dinah, Mike Lesser, and Wendy Lawson. "Attention, Monotropism and the Diagnostic Criteria for Autism." *Autism* 9, no. 2 (2005): 139–156.

Paterson, Don. *Toy Fights: A Boyhood*. Faber and Faber, 2023.

Perazzo, Cathryn, and Sif Dal. "Flash Fiction, Prose Poetry and Ambiguity: The Distinction Between Flash Fiction and Prose Poetry on Ambiguous Terms." *TEXT* 21, no. Special Issue 46 (2017). http://www.textjournal.com.au/speciss/issue46/Perazzo&Dal.pdf

Sima, Richard. "More Than Words: Why Poetry Is Good for Our Health." *International Arts + Mind Lab*, March 11, 2021. https://www.artsandmindlab.org/more-than-words-why-poetry-is-good-for-our-health/

Sohal, Monika, Pavneet Singh, Bhupinder Singh Dhillon, and Harbir Singh Gill. "Efficacy of Journaling in the Management of Mental Illness: A Systematic Review and Meta-Analysis." *Family Medicine and Community Health* 10, no. 1 (2022). https://fmch.bmj.com/content/10/1/e001154

Stone, Hannah. "Review: Oz Hardwick, *A Census of Preconceptions*." *The Lake* (September 2023). http://www.thelakepoetry.co.uk/reviews/sept23/

Suppanen, Emma, Minna Huotilainen, and Sari Ylinen. "Rhythmic Structure Facilitates Learning from Auditory Input in Newborn Infants." *Infant Behavior and Development* 57 (2019). https://doi.org/10.1016/j.infbeh.2019.101346

Wing, Lorna. *The Autistic Spectrum: A Guide for Parents and Professionals*, 2nd ed. Robinson, 2021.

4 "Me Here—You There":[1] Writing Contrast without a Self

K. IVER

Trigger Warning: this chapter briefly mentions suicidality rates among writers.

I write because life is claustrophobic. No to-do list, scheduling, or organizational hack can offer the order my brain lacks. Endless attempts at controlling the entropy thrown at me might lend structure to my external world, but the interior needs a different kind of sorting, editing, rearrangement. I'm writing this essay having just read a neuropsych testing report that confirmed why my brain has fifty tabs open instead of one: ADHD. Below were some comorbidities: PTSD with dissociative traits, alcohol use disorder in remission. A bigger, scarier diagnosis headlined all of them, one the clinician found "more pressing." For me, it's reality altering. A reason for writing underneath reason No. 1.

The testing began in May with a two-hour virtual interview. Mr. C, a medication provider, thought I had too many diagnoses and wanted clarity. He suspected something neurodevelopmental—autism and/or ADHD—and PTSD. I was hopeful that a testing clinician trained in data analysis would simplify my chart. She introduced herself as Dr. F. From the screen, she looked tiny, was white, had dirty blonde hair and high vocals. Her accessories: pearl earrings and a fern neck tattoo. New to New England, I wondered if she was what people meant by *WASP*, updated for 2024. My hope deflated a little, but I checked my assumptions, remained open.

At the end of the interview, she said, "I'm not going to lie, you're a bit of a complex case, but I like a challenge." A young part of me, one that survived on stories of specialness, inflated. The testing had to wait until August. Under a painfully bright overhead—no contrast in sight—I delivered word associations, arranged blocks diamonded by red and white, drew an abstract shape from memory. After the cognitive portion, Dr. F asked a series of questions beginning with, "Do you feel real?"

Too often I interrogate language, a word's nearness to the elements, what anyone intends to translate of their experience. During the vocab portion, Dr. F repeatedly

---

[1] The first part of the title comes from Mary Ruefle's lecture titled "Poetry and the Moon" from her collection of lectures titled *Madness, Rack, and Honey: Collected Lectures* (Wave Books, 2012).

asked me to say more words whose definitions I'd distilled too much. But when asked "Do you feel real?" I was surprised at the certainty filling and leaving my mouth:

"I do not."
"Do you feel empty?"
"Yes."
"Do you feel real?"
"No."
"Do your surroundings feel real?"
I paused. *"Sometimes."*
"Do you feel real?"
"I don't."

A history of my critical decisions began montaging from the hippocampus as I walked to the car. Even without a diagnosis, this news clarified every lens of my life. "No wonder," I said to the parking lot, to memories, to versions of self I'd rather forget—a plot twist for the memoir I'm writing about desire, addiction, and recovery.

How does one inhabit realness?

I wake up daily with the sensation of floating. Meditating with eyes closed defeats the purpose. What invites me to presence, to gravity: a small candle stick that burns for twenty minutes. I turn off the lights, so the flame's edges have definition. The air around the flame feeds it, lends some light, but they both present themselves as light and darkness, heat and less heat, here and above. The small ceramic cradle a reminder of the wood planks holding my body up, my own bones holding my body up. I cannot soften, become aware of what's tender in my body, without attention to its scaffolding. When the flame reaches its last bit of wick, I am watching closely, my eyeball level with the tiny triangle that now looks the way mountains are illustrated: blue with a defined snow peak. This is the tension from which I write.

Mary Ruefle describes the moon as "the first study in contrasts. Me here—you there."[2] I've long been drawn to high-contrast art, easy-to-access geometry, a fairytale's illustrative rendering of the powerful and the underdog. Robert Frost's description of poetry as "a momentary stay against the confusion of the world"[3] discloses that clarity, for him, is rare. If I go too long without writing in poetic form, I ask the world too many journalistic questions, never getting a satisfying response. I need poetry for the same reason Wordsworth did as he watched industrialization's rise, concluding "the world is too much with us."[4]

In writing, music, and art, contrast uses one subject to illuminate another: a shape, color, texture, sound, mood, personality, a position of power. By contrast, I don't

---

[2]Mary Ruefle, "Poetry and the Moon," *Madness, Rack, and Honey: Collected Lectures* (Wave Books, 2012), 15.
[3]Robert Frost, "The Figure a Poem Makes." *Collected Poems of Robert Frost* (Henry Holt and Company, 1939).
[4]William Wordsworth. "The World Is Too Much with Us." *Poems, in Two Volumes,* 1807. Reprint, The Poetry Foundation, https://www.poetryfoundation.org/poems/45564/theworld-is-too-much-with-us

necessarily mean the tension of opposites or a perceived binary, though they are better prompts for beginning a poem than perceived singularity. Sometimes, to see navy, one needs nearness to black. A linocut's two-ness of color, often black and white, can lend a surprising and complex depth and scale depending on the artist's willingness to cut and keep cutting. I am cutting through two-ness while writing this essay, through my first, most enduring contrast.

Some poems use the image, description, sound, metaphor, persona to hide, to lock away a speaker's vulnerability. They take Dickinson's "tell it slant" as a pass on telling the truth at all. I'm most moved by poetry that refuses empty décor so that the reader can confront real emptiness. When an author promotes their work as refusing a trope, a dominant ideology, a corrupt ethics, I'm left wondering what they're embracing. Safwan Dahoul has been painting feminized figures in shades of black and white for decades in what he calls *The Dream Series*. A Syrian refugee, Dahoul forgoes detailed depictions of violence or comfort. What he embraces: a sharp and striking relationship between body and negative space. Years ago, I asked him about his work's engagement with the visual traditions of ancient Egypt. He answered "Perhaps what's more important for me in Pharaonic art is the integration of form and emptiness, which is often the foundation of my work."[5]

Not fullness and emptiness but form and emptiness.

Likewise, Kathleen Pierce's poem "First Lines" uses two-ness to illuminate, then deepen. The first line is the only one of two sentences: "He opens her. She can't have him."[6] A period separates them. Both sentences begin with the pronoun of one and end with the other, the perceived masculine and feminine. The rest of the way, the sentences join but the phrases "He opens her" and "She can't have him" stay intact. The present tense is fixed while the story combusts. "He," the opener, and "She," the can't-haver, take turns beginning each line so the visual and sonic affect is like an argument or a tango thats movements are dramatic enough to keep me watching. The links between the two phrases—"but," "because," "until," "while," "regretful,"—layer the movement with complexity, a bit of softness. This makes the line "She can't have him while he opens her" devastate when it reappears as the only repeating sentence, the final one.

Me here—you there. Appear, reappear.

Dr. F went on vacation for a month before our feedback session. During that time, I wrote into realness as much as possible, drafting an essay about an event as it was unfolding—a break in decades-old patterning. While writing prose, extending thoughts across six and half inches, I missed the shell a poem provides. Now, I was writing the whole beach. It takes a different kind of patience, one that can meet

---

[5]Safwan Dahoul, "Form and Emptiness: An Interview with Safwan Dahoul," interview by K. Iver, *Southeast Review* 38, no 1, https://www.southeastreview.org/single-post/an-interview-with-safwan-dahoul

[6]Kathleen Pierce, "First Lines," *The Oval Hour* (University of Iowa Press, 1999), 47.

overwhelm. How can contrast reside in prose? Beginning with too-muchness? Perhaps by bringing in a third thing.

During the feedback session online, Dr. F named what was pressing: "This is at the level of personality." The "this" didn't meet enough criteria for any personality disorder listed in the DSM (*Diagnostic and Statistical Manual of Mental Disorders*), but there were enough traits for a diagnosis of personality disorder not otherwise specified (PD-NOS), namely traits of dependency: "You had trouble letting reality in when you were a teenager and in your twenties . . . you spent a lot of energy seeking information and help . . . you're able to self-reflect but these traits rise to the level." We didn't have much time left. We'd spent much of it reviewing the cognitive results.

When the written report arrived, I read the interview portion conducted five months prior. There was misinformation that felt critical and a chronology of behavior off by decades. The report pointed to severe childhood trauma as a cause and noted a gap in research for transgendered people. Despite the flawed history of the diagnostic model and the many people it's failed, the text names what no one else has in my forty-two years: "a markedly disintegrated sense of self." How this condition looks in action: "They likely put themselves in situations that confirm their belief that they are damaged and worthless . . . may be unable to access a stable, internal sense of their identity and look to others for direction or information about the world."

The memory of Dr. F's initial comments—*you're a bit of a complex case, but I like a challenge*—began to sting. I thought about personhood, shifted my attention from hurt to the contrast I am now writing and living: not self and other but self and no-self.

Poets have a high rate of suicidality compared with people of other professions. In fact, Tawa's article[7] on this topic discusses a study by Stirman and Pennebaker[8] that found that a poet's abundance of the first-person singular pronoun matches their risk of suicide. The conclusion: language can predict suicidality, and self-referential thought is both a symptom and cause of suffering. This study used John Berryman's work as an example. Louise Glück complicates Berryman's "I" in her craft essay titled "Disruption, Hesitation, Silence" by asserting its instability: "The problem of *The Dream Songs*, the drama of the poems, is an absence of a firm self . . . The proliferating selves dramatize, they do not disguise, this absence."[9] A poem's voice, to me, is not unlike a figure drawing's torso. I modeled for a college class during my twenties. The professor had artists draw nothing but the torso for a month because that's where the distinction of life, of self, is. A roomful of people created representations of my distinction during its most chaotic years, when my behavior was most indicative of a markedly disintegrated sense of self. The professor didn't like some of them. "Too centered," he said behind one student's shoulder. I now read poems in search

---

[7] Renee Tawa. "Scanning Literary Verse for Literal Clues to Suicides." *Los Angeles Times* (August 27, 2001), https://www.latimes.com/archives/la-xpm-2001-aug-27-cl-38798-story.html
[8] Shannon Wiltsey Stirman and James W. Pennebaker, "Word Use in the Poetry of Suicidal and Nonsuicidal Poets," *Psychosomatic Medicine* 63, no. 4 (July 2001): https://doi.org/10.1097/00006842-200107000-00001
[9] Louise Glück, "Disruption, Hesitation, Silence," *American Poetry Review* 22, no. 5 (1993): 31.

of a living torso and teach toward uncovering a voice rather than building one. Who's here, outside one's beauty, likeability, skill as a writer, a sad narrative? What's left from the shedding? That's voice. Glück describes Berryman's voice as "fractured."[10] As a survivor of an attempt, I'm curious if a suicidal writer's repeated "I" points to a search for one, conscious or unconscious, rather than fixation with self.

Stirman and Pennebaker's study, mentioned earlier in this essay, includes a discussion of Sylvia Plath's work.[11] Her poem "The Moon and the Yew Tree" was my first encounter with contrast on the page. Right away I was struck by Plath's tangibility of hereness and thereness, how immersively 3D the twenty-eight lines were. The title's phallic and round shapes both guard and welcome into the "cold and planetary," the repeated "blue," and occasional "black."[12] Each solid form has an edge shimmering with "the light of the mind."[13] Plath accommodates the reader who doesn't have immediate knowledge of a yew tree's evergreen, flattened needles with simple syntax: "The Yew Tree points up. It has a gothic shape. The eyes lift after it and find the moon."[14] She accommodates, then surprises by characterizing the moon as a mother, unruly in her intensity and appearance, careless in her treatment of others.

I was in my early twenties when introduced to this poem, the world and my place in it terrifying. I needed to hear someone say of her own mind "I simply cannot see where there is to get to" and "I have fallen a long way,"[15] even as her images appear findable. Not only could I touch Plath's world, I felt real in it, my body both porous and fully edged.

Who's present when writing? If they're hard to find, below is a list of thresholds, corners to begin searching:

here / there	light / dark	straight / non-linear	grief / joy
round / pointed	soft / hard	fear / want	away / close
cruelty / kindness	ancient / future	outside / inside	skin / internal organ
beginning / end	madness / sanity	art / science	alone / together
funeral / wedding	clothed / naked	victim / aggressor	meaningful / meaningless
open / closed	center / side	beauty / ugliness	speech / silence
work / play	illness / health	real / fake	acceleration / slowness

[10] Ibid.
[11] Stirman and Pennebaker, "Word Use."
[12] Sylvia Plath, "The Moon and the Yew Tree," *The Restored Edition: A Facsimile of Plath's Manuscript, Reinstating Her Original Selection and Arrangement* (Harper Perennial, 2004), 65.
[13] Ibid.
[14] Ibid.
[15] Plath, "The Moon and the Yew Tree," 65.

attachment / detachment	human / animal	shattered / whole	self / other
control / surrender	rise / fall	fight / accept	water / land
sensory / abstract	asleep / awake	feminine / masculine	help / hurt
vulnerability / strength	famous / unknown	numb / raw	binary / spectrum
contrast / singularity	rooted / free	pain / boredom	sitting / lying / standing

I recently heard someone say that because energy is neither created nor destroyed; there's only rebirth. The yoga sutra teaches that the sensory world is comprised of opposites. Our challenge is to see the consciousness that underlies them both. There's pleasure in splitting one's experience in two and a deeper, more sustainable pleasure in complicating the twos. Not emptiness and fullness but form and emptiness. Schopenhauer's contribution upsets the pleasure/pain binary with the argument that "life swings like a pendulum backward and forward between pain and ennui (boredom)."[16] A pendulum means no in-between, only swinging. His solutions are to become monkish—a lifestyle few of us will embrace—or be exposed to art and create. Reading and learning will also ease suffering.

Developing minds learn about their worlds using the sorting of opposites. In his book *The Inner World of Trauma*, Donald Kalsched theorizes that if withdrawal from a traumatic experience isn't possible for an infant or child, the experience remains unprocessed: the psyche must split into parts whose purpose is to protect the self. According to Kalsched, a "diabolical" part will sabotage efforts toward stability, will safeguard the psyche from prolonged positive feelings and drive it toward fantasy—which Kalsched distinguishes from imagination—and addictions. According to Kalsched, patients with these "daimons," which takes its meaning from "divide" or "lacerate," will improve, then plateau, then regress unless the daimon is transformed.[17]

Vievee Francis' poem "I've Been Thinking About Love Again" clarifies presence, splits it, sorts it, then complicates it.[18] I always know where I am, what she wants me to see, until the very end. Francis rouses curiosity with a conversational title and a two-kinds-of-people opener. The split of predator and prey, talon and fur, snow and cardinal, is striking enough to hold the eye. That lucidity dissolves suddenly with the last line: the speaker is certain which animal she is but will not tell us—a profound and disorienting split. It's tempting to wonder if she's eagle or rabbit. What this poem invites me to accept is my own bothness: the need to get and give. It's a tough

---

[16]Arthur Schopenhauer, *The World as Will and Idea* (London: Kegan Paul, Trench, Trübner & Co., 1909), 402.
[17]Donald Kalsched, *The Inner World of Trauma: The Archetypal Defenses of the Personal Spirit* (Routledge, 1996), 13.
[18]Vievee Francis, "I've Been Thinking About Love Again," *Poetry Daily* (May 20, 2022): https://poems.com/poem/ive-been-thinking-about-love-again/

universe, wandering out without awareness of my capacity to take and be taken will make it unnecessarily tougher.

A cloudless noon sun provides no contrast. Under it, I don't see shadow or definition, much less a focal point. It fades a maple's leaves at their greenest and renders them edgeless. Neurodivergent life, at worst, can feel this way. Can leave a metaphorical eye simultaneously wanting more and less, and in search of relief. Under clouds, however, a spring forest brightens. During and after rain, its texture glistens with the palpable. A poem can have such an effect. It can clarify what's here and vary its tone with dusk-like softness. A setting sun powders the view, rewarding the viewer for their day of attention with an in-between.

A tension: a clinical psychologist interviewed and tested me for ten eight hours all together, revealed something I could not see before: my defenses would not allow it. Others have warned against overidentifying with a diagnosis. Some loved ones expressed anger toward Dr. F, insisted she misunderstood me, rejected her report. My sober friends point out that maladaptive perception and behavior is part of the addict's personality, and I'm in recovery programs that require both rigorous confrontation of these traits and daily practice of their opposites. This diagnosis, according to them, is not useful. "You *are* what you *do*," my friend Erin says. When I bring it up, she routinely says, "Oh yeah, the personality disorder you don't have?" My addictions formed very early in life when they were low stakes: to fantasy, television, sugar, attention. One could say I formed a personality around them. While I now make decisions rather than being along for the ride of my desires, I felt as if Dr. F could see my insides. I've never been more independent than today. But, during certain hours, I can still *feel* dependent, unreal, as if no one's here. Written down, the traits are both lookable and glaring. My writing practice depends on a willingness to be vulnerable. I'm unsure how to draft from clarity's shock after so long of using language to turn on the lights. The contrast between light and light? A noon sun upside down?

A few years ago, I sent "The Moon and the Yew Tree" to Kaitlin, a friend twelve years my junior. Kaitlin was navigating a youth like mine, and we were both recovering from emotional orphanhood, both trying to build a logic where there was none, both about to make life-altering decisions. She memorized the poem before our backpacking trip in which everything that could go wrong went disastrous. The water sources dried up. Bees found us threatening. Our own decisions hurt us. Kaitlin was convinced we should tie up our food the way professionals on YouTube demonstrate, the impossible way, and I heavied our bags with too much food. Both of us grew dehydrated, and I became dangerously dizzy from strep throat antibiotics. One night, a full moon offered some relief. We stood on a large rock, removed our clothes and cleaned off the day's sweat with biodegradable wipes. Kaitlin looked up at the light, its perfect roundness, and spoke: "This is the light of the mind." I finished the line: "cold and planetary."

> Kaitlin: The moon is no door.
> K: It is a face in its own right.

Kaitlin: White as a knuckle and terribly upset.
Kaitlin: It drags the sea after it like a dark crime.
K: It is quiet.
Kaitlin: with the O-gape of complete despair.
K: I live here.
Kaitlin: The moon is my mother.
K: She is not sweet like Mary.
Kaitlin: Her blue garments unloose small bats and owls.
K: How I would like to believe in tenderness.
Kaitlin: The moon sees nothing of this.
K: She is bald and wild.[19]

Last year, Kaitlin debuted her publishing career in *Poetry* with the poem "Epitaph as My Mother's Daughter." The final sentence: "I'm sorry, / the world makes more sense without her."[20]

An ADHD diagnosis increases the likelihood of a personality disorder diagnosis. Having either increases the likelihood of addiction. People with highly masked autism who've experienced parental abuse and neglect are often diagnosed with a personality disorder. Dr. F didn't explain my sensitivity to sound and reported that I did not appear pained by the overhead light. But I was very pained by the light, waiting until getting a migraine before asking her to turn it off. People with ADHD and autism also report feelings of unrealness. For a week, I've been on a low-dose stimulant, and I'm now writing this essay with one tab open instead of fifty. I also feel more present, less empty, more *a part of*. It's true that I have treated some of the traits Dr. F listed as addictions from which to recover. She's also right about them being pressing. They almost cost me my life, several times. In recovery circles, it's often said our addictions never stop doing pushups, and I believe we don't know that our rock bottom is *the* bottom. A tension: Dr. F's recommended treatment—dialectical behavioral therapy—was inspired by Zen Buddhist practices. The Buddhist doctrine Anattā translates to "no self" or "no soul." The five aggregates of a person—form, feeling, perception, mental formations, consciousness—are always changing. Anattā parted from Hinduism's Atman—the self—the belief in which causes suffering according to the Buddha. In a more collective culture, would a disintegrated identity be maladaptive? Does a nation of 300 million rugged individuals contribute to my suffering? Can one be too dependent where the disabled, vulnerable, and family-less receive care from institutions and communities? Perhaps the problem is a psyche that thinks of itself as separate from and dissolved into the world in all the maladaptive ways and none of the helpful ones. A possible solution: building containers that open and close when they need to. This would mean learning to write from presence rather than the default: desperation, intensity, boundarylessness.

---

[19]Plath, "The Moon and the Yew Tree," 65.
[20]Kaitlin Rizzo, "Epitaph as My Mother's Daughter," *Poetry* (July/August 2023): https://www.poetryfoundation.org/poetrymagazine/poems/160482/epitaph-as-my-mothers-daughter

A tension: as a child, I learned to float in fantasy. Today, it's difficult to feel my feet when walking. I didn't know this until my first trans therapist asked if I'm aware of my feet when walking. They suggested earth shoes and cold showers, both of which help them inhabit their body. Every moment we're strengthening neuropathways, they said. In the shoes, the feet welcome new contact, feel massaged by varied textures. The feet don't register as mine yet, but the ground feels like the ground. Reality, so intolerable in my youth that fighting it became a default, is my only option. This again complicates writing, as my work has been rewarded for fantasy, obsession, and overthinking.

Drafting this essay is like learning a new instrument. How to write from a recovering body? Studying the elegy helped me find my voice on the page. I now understand that fact as a practice in locating a self: grief finding its location. Embedded in the elegy is contrast. Death epiphanizes life. A Japanese death poem,[21] the last words of a monk or a haiku poet, holds and cuts that tension, countering the Western elegy. Holds and cuts it again. People who've meditated much of their lives are fully present for their dying even as they language it. A new tension toward which I want to write.

At a writer's conference some summers ago, my mentor Eduardo C. Corral read the erotic poems I'd been drafting for a new collection. Their twoness: an "I" and a lover. Corral suggested poems that take on other points of view and an exploration of the autoerotic. That would require the speaker's body to hold all the tension: a self and other, maybe more, inside. This work, holding and owning what's here rather than throwing desire onto another person, is also the work of my recovery. As self-concept settles into its new lens, as it reaches from the unreal to hereness, a contrast poetics is scaffolding my prose. If one's default is feeling lost, a sentence is an opportunity to remember gravity has never left. And to remember that the distinction of beginning from end is made up: life is a series of beginnings. Both the breath and silence of a poetic line wait for the reborn.

Bibliography

Dahoul, Safwan. "Form and Emptiness: An Interview with Safwan Dahoul." Interview by K. Iver. *Southeast Review* 38, no 1. https://www.southeastreview.org/single-post/aninterview-with-safwan-dahoul

Francis, Vievee. "I've Been Thinking About Love Again." *Poetry Daily* (May 20, 2022). https://poems.com/poem/ive-been-thinking-about-love-again/

Frost, Robert. "The Figure a Poem Makes." *Collected Poems of Robert Frost*. Henry Holt and Company, 1939.

Glück, Louise. "Disruption, Hesitation, Silence." *American Poetry Review* 22, no. 5 (1993): 30–32.

Kalsched, Donald. *The Inner World of Trauma: The Archetypal Defenses of the Personal Spirit.* Routledge, 1996.

---

[21] An excellent example of Japanese death poems is Yoel Hoffman's collection titled *Japanese Death Poems* (Tuttle Publishing, 1986).

Pierce, Kathleen. "First Lines." *The Oval Hour*. University of Iowa Press, 1999.

Plath, Sylvia. *Ariel: The Restored Edition: A Facsimile of Plath's Manuscript, Reinstating Her Original Selection and Arrangement*. Harper Perennial, 2004.

Rizzo, Kaitlin. "Epitaph as My Mother's Daughter." *Poetry* (July/August 2023). https://www.poetryfoundation.org/poetrymagazine/poems/160482/epitaph-as-my-mothers-daughter

Ruefle, Mary. "Poetry and the Moon." *Madness, Rack, and Honey*. Wave Books, 2012.

Schopenhauer, Arthur. *The World as Will and Idea*. London: Kegan Paul, Trench, Trübner & Co., 1909.

Stirman, Shannon Wiltsey, and James W. Pennebaker. "Word Use in the Poetry of Suicidal and Nonsuicidal Poets." *Psychosomatic Medicine* 63, no. 4 (July 2001). https://doi.org/10.1097/00006842-200107000-00001

Tawa, Renee. "Scanning Literary Verse for Literal Clues to Suicides." *Los Angeles Times* (August 27, 2001). https://www.latimes.com/archives/la-xpm-2001-aug-27-cl-38798-story.html

Wordsworth, William. "The World Is Too Much with Us." *Poems, in Two Volumes*, 1807. Reprint, *The Poetry Foundation*. https://www.poetryfoundation.org/poems/45564/the-world-is-too-much-with-us

5 Theory of Whose Mind?:[1] A Very Late-Diagnosed Autistic Writer Claps Back

JULIA LEE BARCLAY-MORTON

Autism is core to my being. . . . Autism is my rhetoric. What is at risk here is who tells my story, who tells the story of my people. What's of concern is who gets to author our individual and collective identities . . . whether we are even allowed to call ourselves human.[2]

"Theory of whose mind?" asks M. Remi Yergeau in *Authoring Autism: On Rhetoric and Neurological Queerness*,[3] questioning the foundation of Simon Baron-Cohen's 1985 article,[4] which claims that autistic children have no "theory of mind," a concept which can be defined as "the understanding that others have intentions, desires, beliefs, perceptions, and emotions different from one's own and that such intentions, desires, and so forth affect people's actions and behaviors."[5] But as it turns out, the results of Baron-Cohen's study, which only involved twenty autistic children, have never been successfully replicated. Ever. However, instead of concluding this might not be an accurate assessment of autistic children, Baron-Cohen and others doubled down and redesigned the test—again and again. In every case—even if a new test initially supported his theory—it could *never* be replicated. Ever. This did not stop him from writing *Mindblindness: An Essay on Autism and Theory of Mind*[6] in 1995, collating these skewed findings to declare his theory accurate.

In the years since, researchers, for example Gernsbacher and Yergeau,[7] have dissected Baron-Cohen's flawed research. In *Imagining Autism: Fiction and*

---

[1] The first part of the title comes from M. Remi Yergeau in *Authoring Autism: On Rhetoric and Neurological Queerness* (Duke University Press, 2018).
[2] M. Remi Yergeau, *Authoring Autism: On Rhetoric and Neurological Queerness* (Duke University Press, 2018), 21.
[3] Ibid., 31.
[4] Simon Baron-Cohen et al., "Does the Autistic Child Have a 'Theory of Mind'?" *Cognition* 21, no. 1 (1985): 37–46, https://doi.org/10.1016/0010-0277(85)90022-8
[5] "Theory of Mind," *APA Dictionary of Psychology*, American Psychological Association, effective July 2, 2025, https://dictionary.apa.org/theory-of-mind
[6] Simon Baron-Cohen, *Mindblindness: An Essay on Autism and Theory of Mind* (MIT Press, 1995).
[7] Morton Ann Gernsbacher and M. Remi Yergeau, "Empirical Failures of the Claim that Autistic People Lack Theory of Mind," *Archives of Scientific Psychology* 7, no. 1 (2019): 102–118, https://doi.org/10.1037/arc0000067.

Stereotypes on the Spectrum, Sonya Freeman Loftis asks, "If autistics truly have a deficit in [theory of mind], then why is it that neurotypicals find it so difficult to intuit the intentions of autistic people?"[8] The fact it took thirty-four years for an article to appear in a scientific journal proving the fallacy of an assumption that has dehumanized autistics for decades attests to the length of time it has taken for autistic researchers to be taken seriously in *autism* research. However, the assumption that autistics lack a "theory of mind" persists.

All radical possibilities for autistic futures have and will emerge from autistics researching, writing, teaching, creating, and being given platforms to be heard, seen, and understood. While important ally Steve Silberman helped plow the field with *Neurotribes: The Legacy of Autism and the Future of Neurodiversity*,[9] it's autistics who will tell the story about how we inhabit and build the communities and infrastructure that can offer a way forward. Autistic writers have and continue to bring our unique gifts of pattern recognition, intuition, and heightened sensitivity to the rhizomatic understory of any coalescence to whatever we are creating.

This essay traces how this autistic writer began seeking lines of flight and radical possibilities throughout her creative life, decades before discovering her neurotype. Here she is in 1998, cutting up texts from a theater lab—found texts and participants' own first memories about gender, class, and religion. She is knocking at the prison walls she can sense but not see, listening out for a weak spot, where that weak spot might give:

I speak in language where I am nothing:
closely linked to the point of view of broken
umbrellas

                                         I'm in the death of autonomous lock up—

I'm in the death of action—their theories
positing how long I had been there: infinitely,
no movement, no thought to just FALL DOWN . . .
You can see her almost . . . trapped inside the cocoon, signaling, wanting out, not knowing how, so aware of her need for protection.

The marriage of true tension has
disappeared—   *our heroine now sees that*
my hoping for it has given a framework   *There are multitudes—each one myself.*

She knows—you can hear it—she knows she has to *fall*. She knows the freeze. She knows what it is to be trapped. She knows when she has to play dead. She knows she cannot attack this trap directly. The words direct seem too frightening to share.

---

[8] Sonya Freeman Loftis, *Imagining Autism: Fiction and Stereotypes on the Spectrum* (Indiana University Press, 2015), 10.
[9] Steve Silberman, *Neurotribes: The Legacy of Autism and the Future of Neurodiversity* (Avery, 2016).

Also inadequate. She thinks it's mostly about gender. She is not wrong, but it's also about ancient wounds lodged in the body and unknown autism and never being seen or heard and knowing it but not knowing how to be seen or heard except through masks, and yes Artaud said that masks are what allow truth to come out, but what about when the mask is soldered onto the face for fear of being visible even to oneself? You were able to trick her by the use of cut-ups into writing—into believing *I* existed, even if *in language where I am nothing, closely linked to the point of view of broken umbrellas*, where *There are multitudes—each one myself*. Once she had an inkling *I* existed, she moved from cutting up found text to cutting up her own thoughts and images as they emerged in daylight and in dreams. But until recently you didn't even know who the "I" was.

• • •

Because the history of the silencing of autistics affected me as profoundly as the moon affects the tide—even if unconsciously—let's start with the mid-1980s when Baron-Cohen's theory of autistic mindblindness was published. I'm twenty-one and have attempted yet another failed escape by going to art school in Florence, Italy, which works really well for a few months until I'm left with whomever the mystery shopper is that seems to be me. I'm studying photography, but alongside doodles, I sometimes scribble thoughts in various spiral bound notebooks with enthusiasm for a few days or weeks until I give up and leave the rest of the pages blank:

> *Nov. 9, 1984*
> *Florence, Italy*

> *I'm moving today. An appropriate landmark to be writing in my journal—finalmente . . . It's hard to write now—many ... folks here. I wish I could live with Italians—need to learn—more. Had my first Italian dinner Wed night. Was incredibly depressed beforehand. Reagan—again. It scares me. There are people here ... who are pro-Reagan. Found out my age group is a strong supporter of him. I have to live with these people. I feel a bit in exile. Disgusted with U.S.—not wanting to be [t]here—but knowing here is not my home. A beautiful resting spot—lotus blossoms—but not my home. I wonder where is? Does a home exist for me. Can I create one. Even here I move. No where to run. No where to hide. No where to sway but side by side. Tell me is it true? What shall I Where shall I Why shall I do? (just read T.S. Eliot)*

> > *There will be time. There will be time*
> > *To prepare a face to meet the faces that you meet.*

> *Restless. Eternally restless. More patience—perhaps? Or is it better this way. If the shoe never fits—I'll never have to wear it. Freedom—but it gets cold outside (don't forget your mittens).*

> > *I want to write now. Like I am, but more. I want to do so many things. A large part of me doesn't want to master anything. Eternal beginner. Raw Vision. To*

master is to destroy. To play is grand. I fear "adulthood" more than I ever will admit. Like self-determination — hate decisions . . .

I want to scream — silently. Wish I could watch the world without it watching me. I space-out a lot. Sit on the bus + watch — no awareness that other people see me. I hate mirrors. They remind me of my corporal, tangible presence. The photographer not the photographed. But then I become obsessed by them — mirrors — because I see myself. I don't mind <u>me</u> looking at me. But anyone else — it makes me nervous — unless I'm "on" — laughing, walking — in control. Such a strange child . . .

Revisiting this diary entry years later, what jumps out is the phrase *Wish I could watch the world without the world watching me.* Alongside the poetic echolalia (Eliot, Anderson), this reads like a dictionary definition of autism — and is why I was a theater director rather than an actor or even a writer, letting other people's bodies and words be visible, me behind the scenes manipulating the world but not seen, invisible even, not causing attention to myself. Screaming — *silently.*

• • •

I made some stabs at writing prose in 1992 — around the time Donna Williams' unmasked account of growing up autistic, titled *Nobody Nowhere: The Extraordinary Autobiography of an Autistic Girl*,[10] was published. I oscillated between directing theater and trying to write a novel. I didn't think of writing plays, perhaps because my then husband, a few friends, and one of my stepfathers were all playwrights. I was the director. I didn't want to compete.

During Williams' book tour in the United States for *Nobody Nowhere*, she met autistic writer-activist Jim Sinclair, whom she had connected with on a mailing list. Their meeting, and the revelation of the ease they felt when hanging out and enjoying each other's company, led to the creation in the mid-1990s of Autism Network International, the first ever autistic-led organization. The Internet allowed autistics to finally find each other; they discovered when communicating with one another they no longer felt disabled or misunderstood. This connection began to undermine the internalized ableism of those who found each other and was — and still is — profoundly healing.

In Silberman's *Neurotribes*,[11] he discusses pivotal moments in the year 1998. For one, Laura Tisonick creates an official-looking website for the "Institute for the Study of the Neurologically Typical." The FAQ reads: "Neurotypical syndrome is a neurobiological disorder characterized by preoccupation with social concerns,

---

[10]Donna Williams, *Nobody Nowhere: The Extraordinary Autobiography of an Autistic Girl* (Doubleday, 1992).
[11]Steve Silberman, *Neurotribes: The Legacy of Autism and the Future of Neurodiversity* (Avery, 2016).

delusions of superiority, and obsession with conformity . . . There is no known cure."[12] Also in 1998, the term neurodiversity is published for the first time in an article in *The Atlantic* by Harvey Blume, who writes that "neurodiversity[13] is as important as biodiversity."[14] These shards of light poke through the foggy murk created by decades of misguided, so-called research. Autistics had begun to clap back.

• • •

I spent 1998 writing down all my childhood memories alongside global political events from 1963–1980, because I knew even then we're not made up only of our own little lives, monads independent of influence from (or of) the larger whole. Each daily one-hour session was excruciating. Only people pathologized as having "abnormal" focus, "fixation," or "restricted interests" would torture themselves this way. But I knew I had to do it. This is such an autistic project it's comical.

The Yoga-sutra says some suffering can be averted through understanding its root cause.

I do not know this yet.

But you *knew* that.

Because I was moved frequently as a child and had many different caretakers, I told people who asked why I'm doing this: *My memories are my hometown*. I did not yet know how to save things properly on my computer, so I kept losing writing. I began printing it out to save it. The pages fill two three-inch-thick binders. The losing of my writing seems related to the project—the impossibility of capturing memory, the way it slips through our hands no matter what, how it's always partial. The cut-up for the theater lab, which I created this same year endures, serves as perhaps a more accurate record:

> *Discovers, like chameleons,*
> *she can change color to match many dark rooms,*
> *from drab to psychedelic in a matter of*
> *moments. They can even grow skin to better*
> *mimic laced rooms. The camouflage is both*
> *defensive and offensive.*
> *They are centaurs, ambush hunters,*   *Another type of dissertation?*
> *forced to loving.*

I had begun an experimental lab the year before, asking what theater could do in 1997. We broke down aspects of the theatrical experience: levels of address and

---

[12]Laura Tisonick, "Institute for the Study of the Neurologically Typical (website)," 1998, quoted in Silberman, *Neurotribes*, 435–450.

[13]While the origin of the word "neurodiversity" is in dispute because it developed within the autism community in list-serves, it was first used publicly in Blume's article.

[14]Harvey Blume, "Neurodiversity: On the Neurological Underpinnings of Geekdom," *Atlantic*, September 1998, https://www.theatlantic.com/magazine/archive/1998/09/neurodiversity/305909/

presence, cliché and idiosyncratic speech—in order to cut up *ourselves*, trying to unearth the conscious and unconscious roots of how we defined gender, class, and religion in the United States, anthropologists of our own bodyminds. We created cut-ups to have text we could use to explore these concerns. Here is an example:

> *Here I was, walking around disguised—*
> *consumed by the feminine. A freak from hunger,—*
> *I had slept in men's literature—*
> *those eternally recurring fogs—*
> *read till my eyes fell out—*
> *where they were windows.*
>
> *I'm in the death of literature which*
> *attempts to grasp fists—so help me God—*
> *getting out.*

Artistic Director of The Present Company, John Clancy asked me to articulate my vision for the theater to see how he could support the experimental theater lab. My answer would be published in the intro to my first stage text, titled "Word To Your Mama."[15] It also became the basis for my practice-as-research PhD in the UK and the mission statement for Apocryphal Theatre:

> creating theatrical pieces that uproot the static nature of language, gesture, character, etc. in such a way as to bring about this process of becoming: first in our own bodies/souls/minds as players/writers/designers/choreographers/directors and thence into the bodies/minds/souls of the audience.[16]

> . . . to make visible the construction of the language with which we create the world we perceive; to allow us a moment in the gap between the understood and the unknown, to listen for the voices which have not yet formed, not yet been heard but still call to us in an undefined language which is perhaps no less real or pressing for being as yet unwritten.[17]

• • •

In 2023, while searching for any writing by French philosophers Gilles Deleuze and Felix Guattari related to autism, I discovered philosopher Erin Manning. She was writing about Ferdinand Deligny who, while creating a refuge in the 1960s for non-speaking autistic children to roam in an encampment in the Cevernnes mountains where no one tried to "fix" them, inspired key concepts of Deleuze and Guattari such

---

[15] Julia Barclay, "Word to Your Mama," *Plays and Playwrights 2001*, ed. Martin Denton, New York Theatre Experience, 2001: 149.
[16] Julia Barclay, "Apocryphal Theatre: Practicing Philosophies," PhD diss., University of Northampton (UK), 2009.
[17] Julia Barclay, "Apocryphal Theatre (2003–2011)", https://www.flyingoutofsequence.org/Apocryphal_Theatre/about.html

as "rhizomatic patterning" and "lines of flight," which had informed my research. Manning, like me, had discovered only a few years prior that she was autistic. Years earlier, she conceptualized autistic "languaging," which resonates uncannily with my theatrical manifesto:

> This language of wonder is with, not about. It exists across, in the thinking-feeling. And it worlds, refusing to categorically distinguish between form and forces . . . Human, object, environment, tone, color, sound, what makes its way into communication is not first and foremost the monadic nature of forms but the transversal forces of the as-yet-unthought in the thinking . . .
>
> But even where language is not-yet, there is nonetheless within thought-thinking a drifting, a rhythmic shifting, a polyphonic multiplicity in germ ready to be activated, to be articulated, be it in words, in movement, in gesture . . .
>
> In this regard, autistics are indeed otherworldly (in a way we would be wise to follow): they lead us toward an otherness of worlding . . .
> It composes-with experience, refuting the notion that the world is already known, pre-formed . . . This worlding is thought in motion . . . What is singular about the autistic experience of and in language is that it emphasizes this tuning of language across difference . . .[18]

When my stage text "Word To Your Mama" was first performed in 2000, I puked the whole night beforehand and could not attend my own open dress rehearsal. I couldn't move, but I made a miraculous recovery when John Clancy called and left a long message on my answering machine praising it. I had been heard and seen. No one died. People seemed to even . . . like it. The actors were concerned that the use of sometimes incongruent gestures and focuses on levels of address that were not in direct accordance with the lines would somehow obscure the text. I assured them that the words were just part of the material, that the gestures and relations to the audience and the rules of the room were equally important. It was about unearthing how the reality was being shaped.

By the time I founded Apocryphal Theatre in 2003, the experimentation had gone even further, inspired by the experience of living in New York City on September 11, 2001. I asked actors to improvise their ways through the texts so that who said what line and how would be decided in response to the moment using tools we had created in the experimental theater lab. The world had exploded, nothing was permanent, so why should theater be any different? The actor-artists created a living language that shifted every night, amongst themselves and the audience and the space. Similarly, Manning writes:

> The making-collective of language is an ethics. Think-with, feel-with, autie-type says. Experience the force of expression. Compose-with, participate at the edge

---

[18]Erin Manning, *Always More Than One: Individuation's Dance* (Duke University Press, 2013), 169.

of meaning where language no longer holds together. Learn to listen across registers. Dance the dance of attention of polyphonous expressibility.

The between of words is what is continuously at stake not only in the language of autism but in all language . . . Language is always collective . . . All writing, all speaking, is a collective individuation . . . Language is not an accessory to experience.[19]

My theatrical work not only relates to the collective creation of language but to the framing of it as an ethic—guided by that desire to *(en)act* ethically. In other words, even before my diagnosis, I had been engaged in work that attempts to liberate and make visible autistic perception for like a while.

• • •

In 2021, soon after being diagnosed autistic at fifty-seven, I was in search of what unmasked autistic writing might be. I knew by then my very late diagnosis had to do in part with my ability to mask—so this felt urgent. This led me to the book *Authoring Autism* wherein Yergeau describes the rhetoric/s unique to autistic bodyminds. I began to understand that my own stuttering texts—these words I had been writing for over twenty years—were in fact what Yergeau refers to as "autistexts."[20] So, of course, my response to diagnosis was to write one, which opens:

A moment: maybe stage text/maybe memoir/maybe both . . .

There is this moment when you find something. This thing that you knew and didn't know. That gives a key to who you are, one that was missing for years.

And there is elation.

And a sense that it All Makes Sense now.

A relief.

An exhalation.

And then?

You already know.

Yes.

Clunk.

Because while it's true, now you Know this thing and it's a Big Thing, you are still you. And while it may make sense of it All . . . it doesn't make the Situation on the Ground that much better.

---

[19] Erin Manning, *Always More Than One: Individuation's Dance* (Duke University Press, 2013), 168.
[20] Yergeau, *Authoring Autism*, 20–24.

Except it does.

Yes. It definitely does.

It does and it doesn't.

Right.

Yes

Like say finding out you have been going in the wrong direction for oh say over half a century and realizing now why all the landmarks are funky and somehow don't make sense because you Are Not Where You Thought You Were Going.

Or should be.

Right.

Because you did All The Things You Thought You Were Supposed to Do but then . . .

Back of a Dunkin Donuts parking lot at 3am or whatever.

As a metaphor.

Duh.

And so this Thing you discover answers the question of why the Directions you read led you not to the ocean front home and your dream life full of Art and Friends and Success but instead to the vacant parking lot in the wee hours of the night.

Alone.

Staring at flashing neon sign with letter missing and hearing a cat wailing behind the dumpster.

Stone Cold Sober.

Right. That's the best part!

Sober as a Judge. Totally Fucking Sober.

Could not be more fucking sober.

So this is no dream or hallucination. It's just reality.

You and the open tuna can.

Or whatever.

Right.

In your own noir film but it's not a film.

Or a Hopper painting.

Just your fucking life laid out etherized upon the table and etc.

Not TS Eliot either I'm afraid.

OK, whatever.

But it's like you can See what your life is now, like a map is on top of what had seemed a confused mess, like a tangle in your hair is suddenly visible, each strand, how it's bunched up and why.

So clear.

All those twists and turns, the meltdowns, the freakouts, the escape routes, the paralysis, the submission, the fighting, the desire to die whenever anyone puts on an overhead light, the need to flee into another room whenever you are at a party even if it's your own and you love everyone there, the passions you can't release, the bullheadedness, the hatred of change but also the hatred of repetition but the need for it all at the same time.

Autistic.

Fucking Autistic.

Autistic?

Are you SURE?

You don't LOOK autistic?

glares then laughs . . .

In analyzing this "autistext," I now wonder if I engage with "second persons" because I've always seen myself from the outside as much as the inside because that's how autistics are regarded? In the same way Genet was accused as a child of being a thief when he hadn't stolen anything and then became a thief as an adult. How we are *seen* into the world affects how we see. These dialogic voices come in and out of my prose now, too. I can't *not* see from that point of view. It's not *intellectualizing*; it's not dissociation. It's instead allowing for the *importance of second-persons*. Sometimes the outside viewer is generous, sometimes hostile, perhaps a judge—it morphs, just like my relationship to myself morphs from moment to moment as does my place in the world amongst others. We aren't monads. We swim in a sea of the social as it shifts, along with the wind and rain and tides. We are not *not* affected. As Manning says, in part quoting Deleuze,

> Here, in the midst of life-living, artfulness reminds us that the "I" is not where life begins, and the "you" is not what makes it art. Made up as it is of a thousand contemplations, the art of time reminds us that "we [must] speak of the self only in virtue of these thousands of little witnesses which contemplate within us: it is always a third party who says 'me'" (Deleuze 1978: 75). This is why artfulness is rarer than art.[21]

• • •

---

[21] Erin Manning, *The Minor Gesture* (Duke University Press, 2016), 63.

As part of the book launch for my hybrid collection *The Mortality Shot*[22] in 2022, I saw words of mine performed on a stage for the first time since coming out as autistic—and I spoke to the audience afterwards. Back to the sanctuary. Feeling heard, feeling exposed, feeling all of it.

The next day?

Burnout.

Inevitable yes, but it's the reason I haven't built the career I'd hoped in theater or writing or anything really. Because no matter what I do, after I put myself out there, I then have to hide. What I'm supposed to do is stay visible, follow up, and make shit happen, but I can't. Part of the burnout involves shame because of this—knowing what I should be doing, and seeing people talking about the need to do x and y, and barely getting to b or c. A sense of being chronically behind. This can then lead to gerbil wheel workaholism for a few frantic hours or days that produces nothing except an even worse burnout.

"Just connect," we are told. Yes, but how, when the onus is all on autistics to mask enough to fit in with the rest of you? How is that connection? It's not. It's only passing to get an invitation to the party. The fact is: even at this event where my own words are being read by fabulous actors and the audience is responsive and kind, I know I'm masking. It's necessary masking. Even the neurotypical mask this way to some extent. It's the mask of The Professional. During the talkback afterwards, I feel pressure to put on an increasingly uncomfortable mask of "someone who knows something about something," even when talking about my own writing.

While I'm doing a fairly convincing job of saying things that appear to make sense to people, I'm simultaneously wondering: *Is that really true*? *Do I feel that way*? *Is that why I wrote that*? So, I begin to add this questioning of myself into my answers. But then Adam, who wrote the foreword to the book and is moderating the discussion, says "but you seem to make some declarations in the book"—and I have to admit yes, that's true, too. In the essays, and even in the stage text, I do sometimes speak from a place of authority. Only after the event do I remember that in the stage text especially but even in some essays, I interrogate those moments, but I forgot that when we were talking in public. When I'm masking, the energy to keep the seams from showing means I can forget crucial information and stop knowing what I feel. The reality is that many autistics mirror others' words and gestures. This makes sense when you realize that trying frantically to fit in and be discernible to others will take you so far outside yourself that this can become your last resort. It feels natural in the moment, even as if it's a *connection*, but it's not. Because the connection is with a mask, one that has morphed somewhat ingeniously to mirror you in a favorable light so you will like me. When I feel accepted as I am (a rare event—usually only in the company of other autistics), I don't have to lose my own point of view and panic-agree with what's being said.

More than one therapist over the years has suggested—after I've said *I don't know* reflexively—"Maybe you *do* know." And I *do* know, but the kind of knowing that

---

[22] Julia Barclay-Morton, *The Mortality Shot* (Liquid Cat Press, 2022).

is lodged in my body, that doesn't have words, the one with all the instincts I was told to distrust by everyone's reactions to me from when I was an infant onward. How can I *know* that I know? Have confidence in this? How can I give words to an unshared experience, one that when I try to give words to is met with incredulity or shaming? Recently in autistic groups, my unmasked self was met for the first time with nods and understanding, a deeply healing experience, but one that is very new. Over five decades of encoded shame and doubt do not evaporate overnight.

Autistic burnout comes from all of this. The masking, the questioning, the not knowing, the knowing, and maybe not wanting to know what I know in equal measure. Because what I do know is this: there is no one way to be or one thing I'm saying. I know there is pressure in this capitalist world to "brand" oneself—to do One thing and be Known for it—which I've never had any interest in doing, so I pay a high price as a consequence. Whenever I *have* tried to mold myself to these market forces, I've failed spectacularly, under the weight of my own self-doubt and self-hatred—because I know it's false. This is another autistic trait I experience: the need to act with consistent ethics in all things accompanied by a visceral feeling of *Wrongness* when not doing so. While I'm sure many will say, *Oh I feel this way, too*, what I've discovered while talking to other autistic adults is that we feel it to such a degree it can make us sick. All the happy-clappy excuses used to weasel around integrity in the allistic (non-autistic) world, like "compromise" and "nuance," make my entire being revolt.

This is why I'm so bad at marketing my stuff. I can't do all the things you're meant to do. Anytime I do even the basics, I feel slimed. Or I just freeze and can't bring myself to do anything. All of this is why when I *am* in a productive workflow and can bring myself to do any of these things, I don't let myself stop until I collapse, because I'm afraid that I'll never be able to do it again. This is autistic inertia. And guess what? That turns out to be another form of autistic masking: working past exhaustion, not allowing rest, because of this sense of having to prove oneself to the world: an involuntary, relentless drive to achieve in order to make up for what allistics judge as my consistent failure *to connect*.

In 2022, Leah Lakshmi Piepzna-Samarasinha's work, titled *The Future Is Disabled: Prophecies, Love Notes and Mourning Songs*,[23] was also published, which not only dissects this problem but proposes solutions. They offer a vision of a radical future, inclusive of new rhetorics, mutual aid, and new ways of understanding disability. Their refusal to temper how they write to accommodate a neuro-normative, non-disabled, white audience is a breath of fresh air and feels like being given a permission slip to *do whatever the fuck I want* with my own writing. It reminds me to hold to the original vision of non-linear, rhizomatic "autistexts" and to not give in to rules created with the faulty assumption that there is a universal human experience we can just "show" without telling.

---

[23] Leah Lakshmi Piepzna-Samarasinha, *The Future Is Disabled: Prophecies, Love Notes and Mourning Songs* (Arsenal Pulp Press, 2022).

One way to recover from masking burnout is spending time in closeknit autistic communities, including the book club in which we read this book. Piepzna-Samarasinha's hope is infectious as is their embrace of their disabilities, including understanding themself as autistic later in life. Their writing is an embodiment of a fact: *we* are the experts in this, no one else. Listen or don't, understand or don't, but we aren't waiting for you to come around anymore:

We aren't waiting.

We are here.

She is.

They are.

I am.

You are.

Yes.

But we must care for one another, and bear witness to one another . . .

*Yes, she thought, laying down. The water
reflects my vision.*

                                                Enigmatic, no liturgy: it would be destroyed.

We build worlds in the darkness of that cupboard.[24]

Yes.

We are building worlds.

Or we are perhaps recognizing worlds already there that have been buried and forgotten, hidden away from us, by others and by ourselves.

But the thousand little witnesses . . .

Yes.

Bibliography

Barclay, Julia. "Apocryphal Theatre: Practicing Philosophies." PhD diss., University of Northampton (UK), 2009.

Barclay, Julia. "Word to Your Mama." *Plays and Playwrights 2001*, ed. Martin Denton. New York Theatre Experience, 2001: 147–168.

Barclay-Morton, Julia. *The Mortality Shot*. Liquid Cat Press, 2022.

Baron-Cohen, Simon, Alan M. Leslie, and Uta Frith. "Does the Autistic Child Have a 'Theory of Mind'?" *Cognition* 21, no. 1 (1985): 37–46. https://doi.org/10.1016/0010-0277(85)90022 8

Baron-Cohen, Simon. *Mindblindness: An Essay on Autism and Theory of Mind*. MIT Press, 1995.

---

[24] Excerpt from cut-up by the author, Julia Barclay-Morton, of words and phrases by autistic writers.

Blume, Harvey. "Neurodiversity: On the Neurological Underpinnings of Geekdom." *Atlantic*, September 1998. https://www.theatlantic.com/magazine/archive/1998/09/neurodiversity/305909/

Gernsbacher, Morton Ann and M. Remi Yergeau. "Empirical Failures of the Claim that Autistic People Lack Theory of Mind." *Archives of Scientific Psychology* 7, no. 1 (2019): 102–118. https://doi.org/10.1037/arc0000067

Manning, Erin. *Always More Than One: Individuation's Dance.* Duke University Press, 2013.

Manning, Erin. *The Minor Gesture.* Duke University Press, 2016.

Silberman, Steve. *Neurotribes: The Legacy of Autism and the Future of Neurodiversity.* Avery, 2016.

Williams, Donna. *Nobody, Nowhere: The Extraordinary Autobiography of an Autistic Girl.* Doubleday, 1992.

Piepzna-Samarasinha, Leah Lakshmi. *The Future Is Disabled: Prophecies, Love Notes and Mourning Songs.* Arsenal Pulp Press, 2022.

Yergeau, M. Remi. *Authoring Autism: On Rhetoric and Neurological Queerness.* Duke University Press, 2018.

Part 2 Views from the Inside: Writers Confronting Stigma, Exploitation, and Ableism

6   There Is a Charge for the Eyeing of My Scars:[1] Writing the Neurodivergent, Disabled Body for a Dominant Audience

GRACE QUANTOCK

When another student handed me a copy of the mental health magazine, she was excited. She wasn't the first. That morning on the train, my email and phone had pinged urgently. I had been writing, my laptop balanced on my knees as my wheelchair rocked with our movement over the tracks. I saw the enthusiasm, the recommendations hitting my notifications. I still didn't look. Not only did I not rush to see the first issue on counseling and disability, I looked away. I grew up with physical difference, becoming disabled at thirteen years old. I craved nuanced and insightful literature around disability, chronic illness, and neurodivergence, yet I found mostly silence, with occasional cloying highlights of "inspirational" stories. These stories often increased bullying, perhaps because disability had been highlighted, perhaps because I was insufficiently inspirational.

In the lobby of our therapeutic training college, I thanked my peer and looked over the magazine. I still didn't open it. I didn't want to see my experience reduced to pap, to pity and simplicity, which seemed to be the only content featuring us that non-disabled people would consume. I suppose, with so much of disabled history hidden, with our very bodies still segregated in many ways from benefit-induced poverty to lack of access, most non-disabled people had no understanding with which to contextualize and process the nuances and tensions our lives stretch across.

My ingratitude was noticed in the classroom, commented upon, and I didn't have a way to explain it. As other students filed in, I thought about when I had been excited for representation. I read magazines and newspapers and couldn't understand why the stories were so one-dimensional, when they appeared at all. I took classes in writing, in how to pitch, in framing my story in a way that could catch attention, could hold it, could be remembered. I sent out pitches, carefully honed. Like many writers, I heard nothing. At one workshop, with the former editor of one of the largest daily newspapers in the UK, I found something approximating an answer.

---

[1] The first part of the title is composed of inverted lines from Sylvia Plath's poem "Lady Lazarus," which was first published in Plath's posthumous collection *Ariel* in 1965.

"We are teaching you this, because you never went to Eton, but you are up against people who did. I'm going to teach you how the UK media landscape works," he began. We were a group of women interested in social and political change; this workshop was to help us make our points in print.

"What you have to understand is that newspapers in the UK will boil down a story to its very essence, to its basic facts. Then they will exaggerate those facts. That's how it works."

I started to see why my complex pitches were missing the mark. My stories were all conflict, but the wrong kind. I didn't want to write about love overcoming disability but about living well when you're under pressure to keep seeking a miracle cure, the strength it takes to refuse another round of rehab when you're young enough to be expected not to give up and put your efforts into walking again, not living in your body as it is. Or exploring the tensions between, say, needing to attend to my body to take care of it in a collapsing National Health Service (NHS), and needing to dissociate from it because my body is where the pain and trauma reside.

The workshop offered a space to work on pitches, and I asked about getting commissioned without any contacts or journalism background.

"Some editors will accept pitches from new people," the former editor explained.

"There's an editor on Twitter, she's always tweeting about how not enough women pitch her. How she wants to commission women and says we shouldn't be so worried and should send in simple pitches, like men do, and . . ." I held out my phone to him.

"Look, I know the editor you're talking about. You're right, if you've pitched her, she should have at least replied to you." He scanned the pitch on my phone.

"It's that." He pointed at a word on the screen.

"What?" I leaned forward to see. He was pointing at the word "intersectionality."

"That word will never be printed in a British newspaper," he said.

I realized the reason I didn't see the kind of articles I craved was not because no one was writing them, but because no one in the mainstream media would publish them. I simplified my pitches and subjects; I kept trying. Through early 2020, I pitched many stories including:

- How disability thinking has invisibly innovated life through Covid-19 and lockdown, charting the ways disability culture and technology have supported the majority during Covid.
- A therapist's guide to navigating tricky conversations on Zoom, drawing on my experience being housebounx'd for many years, bringing professional and personal experience of having to navigate tough talks digitally.
- Surviving working from home from the perspective of a disabled woman housebound for six years, as without realizing it, years of being housebound and bedbound were giving me valuable pandemic coping skills.
- How to shift gears to live well in this new normal, as many do, when newly diagnosed with chronic illness or injury.

- Finding joy when stuck at home, based on my ebook, titled *Beyond the Boundaries: Finding Freedom and Fulfilment Within Four Walls*, which contains a list of 500 things to do when stuck at home and struggling.
- Surviving emerging from lockdown, drawing on my experience supporting disabled clients emerging from being housebound, bedbound, or long hospital treatments, as much of isolation and emergence around Covid parallels chronic illness and disability experience.

None of these pitches were responded to or picked up. But as article after article was published by people with no experience of living well inside, I finally realized that the editors didn't want to hear from disabled experience. They didn't want to be like us. Maintaining distance between themselves and what Susan Sontag terms the "kingdom of the sick"[2] had become even more imperative during a pandemic, when those boundaries were blurring and so many were being pushed into our world.

I realized there are parameters, by dint of my disabled body and mind, that I will always fall outside of.

The reasons I received for why my writing about disabled experience was turned down included the following: a) it's too academic, b) readers want something cheerful, and c) it isn't relevant to a general readership. Now, these may be true, but there are 16 million disabled people in the UK.[3] Additionally, the Office of National Statistics released new data in November 2022, showing a half a million increase in the number of people not in work between 2019 and 2022,[4] with long-term illness being the reason some researchers give for this increase. Furthermore, there's been a 41 percent increase in the number of people leaving work due to health problems and disabilities since 2019.[5] When you consider these significant numbers, I have to wonder if worries about lack of readership are actually code for "I don't know any disabled people, so I can't picture the reader." I feel like I know the readers because I live among them, because I am of this community, and I know how vast we are. I also wonder if academic is code for "not sufficiently inspirational." It is true that I resist inspiration with every part of me. I find it creepy that people emotionally get off on the labor I have to expend just to get through the day.

When I read a story about a child who mowed lawns to fund a prosthetic limb for their disabled schoolfriend, it doesn't warm me. I don't coo over human kindness and ingenuity but question why we are celebrating child labor funding essential medical

---

[2] Susan Sontag, "Illness as Metaphor," *The New York Review*, January 26, 1978, https://www.nybooks.com/articles/1978/01/26/illness-as-metaphor/
[3] "Disability Facts and Figures," *Scope*, accessed May 28, 2024, https://www.scope.org.uk/media/disability-facts-figures/
[4] "Half a Million More People Are Out of the Labour Force Because of Long-Term Sickness," *Office for National Statistics* (ONS), accessed November 10, 2022, https://www.ons.gov.uk/employmentandlabourmarket/peoplenotinwork/economicinactivity/articles/halfamillionmorepeopleareoutofthelabourforcebecauseoflongtermsickness/2022-11-10
[5] Ibid.

supplies. I wonder about the profit made on the prosthetic limb and which companies were exempt from their responsibilities due to the labor of that child. This isn't intended to be a bitter story about lack of success as a writer; I've had stories picked up by *The Guardian*, *The Metro*, *The New Statesman*, and many more. But I'm interested in which stories get printed, which ones get ignored, and how it impacts us as disabled artists to be writing with the non-disabled gaze in mind.

In my experience, expectations of disabled writing are often bizarrely skewed. There's anticipation of writing of our pain, our loneliness, our decrepitude. But not of the difficulties many of us actually experience—mourning and raging at the lack of access, rather than the experience of pain. Of course, often it's both, but I experience my body as one part of a wider eco-system, so it's not simply the pain I carry but how my body, as it is, interacts with the society we have built. This includes the stares when I'm outside, the stairs blocking my route or having to give twenty-four hours' notice to get ramp access to travel on a train. It also includes frustration at the lack of research funding into often very prevalent conditions, such as endometriosis and adenomyosis. The interplay between our bodies and our environments is complex and, to me, fascinating.

But I've been told when being commissioned to write a piece that I mustn't "get political," especially about "the appalling lack of provision for wheelchair users to access the countryside." I don't expect hills to be equipped with lifts (although yes, level access paths and accessible gates in good repair would be helpful). I don't expect the natural world to be made fully accessible to me. I expect a government which holds water companies to account and doesn't vote to allow dumping of raw sewage into rivers,[6] polluting the sea with feces to the extent that they can kill wild swimmers.[7] I used to be able to swim in the sea because I'm at less risk of an airborne infection in the open air. Plus, the local swimming pool is so unclean I got infections every time I swam until my medical team advised me to stop. But the sea is now so unclean, I can't swim there either. My mother advised me to go up to the top of the mountains and swim there in a pond filled from the mountain springs, which flow directly out of the rocks. It has white clawed crayfish, which are often a sign of clean waters. Yet maybe this is exactly what is too political, and I should stick to describing wild swimming in terms of how it feels to move freely through the water when I can't move easily on land. But that's denying my reality and focusing on a situation in which I am less disabled, because the water supports and holds me. I can't share that without sharing why I am no longer able to access those waters. I'm always fascinated by which aspects of my writing are most popular with disabled and nondisabled readers.

It's a privilege few get to explore as, too often, the most popular books about disability are by non-disabled authors, for example in *The Guardian*'s list of The Top

---

[6]"Tory MPs Defend Votes After Uproar Over Sewage Proposals," *BBC News*, last modified October 25, 2021, https://www.bbc.com/news/uk-politics-59040175
[7]Emily Gudge. "River Thames Pollution 'Devastating'—Oxford Wild Swimmer." *BBC News*, last modified April 28, 2024, https://www.bbc.co.uk/news/uk-england-oxfordshire-68855301

10 Books About Disability,[8] which includes *Of Mice and Men*, *The Curious Incident of the Dog in the Night-time*, and many more classic novels. Often, disabled experience is seen as more palatable when translated and expressed by a non-disabled person. They don't even have to draw on research, as Mark Haddon, the author of *The Curious Incident of the Dog in the Night-time* wrote:

> I did no research for Curious Incident (other than photographing the interiors of Swindon and Paddington stations). I'd read Oliver Sacks' essay about Temple Grandin and a handful of newspaper and magazine articles about, or by, people with Asperger's and autism. I deliberately didn't add to this list. Imagination always trumps research. I thought that if I could make Christopher real to me then he'd be real to readers.[9]

It's noteworthy that another's interpretation of author Temple Grandin's experience is cited first. Temple Grandin is a prolific writer and speaker. Having spoken alongside her on a panel, I have experienced her speaking and cannot imagine wanting to add any filter to such erudition. The work of neurologists like Sacks is necessary, and Grandin has written of how he changed her life: "He just gave people so much insight into how the brain works . . . he got inside my mind."[10] But I don't see his insight as a substitute for listening to Grandin's own experience. Perhaps it's because my first training was as a historian. Firsthand source material matters, as does the interpretations of it and the biases of the interpreters. Or maybe it's because I don't want my meaning mangled by someone else when I am here speaking. Our voices have value: I don't want my words to be shorn of my history or filtered for an audience unready for disabled reality.

Disability is hidden through our history as well as our literature, just as we, as disabled people, have been hidden too. For much of our history, disabled people were not at liberty, we were in institutions.[11] I often feel this lack of familiarity with disability when I am in public. As a wheelchair user, with an obvious mobility aid, I can never blend in, in public. My appearance attracts enquiry. On the way to college one day, I was stopped in the street by a stranger: "What's wrong with you? You're too pretty to be in that wheelchair." I was wearing a vintage shooting skirt in soft brown tweed; I love it because it has pockets (originally for shotgun cartridges). I'd paired it with an apricot silk blouse and a blonde straw hat to guard my sensitive skin against the blazing sunshine, even late in the autumn. I've already been told I look like I am from the past three times today. This is not quite true; if I was from the era my clothes

---

[8] Philip Wilson, "The Top 10 Books About Disability," *The Guardian*, last modified July 3, 2013, https://www.theguardian.com/books/2013/jul/03/top-10-books-disability-paul-wilson
[9] Mark Haddon, "Asperger's & Autism," MarkHaddon.com, July 16, 2009, http://markhaddon.com/blog/aspergers-autism
[10] Sarah Zhang. "Temple Grandin on How Oliver Sacks Changed her Life." *Wired*, last modified September 1, 2015, https://www.wired.com/2015/09/temple-grandin-oliver-sacks-changed-life/.
[11] Tom Shakespeare's *Disability: The Basics* (Routledge, 2017) provides an excellent overview of the historical and cultural contexts of disability.

evoke, I would not be at liberty to travel through this city—to study, to work, to be free. But my clothes are neatly pressed, and I smell like roses thanks to the golden hued rose maroc oil dotting my pulse points. In this way, I am confusing—disabled but styled. Impaired but invisibly so, beyond the wheelchair, or perhaps, beyond first glance. My internal impairments—my autoimmune illnesses, multiple neurodivergences, chronic pain—are all invisible under my carefully styled hair and make-up.

People prefer it when I wear make-up; my fellow students make comments that I might be recovering. They know recovery is impossible, or they should if they have listened to my answer the first time they asked that question. But I have learned it is more comfortable for people around me if I look as far from sick as possible. I resent the extra labor because I still feel the same no matter how I present. But I cannot have more conversations about potential cures today, so out come the beauty blender, Lily Lolo Vegan Mineral Foundation in China Doll, and the Cloud Paint Puff Blusher shaped like a tube of watercolor paint.

This is what I say, when people ask what's wrong with me (although maybe I shouldn't):

For the eyeing of my scars, there is a charge

For the hearing of my heart——

It really goes.

And there is a charge, a very large charge

For a word or a touch

Or a bit of blood

Or a piece of my hair or my clothes.[12]

I don't assume most people understand this, as a response, or pierce through the layers of reference I've interwoven in my relationship to Sylvia Plath's poem, "Lady Lazarus," over my years of illness, near death, and dealing with what happens when we don't die—or live—as expected.

I live as a disabled woman and therefore, to many people, I live in between. Not fully alive, as I carry pain and impairment with me, reminding those around me of the fallibility of the human body, the limits of medicine, and the human suffering which exists around, through, and sometimes because of our technological advances. I transcend the binaries with my wheelchair, which I relate to as a part of my body, with my wearable technology which modulates and supports my body into being. Too inconvenient, I won't be fully whole or politely die. Nor will I be a pitiful human or fixed by technology. Instead, I straddle the boundaries, the binaries, and exist not in spite

---

[12]Sylvia Plath, "Lady Lazarus," *Ariel* (Faber & Faber, 1965; repr. in *The Collected Poems*, Harper Perennial, 2018), 244–247.

of the disbelief but disregarding it. Because I, like many disabled folks and LGBTIAQ+ folks, live a whole and delighted life beyond the understanding of many people who live closer to the mainstream. And it's the mainstream I have no appetite for. While they pity me for not being like them, I can't imagine living simply on the surface of such a vast and compelling world.

The charge for the eyeing of my scars is one that I pay first. It costs me to share these things with people, costs me because I relive, technically become re-traumatized, when I open up the memories, the wounds again. Because seeing people's response tells me something about them, about our societies, and about what I did and did not get the day I received that wound first. It too often tells me that they are using my scars to mark my otherness, my difference, my distance, and to reassure themselves that they will never end up in my position. I make that as difficult as I can for them because it's untrue.

It's disguised as "listening to lived experience," but there are only certain experiences they want to listen to; it's an updated freak show. Consider my intersections: I am disabled, neurodiverse, a wheelchair user, a trauma survivor, a woman, petite, intellectual, and academic. These qualities combined break the dominant narratives. But it's not only my voice and the stories I tell which are policed; disabled bodies are policed for confronting the ableism non-disabled people embody and in the structures they build. I don't even have to say anything. I just have to turn up and need to use the loo. The one that's "totally accessible, there's just a small step. Derek here will carry you over it." Uh, no, I'm not going into a bathroom with Derek, sorry. "Oh, and the lightbulb is out, no one here uses it, you see. But you can pee in the dark, right?"

Disabled women are still welcomed for our shock value, disguised as "listening to lived experience." Tell us of your terrible experiences, so we can nod and gasp, while disavowing how we are contributing to othering in this very room. When you are only asked to speak on what you've suffered, not your expertise, craft, art, possibility. What we are *not asked* has an impact on how you experience yourself and the direction of your work in our world. I'm fed up of being a cautionary tale. I don't want shock and sorrow; I want you to be awake. If you've never heard of these struggles before, how have you managed to insulate yourself from them? Don't you have disabled friends or family? Or maybe you aren't the kind of person such painful things can be safely shared with.

I'm afraid to say, by now, I turn it around, and if they demand to see, I make them pay. I sell access to my body and experience for cash because I need to be paid, and that's what people will pay for, disregarding my expertise of course, because how could I have any of that? I'm comfortable with this because I was already inured to the cost of marginalized labor: how often I calculate my hourly rate and comfort myself with what I am being paid to listen to a man explain to me not only what I already know but what I have already fixed for him. But it's too tempting for them, it seems, to lean over me, a petite woman with long hair in my wheelchair, bending down and explaining paternalistically.

On different days, my different roles are a writer and then a therapist; as a writer, I show my scars, and as a therapist, I witness the scars of others. Therapists sell therapeutic love by the hour. Part of my job is to sit in the room, to cherish and therapeutically love, to risk merging with, to be incredibly vulnerable with, to fully sit with, take in, listen to, and psychologically hold whoever comes through the door. When I became a therapist, I could set boundaries for people to tell me of their pain, to reach into my own scars and pull out the experience and wisdom I had accrued there and draw on it to sit alongside someone lost in the depths of their own suffering. I could know that the suffering is true and that there is also a future, that the pain may go on, but that life can be worth going onwards for.

Our disabled pain is too often seen as educative. We are called upon to share because there is a persistent belief that if people know about a problem, this will cause the problem to be fixed. I have yet to see this work. I have absolutely seen people create change through concerted, collective effort, but there isn't a tipping point where awareness becomes action. That's why I am reticent about sharing my scars for "awareness" because I have shared so many times and not seen the shifts I was promised. This isn't to say all trauma is recognized; it is not, but our pain is privileged above our joy. I write bracing myself for the cloying chloroform sympathy, knowing I am being harmed in sharing but speaking out because I hope to stop future harm to those coming up behind me, and because quite frankly, seeing my scars is still all that many are willing to pay for. It makes me complicit in my own oppression—I need to eat. That's what comes of a benefits system riddled from a decade of the UK government's austerity program. There are places we are all most familiar with on the spectrum of degradation, and the showing of my scars for pay is the one I know most intimately. But there is a charge.

When we are only asked to speak on what we've suffered, not our expertise, our craft, our art, that has an impact on how we experience ourselves and the direction of our work. The wider implications for disabled, neurodivergent, and chronically ill creatives, and for our literary canon itself, is that we are writing for non-disabled gazes, mired all too often in outdated stereotypes of what disabled experience is like and skewed by the fear of disability, impairment, and death. In Virginia Woolf's 1925 essay titled "On Being Ill," she asks why "illness has not taken its place with love, battle, and jealousy among the prime themes of literature."[13] It's a question we are still asking: whose stories we do (and don't) tell and what counts as literature? Where we turn our gaze impacts the literary canon, which in turn impacts people's perceptions and the policies we live under, the care we have access to, the futures we can dream into being, and the treatment we receive in the street. What is the impact when you experience your pain every day and see it amplified to such an extent that it overshadows every other aspect of you, and you are reduced to your pain? But, crucially, told that this is a kind favor the publisher is doing for you, because you said

---

[13] Virginia Woolf, "On Being Ill," *The New Criterion* (January 1926): 32–45.

you wanted to see your stories told and included, didn't you? And isn't this your story? This reality is so insidious, and it's happening all the time.

To combat this, writing joy is absolutely necessary, and joy can be tricky for trauma survivors and marginalized folks. Joy draws attention; it can even feel like it will make a bad thing happen, that the other shoe might crash down. Joy can feel like betraying our own and others' struggles. Joy can also feel impossible in this world, with the oppression, the abuse, the cost of living, the climate crisis, not to mention surveillance, state voyeurism, or the threat of it. Centering joy comes with the risk of surveillance. The extent of this surveillance was laid bare in a 2021 report by Privacy International, which exposed the far-reaching capabilities of the UK's government benefits agency, the Department of Work and Pensions (DWP). The report revealed that the DWP's surveillance net extends not just to benefit claimants, including disability claimants, but to their social circles, as well.[14]

I teach a workshop on writing joy for marginalized folks. In our workshop, we make a Joy Journal, which we begin by noticing where we experience joy in a world that dismisses our pleasure. We develop the practice of noticing and describing pleasure, even in a world that tells us we cannot and should not. Writing joy is absolutely necessary, just as disabled voices—and our authentic, complex experiences—are necessary in literature and in the media to ensure disabled futures.

Bibliography

BBC. "Tory MPs Defend Votes After Uproar Over Sewage Proposals," BBC News, last modified October 25, 2021. https://www.bbc.com/news/uk-politics-59040175

Gudge, Emily. "River Thames Pollution 'Devastating'—Oxford Wild Swimmer." BBC News, last modified April 28, 2024. https://www.bbc.co.uk/news/uk-england-oxfordshire-68855301

Haddon, Mark. "Asperger's & Autism." MarkHaddon.com, July 16, 2009. http://markhaddon.com/blog/aspergers-autism

Office for National Statistics (ONS). "Half a Million More People Are Out of the Labour Force Because of Long-Term Sickness." November 10, 2022. https://www.ons.gov.uk/employmentandlabourmarket/peoplenotinwork/economicinactivty/articles/halfamillionmorepeopleareoutofthelabourforcebecauseoflongtermsickness/2022-11-10.

Plath, Sylvia. "Lady Lazarus." *Ariel*. Faber & Faber, 1965. Reprint in *The Collected Poems*, Harper Perennial, 2018.

Privacy International. "Shedding Light on the DWP Part 1—We Read the UK Welfare Agency's 995-Page Guide on Conducting Surveillance and Here Are the Scariest Bits." Privacy International, 2021. https://privacyinternational.org/long-read/4395/shedding-light-dwp-part-1-we-read-uk-welfare-agencys-995-page-guide-conducting

---

[14]Privacy International. "Shedding Light on the DWP Part 1—We Read the UK Welfare Agency's 995-Page Guide on Conducting Surveillance and Here Are the Scariest Bits." *Privacy International*, 2021, https://privacyinternational.org/long-read/4395/shedding-light-dwp-part-1-we-read-uk-welfare-agencys-995-page-guide-conducting

Scope. "Disability Facts and Figures." Accessed May 28, 2024. https://www.scope.org.uk/media/disability-facts-figures/

Sontag, Susan. "Illness as Metaphor," *The New York Review*, January 26, 1978. https://www.nybooks.com/articles/1978/01/26/illness-as-metaphor/

Wilson, Philip. "The Top 10 Books About Disability." *The Guardian*, July 3, 2013. https://www.theguardian.com/books/2013/jul/03/top-10-books-disability-paul-wilson

Woolf, Virginia. "On Being Ill," *The New Criterion* (January 1926): 32–45.

Zhang, Sarah. "Temple Grandin on How Oliver Sacks Changed Her Life." *Wired*, September 1, 2015. https://www.wired.com/2015/09/temple-grandin-oliver-sacks-changed-life/

7 When Methods Fail: A View from the Perspective of a Dyslexic Writer

SAUL LEMEROND

So, I have a story that always kills at readings. It's called "That Day in the School Yard." This is how it begins:

> Marcus lays flat on his back writhing in pain, whimpering. Janet levels her pistol at Dave.
> "I have to do this," says Janet. "Your snakes for arms are biting too many people."
> "I didn't ask for these!" Screams Dave, tears streaming down his eyes. "I never asked to have snakes for arms!"[1]

This piece is one of many stories I have that features absurd alienation. I like writing stories like this. Something of which I am sure is in no way connected to my dyslexia, which is something that in no way shaped the person I am today. Just kidding, that was a joke. For a very long time I was undiagnosed, and contrary to what I just said, my dyslexia actually had some pretty profound effects on my life, and I'm going to address some of those effects now. I was a deeply unhappy child. It would be an understatement to say I struggled in school. This was partially in the 1980s but mostly in the 1990s. I'm sure it's different now, and there are people who care about kids with learning disabilities like mine. How different this makes their learning environments, I do not know, but imagine whatever the difference, it's not enough. I say this because of my history with undiagnosed dyslexia, and because I'm an educator now.

Maybe you're an educator, too. If you're not, it's a safe bet you were a student once. So, as a student and/or educator, I can see you and I have a lot in common, and I'd like you to join me in a little exercise. I'd like you to pretend you're me. Not me today but me in kindergarten. You are kindergarten me. You are mild mannered, like to make jokes, and are obsessed with the Teenage Mutant Ninja Turtles, mostly Michelangelo because he's the coolest. You and the rest of your kindergarten class are doing a workbook exercise. You're practicing your letters. Copying them over and over again, and it's apparent that you have very sloppy handwriting. Maybe the

---

[1] Saul Lemerond, "That Day in the School Yard," *Intrinsick* (April 16, 2025), https://www.intrinsick.com/stories/pterrorshark-vs-sharkadactl-that-day-in-the-school-yard

sloppiest. You can tell because you look to your right and left and see your peers and the job they're doing, making beautifully straight lines and elegant curves for the shapes of their letters. Your letters are all crooked and bent in ways they're not supposed to be. It's clear from the workbook pictures you're doing it wrong. You can't get your lines to go straight up and down, and you can't get your loops evenly round. You are concentrating. You are trying hard, and it is not working.

The teacher, who is smiling at each classmate's work as she walks past, stops smiling when she looks at yours, sees you're struggling, and gently says that you need to slow down. You're going too fast.

So, you slow down. The other students aren't going as slow as you, and they're getting a lot further ahead in the workbook where each page is a new letter of the alphabet. You don't want to fall behind, but you also want to do it right, so you do what your teacher asks. You go slow.

And will you look at that, your letters start to look better. Your teacher was right. It turns out all you needed was a little direction, and now you feel like you're keeping up with the rest of the class, learning to do the sorts of things you're supposed to learn.

Just kidding, that's not what happens.

What happens is your letters don't look any better at all. You were flustered before, and now it is worse. In your distress, you slam your feelings of fluster and frustration together and become fluster-ated. It's bad.

Your teacher sees this the next time she comes around and says, "[insert your name here], I told you, you need to take your time. Your letters will turn out better if you just go slower."

Of course, she must be right. She is the teacher after all. So, now you go even slower, as slow as you can, like, slow motion slow, and while you go slow-mo slow, you to try to pay as much attention as possible to making those lines straight and loops nicely curved. And, after what seems like forever, it finally works. Your letters are good, and the teacher smiles and you catch up with the rest of the class. You had to work harder than the other kids, but your hard work has paid off.

Except of course this is not what happens.

What happens is going slow-mo slow does not help. Your letters very clearly look worse, and you start to get the impression that you're doing all this extra work for nothing, maybe even for less than nothing. You look to your left and right. Your peers, if they're not already done with the exercise, are not going particularly slow, and you wonder why it is that you can't do what they're doing. Why they can make their letters right, and you can't? Then your teacher comes over and says . . .

And I want to stop here because some version of this conversation will happen to you over and over again for the next thirteen years of your life (your entire K–12 experience) anytime letters or numbers are involved:

. . . your teacher comes over and says "[insert your name here], you're not listening. I told you to slow down."

And, your cheeks get red, and you say, "But, I did listen."

Her response?

She just repeats herself, "You need to slow down," then she walks away, and you sit there, humiliated.

This story is emblematic of your entire education. You try to do what your teachers instruct you to, but you can't because apparently, if your teachers are to be believed, you don't listen, or you're lazy, or you have a bad attitude, or you don't take your work seriously, or it's some combination of all that.

When you're in sixth grade, and you've failed another algebra exam, your teacher says, "[insert your name here], you're making too many simple mistakes. You need to make sure to check your work before you hand it in. If you just took the time to check your work, you wouldn't have failed every exam you've taken so far in this class. In fact, you'd be doing quite well."

And you have, at this point in your life, heard this so many times that you know saying, "But, I did. I checked it over and over and over again. It looked right to me. It always looks right," will do nothing. It's never worked before. Why should it now? You know it's pointless, but you say it anyway. You say, "I did check it."

The reply you get most often in times like these is nothing. Silence. Your teachers have nothing to say because they can't help you. They believe in their teaching methods and will not entertain the notion that there are some cases in which those methods do not work. Because of this, they couldn't help you even if they wanted to, though to be clear, they don't. They've convinced themselves you aren't listening to them. That you *won't* listen to them. Or, they've convinced themselves that you do listen to them, but you're just too lazy or otherwise hostile to do what they ask.

If you knew the meaning of absurd at this time in your life, you'd say this was it. It's not like they haven't watched you check your work and watched in real time as you look over your errors with no sense that they're there. Of course they have. They think that you aren't trying. They think that you don't care about school. That it's your fault.

They think you have snakes for arms.

They truly believe, deep down, in a place where thoughts like this crystallize, that if you just slowed down and took your work seriously like all the other twelve-year-old boys you would be doing just as well as them if not better. They think that you're failing your classes on purpose. They really do. You know this is what they think because they tell you that you have an attitude problem. That you don't understand the value of education. They think that you, a mild-mannered kid who has never gotten a single detention; they think that at the age of twelve you've made the very conscious and very adult decision to throw away your education and any sort of future that goes with that. You know this because they make it known.

They say things like, "You're smart enough for the advanced algebra course, but I'm not going to recommend you for it because you're too lazy."

If this sounds cruel, it's because it is.

What's worse is that, eventually, through the magic of reinforcement, they end up being right about you. This is because the amount of anger you have toward school by this time is indescribable, so their opinions become self-fulfilling prophecies, and you stop trying.

You make a calculation. You look at the possible outcomes of putting in effort and not putting in effort, see that the results are the same either way, and decide your time is better spent elsewhere, which, and you can scarcely understand this in hindsight, is the simple and pure escapism of reading for pleasure and the therapeutic release of writing poems and stories. If there happens to be something you want to learn, you go to the library, look it up, and figure it out yourself.

When, for some inexplicable reason, you get passed on to the ninth grade even though you failed nearly all of your classes in middle school, you start high school knowing the next four years are going to be a complete waste of your time.

Before we go on, I want to make something clear. Dyslexia is a weird spectrum and presents itself differently in different people. I have never had much trouble reading. I think maybe because I stumbled into a couple of good coping mechanisms at a young age. But writing and math and drawing are different. Everything comes out wonky all the time. Not sometimes and not a little bit. It's all the time and a lot. For math and writing, I cannot tell why it's wrong by looking at it. It doesn't matter how slow I go or how many times I go over it.

It's not fun. It does not make me an interesting person. It sucks. It will never not suck. It's not fair, and I hate it.

My dyslexia made K–12 a profoundly alienating experience. One whose various cruelties and absurdities completely undermined the entire institution of education, and I still feel this strongly. My life is a constant exercise in looking at something I've composed, knowing there must be errors I cannot see, and wondering just exactly when that embarrassment bomb is going to explode.

Look, I admit I've done alright for myself. I have a PhD. I teach college writing and publish stories, which is pretty cool. But if you were to go back in time and tell an adolescent me that anything like this was in my future, I would have laughed in your face because there were no pathways open for me. Not spoken or unspoken. None. Nothing involving school was an option for me, and I'd known this to be true since the seventh grade.

So, when a miracle happened years after high school, and I learned a few useful coping mechanisms online and decided to go to college for creative writing, I was happy to learn that the structures that ignored neurodiversity and reified neurotypicality, structures that made my learning and writing life such a hopeless, embarrassing existence, had thankfully been dismantled. I was able to pursue my studies without the strong sense of sorrow, shame, and systemic opposition that had hung over me for as long as I could remember.

That was a joke. I'm kidding. Of course that didn't happen. Instead, I learned that there is no aspect of the creative writing industry (academic, publishing, or otherwise) that doesn't severely punish writers who cannot hand in clean work, which by way of the transitive property is another way of saying that there are structures in the creative writing world that specifically target, punish, exclude, and erase dyslexics and those with similar learning disabilities.

I have, in my life, known peers, professors, and editors (people who were often friends of mine) who made it clear to me that I insulted them, personally, for failing to hand them something that was not error free. I once had a colleague ask me if I was drunk when I sent them an email. I have also worked on journals where editors have said to me of others' work, "Well, if the person who submitted the story doesn't care enough to proofread the work, then why should I care enough to read it?"

I did not get diagnosed with dyslexia until I was in my mid-thirties, though I always suspected I had it. Most of the folks on my Mom's side of the family have it. Or, at least that's the suspicion anyway. I come from a working-class culture where you did not pay doctors to tell you things that you already knew. All the coping mechanisms I learned, I learned on my own. I had, and continue to have, friends and girlfriends proofread my stuff. I pay them if I have to. I started using the Google search bar as my spell check when I realized the algorithm understood context better than Word's spellchecker, which is beyond useless for me.

When I felt confident enough, I went to a local tech school in my late thirties because I was pretty sure no college would accept me with a 1.6 high school GPA (grade point average). Then, I transferred to my local university where I discovered the academic world of creative writing. As you might imagine, there were several people in this institution who noticed I had some issues. The same can be said for my master's program, only more so. Even more so for my PhD program.

I got diagnosed with dyslexia at the age of thirty-five, so I could try to pass my PhD comprehensive exams. It cost me $600. As PhD comprehensive exams vary from program to program, I will describe the chosen format at the particular program I attended.

You, [insert your name here], you're on campus, sitting at a computer set in lock-down mode. Lock-down mode means the computer has only one capability, which in this case is Microsoft Word. You are given an envelope with questions in it. The questions can be about anything that was written during the specific area of study you are being tested on. In this case, let's say it's early American literature. This means that they can ask you about any work of literature that was written in America over a several hundred-year period.

You can have no outside help. You can use no sources. You have access to nothing besides the desktop which is functionally a fancy word processor. You have five hours to write eighteen pages. That's all you get. Now, here's some things you should probably know about yourself:

> You make more mistakes the more stressed out you are.
>
> You make more mistakes the more tired you get.
>
> You make more mistakes the more self-conscious you get about making mistakes.
>
> You have no way of seeing your mistakes.

> The exams are graded pass/fail.
>
> You have never written anything worth reading that wasn't heavily dependent on your coping mechanisms: Google, the Internet, text-to-speech, etc., and you have access to none of those things during these exams.

Here's some more things you should know about yourself:

> You fail one exam, twice, which is the number of times you can fail an exam before the program director can ask you to go kick rocks.
>
> Your examiners have pointed to "writing issues."
>
> If you leave the program, you will have functionally wasted four years of your life and amassed an amount of student loan debt that you are, even a decade later, ashamed to talk about.

Effectively, I sought my costly dyslexia diagnosis because it was either that or drop out of my PhD program. As I mentioned, the center that tested me charged $600. This was an amount of money that as a grad student I did not have. Thankfully my credit card company was happy to foot the bill, asking only a meager 21 percent annual interest rate.

At any rate, it worked. I was able to pass my final PhD comprehensive exam with the accommodations I received following my diagnosis; for example, the five-hour exam became a seven-and-a-half-hour exam. I went on to defend my dissertation the next semester and look at me now. For many reasons, I consider getting diagnosed with dyslexia the best decision of my life and well worth the cost and the trouble. This has less to do with my exams and more to do with how I've come to understand myself as a person, how much shame I internalize on a daily basis, how I perceive others' perceptions of me, and a whole lot more. Having said that, I will never forgive the examiners who failed me and failed me again, ever. They, like many people, made assumptions about folks like me and their "writing issues."

This is my academic world. And it's just as alienating as my middle school algebra class. Whenever I hit the submit button on a story, I wonder if I wouldn't have been better off not sending it. This is because if there is a standard that work should be submitted relatively free of spelling and grammar errors, and you cannot see your errors, it means you are fucked. That's what it means. And, I get it. Sort of. I understand why some folks are seduced by these sorts of attitudes. If I didn't understand it, I probably wouldn't be so insecure about it. But, I don't want to opine about whether those sorts of standards are reasonable. That is not why I am here.

I want to make a simple point, which is to say that if these standards were actually true and necessary, then they preclude me from participating. It is that simple. Look, like I said before, I'm proud of who I am and what I've been able to accomplish. I am, despite the acerbic tone of this essay, a positive person whose default disposition mostly includes smiling and laughing. But, I feel this strongly because I know there are a lot of people out there like me who aren't or haven't been as lucky as I've been, and that's not okay. It sucks. It will never not suck. It's not fair, and I hate it.

What's worse is that there is no part of me that thinks any of my past teachers or professors believed cruelty was good praxis. I do not believe any of them knowingly enacted their cruelties upon me. They were trained in certain methods. Those methods were all they knew, and they believed in them. So, whenever they encountered instances where their methods were ineffective, they assumed a willful refusal on the part of the student. It never dawned on them to question their methods. It never even dawned on them that there could be some different dynamic at play. The problem is, and always has been, a systemic one. And that needs to change . . . a lot. It does, it needs to change a lot. I feel like it should be easy, not hard but easy, to accommodate conscientious folks like me. It's not like we have snakes for arms. I'd be willing to bet almost none of us do. Like, maybe it would be okay if we all took ourselves a little less seriously. Maybe then the world would be a better place.

Or, and perhaps more importantly, maybe it's time to acknowledge that normative teaching methods and standards (as well as normative writing beliefs and publishing standards) at their most fundamental levels exist to reward the same sorts of people they've been rewarding for centuries. Maybe then we'd be better off. I know I'd be better off because I can say unequivocally that right now that sort of person is not me. There are, in fact, a lot of people who aren't that sort of person who deserve to be seen and to be read.

Bibliography

Lemerond, Saul. "That Day in the School Yard." *Intrinsick* (April 16, 2025). https://www.intrinsick.com/stories/pterrorshark-vs-sharkadactl-that-day-in-the-school-yard

8   The Breath of the Bird: My Writing Life with Bipolar Disorder

CELESTE MARIA SCHUELER

Trigger Warning: this chapter contains mention of hallucinations, self-harm, and suicide ideation.

Many are painfully unaware that the Americans with Disabilities Act (ADA) includes psychiatric diagnoses in its list of disabilities, including anxiety disorder, depression, bipolar disorder, and schizophrenia,[1] which means that those diagnosed with these conditions should receive understanding, fair treatment, and disability accommodations in writing classrooms, in writing workshops, in jobs, in publishing opportunities, and beyond. Furthermore, psychiatric conditions are far more common than many suspect: the National Institute of Mental Health currently estimates that 2.8 percent of adults in the United States have bipolar disorder,[2] the condition that will be discussed in this chapter. In this collection of vignettes, I recount my journey from a young student-writer to being a professional writer and full-time mother, all the while trying desperately to write and publish poems while blighted by bipolar disorder. I also discuss the stigma I've experienced as well as the accommodations plan that enabled me to finish my education in creative writing. Bipolar is relentless, terrifying, and unfairly stigmatized, but it is also part of my identity and a source of my poetic inspiration.

• • •

The first onslaught of turbulent mood swings I can remember was the summer before I turned fifteen years old. Suicidal ideation rang through my head that summer as I felt completely out of control. I would spend my high school years in and out of hypomania and depression. My mother took me to specialists who only labeled my symptoms as *teen angst*. Nights were spent sleepless, and days left me feeling neurotic, as my mind sprinted from the highest happiness to an uncontrollable turmoil of tears in the

---

[1] "Mental Health Conditions in the Workplace and the ADA." *ADA National Network*. Last modified January 2025, https://adata.org/factsheet/health
[2] "Bipolar Disorder." *National Institute of Health*. Accessed January 23, 2025, https://www.nimh.nih.gov/health/statistics/bipolar-disorder

bathroom. My mood swings were unbearable, and I began to self-harm nearly every day. In high school, I managed to maintain a high GPA taking advanced English and journalism classes and continued to sing in the choir. I had dreams of being a journalist for CNN or working for magazines. However, my unmedicated mental illness would follow me into my college years.

I saw my first psychiatrist during my freshman year at Mississippi University for Women (MUW) in 2007, but I still did not have a diagnosis. I struggled with honors classes, maintaining a social life, and staying on top of taking multiple medications multiple times a day. Brain fog set in as the depression crept into every part of my life. I could not remember to take Depakote three times a day and only take the Xanax as needed. Later, I would try Abilify and have a severe allergic reaction in my early morning history class. Despite my parents' phone calls to professors, seeing a counselor on campus, and remaining under the care of a psychiatrist, no one strived to help me create an accommodations plan at this time. I would lose my scholarship due to a low GPA after my freshman year.

• • •

The first poems I wrote about my mood swings were read by my creative writing professor. After nearly a full semester of reading my terrible poems about mania and depression and noticing my multiple absences, he suggested I take my paperwork and my strife to the department of student affairs. With notes from my psychiatrist and a letter from my new therapist, I had an accommodations plan created that gave me help with my disability. I still did not have a true diagnosis, but it was enough that I could receive accommodations for deadlines and missed classes. Even so, I attempted suicide for the first time in the spring of 2009, and I had to medically withdraw from the university that semester. I remember telling the psychiatrist on call that it felt like birds were inside me. Birds rattling every emotion I ever felt. These birds would reveal themselves in my future poems about my mental illness. Three years later, I would experience psychosis for the first time: in my hallucinations, I beheld bloody and mutilated animals along the walls of my resident hall.

• • •

Three psychiatrists and nearly ten years later, I would finally be diagnosed with bipolar disorder and learn that seasonal changes affect my mood swings. At this time, I was twenty-five years old and living in Oklahoma City with my Air Force spouse. We were sitting in my doctor's office when she told us I should not live alone, yet my husband was about to deploy for months at a time. I had already suffered a severe depressive episode that sent me to the psychiatric hospital earlier that year. After my husband's deployment, I again experienced psychosis: hallucinating dead rats in piles around the house; curbs were full of dead, mutilated cats as I drove around the city. As I would get ready for bed, I had no idea what was real or a nightmare. My hallucinations were jarring and isolating. I would imagine going to sleep and never waking up. Again, I was hospitalized.

• • •

I was not writing from the ages of twenty-four to nearly twenty-eight, though I would begin a medication in 2015 called Latuda, and within three weeks, my life drastically changed. Latuda is a medication specifically created to treat bipolar depression. Stabilization was on the horizon as I applied to graduate with a BA in English and Creative Writing. In fact, I likely would not have finished my education without the accommodations plan that was recommended by my professor years before, which highlights the impact that one attentive, knowledgeable, and caring creative writing educator can have on a student. I had thought all those dreams of continuing my education were gone because of my condition. I was accepted into the MFA program at MUW in 2016 and began writing poems and essays about my experience with mental illness. I was on top of my pillbox and maintaining good sleep and exercise habits. I finally felt happy. I had been stable for over a year, with only a few bouts of depression here and there. The urge to self-harm or suicide was always there when the depressive episodes would reappear. Once again, I had an accommodations plan for my graduate classes, and I felt like I could be more open about my diagnosis, but the stigma was still there ringing in my head. I was afraid to tell other Air Force spouses I met, and birds would wing in my chest whenever I shared a poem about bipolar disorder.

• • •

I was hospitalized four times between 2009 and 2018, and I was in and out of outpatient programs and dominated by endless psychiatric and therapy appointments. My moods would ricochet depending on the seasons and the stress in my life. I gave birth to my twin daughters after my last hospitalization and graduated with my MFA in creative writing in December 2019. Despite these joys, dark periods would follow, and I would struggle to juggle writing poetry with my mental illness and motherhood. We would move from an Air Force base in rural Oklahoma to the hilly metro of Seattle in 2021, and the gray fall and winter would prove to be difficult on my mood swings. But I threw myself into my writing and raising my twins. As they began to grow more independent and started preschool and moved into kindergarten, I found more time to focus on writing new poems and revising older ones. I would attend my first AWP conference in Seattle in 2023 and find joy in a community of other writers and in listening to other panelists share their struggles with mental illness. I did not feel such immense isolation anymore. Later, I would find community in other writers at events in Tacoma as well as Seattle.

• • •

I almost did not write this essay because I almost didn't make it. Summer was fun and easy that year. Endless days of warmth and sunshine always prove to be the best for my mood swings. My first full-length collection of poetry was accepted for publication. I was writing and rewriting poems for my manuscript. My regular therapist was on maternity leave, but I was still flourishing. Until September.

My husband left for flights, and despite years of learning how to navigate throes of depression, I fell into a deep depressive episode and felt the old twinge of suicidal ideation. I started seeing an interim therapist until mine came back from maternity leave. However, there was a Sunday morning where the depressive episode was so consuming that I had to send my daughters to the neighbor's house to play until my husband came home from flying. I spent two hours on the phone with a friend who talked me down from the proverbial ledge.

• • •

It's been twenty-one years since the first ideas of suicide rang throughout my body, and I am still having to reevaluate my medications and therapy appointments. I now see my therapist twice a week and have upped my mood stabilizer. I am still taking Latuda, but now I also take a cocktail of Buspar, Gabapentin, and Lamictal. I never miss a dose. I never miss therapy or psychiatric appointments. But I do not write every day or send out for publication every day because, despite what we're told about effective writing habits, doing so is impossible.

Bipolar disorder affects every aspect of my life, and no matter how many times I read the *DSM-5* or bipolar self-help books, I still don't fully understand how my brain works. My therapist has explained how my brain functions during a hypomanic or depressive episode and how my cognition goes awry. Despite medications and books and DBT and support, I am still learning how to cope with my moods. I am still learning how to take care of myself.

Bipolar disorder touches everything I touch. Those birds still suffocate me at times, and I try to write them out. I still feel shame when I fill out medical forms for anything and have to list medication after medication. Another military spouse friend told me over coffee that bipolar is one of the most stigmatized mental illnesses. I've experienced this stigma firsthand. And every time I share a poem about my experience, I strive to tear down those walls of stigma. The troubled, beautiful birds of my mindbody want to be seen, and have their true song be heard.

Bibliography

ADA National Network. "Mental Health Conditions in the Workplace and the ADA."
    ADA National Network. Last modified January 2025. https://adata.org/factsheet/health
National Institute of Health. "Bipolar Disorder." National Institute of Health. Accessed
    January 23, 2025, https://www.nimh.nih.gov/health/statistics/bipolar-disorder

9 The Gallery Effect: The Visibly Disabled Writer in the Real World

TYLER DARNELL

Disability is not a brave struggle or courage in the face of adversity.
Disability is an art. It's an ingenious way to live.[1]

I've called myself an athlete of the mundane. While my two abled siblings were athletes and competitors in school, I was watching on the sidelines. I spent all my time in hospitals and physical therapy learning how to walk with cerebral palsy. The one thing everyone else around me could do as toddlers.

I didn't remove myself from sports entirely. I served as the water boy for my middle school football team, but I refused to give up my first period English class so that I could join the team fully. I liked being able to read and write in the morning. It set a tone for my day, even then. English as a subject in school was easier than about anything else I could do. I read early and often. I read everything. I went to the library almost as often as I went to church. I could explore these words on paper freely in the ways the physical world would never open itself up to me. Even as others tried to include me, it felt shallow. Any praise for physical ability in sports was rooted not in excellence but in the fact that I tried at all.

The mechanics of writing and stories came to me as I went through school. Writing is a primitive technology, sure, but it gave me access to what was within. The parts not even others could see, which was what was really interesting to me about reading. I wanted to peek in the windows and doors, to see in other people's lives without being rude or disrespectful. Because everyone sure as hell seemed to butt into mine. Parents, family, doctors, nurses, and everyone else in between. I couldn't even make a friend without them asking in the first five minutes what was wrong with me. Of course, I knew. My parents, family, doctors, and nurses had told me (though I have learned this is not a universal experience as some parents avoid the concrete terms), but how do you tell another seven-year-old who's just learned to manage a select few multisyllabic words how to say *cerebral palsy*?

This is why my first novel uses the misnomer *Super Ballsy*. Even as I get older people have a hard time saying the words, but never a hard time asking. It didn't

---

[1] Epigraph is by Neil Marcus, who was widely known to say this at his performances.

come from me. Super Ballsy was from an ex-boyfriend when I was well into my twenties. It was the first time hanging out with his friends, and when I told them my boyfriend drunk slurred "Super Ballsy" so loud everyone could hear, it stuck. Maybe there was something super about it. Others in my life have often gone out of their way to make it sound like lurching out of my house and holding down a demanding job as a high school English teacher had a ring of the extraordinary. Ballsy was a little cruder, maybe, but I guess I didn't let it stop me either.

I call it "The Gallery Effect." Disabled people are always being watched. Always being told by the eyes of strangers that they are doing something wrong. And sometimes they even use words. It is not, primarily, good or bad to be disabled, but it is a hell of a lot harder to get along when all you're trying to do most days is get things done. Not for others' enjoyment like art, but simply living our lives. Not even performance art, just living. There is no other vessel than our body that we can contain our life in. It wasn't a choice.

Others seemed to make much of how I used my time and energy because I was disabled. Because they believed they couldn't if they were in the same situation. As if I had checked a box at birth and made the choice. As if I wanted things more difficult. As if disability would be more fun for me. It does add a kind of texture and strangeness to the world, but only because the world leaves so little room for difference, unless the *difference* can be turned into a commodity for others.

Once, when I was sixteen years old, a complete stranger came up to me, bawling, in the supermarket. She asked if she could give me a hug, her arms already outstretched. She had lost her disabled child whom she swore looked and walked like I did. I didn't know what to do but saying no felt like too much at the time. In my late thirties now, I would simply say, "I am so sorry for your loss, but I am still alive and need to handle my very basic need of school supplies." Not that anyone cares like that now. Middle-aged disability doesn't have the same cachet as youth. I was the cute kid on the Easter Seals Telethon at four years old, after all, leaning into my mother's blouse speaking maybe two words into the camera. As the disabled body ages, it becomes more ignored, less tolerated. I am only somewhat prepared. Perhaps my corpus will one day save me from some of that hassle.

Writing has been a way for me to be invisible. I would read books all the time and awe at the skill, craft, and talent, and know nothing about the writer except a small bio and picture on the back cover. They didn't have to be right in front of me to acknowledge their work. It wasn't questioned because it was already created. I knew they could do it because they did it. I could see it in their work. The work of writing for me has been an effort to maintain this coveted status: appreciated for what's been done but not questioned for my presence.

Then I wrote a whole novel in the pandemic about a young kid in middle school with cerebral palsy. I remember reading as a kid and seeing nothing in the kids' section that looked like me. The closest I got was E. B. White's *The Trumpeter Swan* about a swan who couldn't sing a song like his peers, but with a little help, discovered that he could handle a trumpet and play his own song. Alas, I was not a swan. Just a young boy who went to the Shriner's Hospital for Children to be assessed, poked, and prodded twice a year. Then I got cut open to achieve a more meaningful result than walking aimlessly down hospital halls and assessed for things my damaged brain couldn't control.

I have learned to walk three times in my thirty-something years. Two more times than most people. Without the struggle and pain of those intensive physical therapy routines post-surgery, I wouldn't be walking the way I am today. Full recovery from those surgeries takes around two years, all told. I had to build new brain synapses. The surgery weakened muscles and tendons so I could tell my body more clearly what to do: pick up your foot higher, pull your leg in. Again, again, again. Revision for my body through pain. Each leg muscle weakened so much it burned.

That's what cerebral palsy is—brain damage that the nerve synapses up there work around, however poorly. It manifests physically, but its root is neurological. My case is mild. I can walk, though imperfectly, and am physically awkward. It's a dynamic disability, and others may have different experiences. Where others may have intellectual disabilities as well, I've graduated high school, college, and pursued more than one certification to supplement those learnings. All the while, writing felt like a type of magic. Then I discovered people got paid to do it. My English teacher told me most of the writers we read were already wealthy. For instance, *Frankenstein* was conceived by Mary Shelley surrounded by wealthy peers. Writing then was just a fun hobby for the elite. The disabled were too busy being institutionalized or left to wallow in filth on the street in the nineteenth century.

Even so, at eighteen years old, I asked to use my dad's credit card and ordered $100 worth of books on writing and craft. I remember almost none of what I read now, but I know I was earnest, and some seeped in. My first forays into writing were fitful, and I didn't always know what I was doing, but I always came back. Like a duck to water. Or maybe like a swan, who wrote instead of playing the trumpet.

In my second year of college, I exhausted all avenues for "respectable" degrees because I was godawful at math. I switched to English for a semester and a half without telling my dad, the engineer. He was surprised but agreed to continue funding the endeavor. I wanted not to flunk out of college taking math courses I didn't understand. I took a logic course instead and passed with a C, which counted as math under the liberal arts requirements. My first workshop was poetry, which let me hide under a veil of words and phrases that maybe did or didn't have meaning. It wasn't my first choice, but fiction was full that semester. I enjoyed reading *The Dream Songs* of John Berryman, even if the ultimate end was morose. It did the job of putting me off from being a poet for the most part. I was cheerier than that. My poems didn't feel like a risk because I didn't feel seen. That summer, I worked as a camp counselor at my local YMCA and was full of stories. I wrote my first fiction workshop piece about foursquare and drama between kids. In hindsight, maybe this was my first clue that I would write children's fiction one day which also included a red rubber ball. While it was loosely based on my experience the summer before, my disability didn't carry over. I focused on the kids' drama and not my own experience.

It wasn't until I took a risk and wrote from my disabled experience as a post-surgery teen trying to find love in a hospital room that it really hit. It made sense that my first girlfriend was fictional. I didn't know what love was or that I wanted to acknowledge that I was gay. I was just parroting what all the straight greats were doing minus disability, of course. Eyes lit up, there was a note from my instructor that said *you should write about this more*. I had lifted the veil. Of course, I was still disabled in the class. I lurched in like I always did, but I was assessed on the value of my prose. I didn't write about my disability again for over a decade, however. I didn't believe it mattered yet. That who I was could reflect in the work I made. The entire canon of literature I was exposed to was mostly straight, white, abled, and male. I was only some of those things. I took a sinister solace in that for the future writing career I imagined but never pursued until I found better stories to tell.

By 2010, I had graduated college and was working at a pharmacy. I worked all year except for one week when my alma mater hosted a writing conference. I would save up the few hundred dollars, so I could stay on-campus. I was in workshops led by grad students. If I wrote only once a year, it was in the few weeks before and during that time. It kept me going even as other parts of my world crumbled. My family's homophobia would not back down, which felt even more jarring as they had always supported me with my cerebral palsy. What was one more difference? My disability was never framed as a sacrifice, though I knew it was, but my sexuality was too much for them. They told me my life would be miserable, by which they meant they would do their best to make it so. After watching my two straight siblings get married with their love and support, it felt like I was in a bizarro world.

"The Importance of Tractor Beams" was the first story I wrote that felt honest. It's never been published, but it did its job. I got a first-floor garage apartment in a gentrified city neighborhood in Houston for a reasonable monthly price. I watched million-dollar homes rise up in my four years there as I built a small oasis of my own. My writing community showed up because I was brave enough to show up on the page. I watch *Bob's Burgers* now, and it reminds me of that garage apartment, tucked in the back at the end of a driveway, impossible for delivery drivers to find. Neon green with yellow trim. My husband called it the Sprite can house for its color when he moved me out into our shared apartment. It was what I needed at the time, an apartment in a city neighborhood with some sense of decency toward difference for under a thousand dollars per month.

To be observed as a writer is to be observed on the page. In this space, my physical body is not as important as my body of work. Words are like passports to my intellectual integrity. Instead of being looked at and questioning my value, I can be announced to readers before I enter. Words will last longer than our bodies. More fragile in some ways, but sturdier in others. Multiplied in publication, like clones, finding their way into readers' minds. Shaping them. And maybe that's where the conflict lies for me. Are people willing to be shaped by a disabled writer's words like they will inevitably be shaped by our bodies?

The disabled body is a spectacle because the abled person will always want to work against it. The disabled writer being observed in workshop or elsewhere can be seen as an enemy in the same way that the literary canon tries to edge all others out. Because what is good only looks and behaves one way. And the best good in the body, pristine health, is all that deserves to be honored: perfection to form defined by those who have it. This doesn't even consider the invisible disabilities so many live with that can be hidden, unseen, or ignored. We do this disservice to our bodies and our writing by pretending disability doesn't exist. Instead of honoring our energy and expertise in our bodies we try to push through, whether it's in workshop or roadblocks in personal writing time.

I've been to high-profile readings and seen authors get that question the interviewer always asks: how do you write? And the answer is always some weird quirk that most folks could never remake in their own life, especially if this person is already a best-selling, full-time author, a unicorn, and disabled people are rarely unicorns. We are a large, marginalized group often with limited access in different ways. That's a whole lot of people who may not get the same consideration because our process and stories may be different.

Aspiring writers come to the page with a few assumptions. These were mine: first, I believed if I had a few hours, I could just sit down and write a decent story. The truth was, even when I had that kind of time, my body didn't respond that way. I got uncomfortable easily sitting down for too long. I need to be able to change things up, and I will rarely sit and write a whole story or chapter. I need to give myself permission to come back. I need to be able to live my life *and* write. Most of us are writing on an idea we hope makes it to publication, and there's no guarantee, but if we can live our lives in the process, we're bound to get through it better. Coming back after some time away improves my writing every time.

Second, I thought "I'm a minority in sexuality and disability, and nobody wants to read about that." This was one of my most pervasive lies. But I needed more than a pep talk. I needed it modeled. I got on the social media site formerly known as Twitter and started following writers because I didn't know what else to do. I was fascinated by a few debut authors I saw promoting their books. These books were very gay, very niche, and very young adult. Over the span of three to five years, I watched these books sell and build a following. One book became five books very quickly. Each of these debut authors I followed was building a career right in front of me. If they could tell their stories, maybe I could too. Disability was missing in the canon, and I had access to that experience.

The need for disability writing was confirmed for me in the work of writers like Ryan O'Connell, who is gay with cerebral palsy, as well. I heard about his book of essays on the *Other Ppl* podcast and ate them up. He said his work was in pre-production to become a TV series. It took years for it to come to pass, but his show *Special* on Netflix, which ran from 2019–2021, starred Ryan O'Connell as a fictional version of himself. In the first episode, he falls in the opening scene in front of a young boy on a scooter. He fell just like I do. I felt so euphoric seeing it on-screen. That's me. That's how I do it. I never thought I would see anything like that. It was real and honest, and it was because it was the disabled actor doing it. In the rest of the scene, Ryan gets up in that strange disabled way I also do. The young boy asks him if he needs to go to the hospital and says he can get his mom. Ryan says he's fine and begins the tedious process of explaining he has cerebral palsy, a neuromuscular disease which obviously sounds scary because the boy screams and rides his scooter away from him as fast as he can. The boy would've been more comfortable with a scarier story rooted in fantasy. Maybe others would, too. Horror may be more acceptable, but what if we're not afraid? That scene follows with a montage of O'Connell walking in his own way down the street, multiple shots, different pants or shoes, his life moving forward like it does—disabled.

His work illustrates disability is seen in a certain way, even by children. It's a scary unknown thing. Not a lived reality to most, at least not yet. Most people, if they live long enough, end up as part of the disabled community. It cannot be escaped, only lived through. Some of us just got here a lot sooner while others take short stays with broken legs or arms or operations, until they finally get their extended stay disability. It's just a matter of when.

Maybe that's my problem. Maybe that's why Super Ballsy happens. Four syllables. More common words. A little sophomoric, maybe. Ballsy will make some kids giggle. Maybe one day they will read my novel and chuckle, maybe it will be the gateway to those other words: Cerebral Palsy. They will know the name. They will know a character. A person with a disability. How they think and feel and want to be perceived in the world. Not every disabled person, of course, but just one, informed by my experience. The way Ryan O'Connell's work is informed by his. Whether it's on television or words on the page. Maybe because of our work, people who are like us will be observed in a new way as full, complex people equal in respect and dignity—able to make mistakes as well as be lauded for our true accomplishments that have little to do with how we navigate the world. Maybe, the gallery will be closed. And our humanity will be opened.

10 What Do You Really Want to Say? A Creative Writing MA Student's Experience with Rejection Sensitive Dysphoria (RSD)

BETH REES

"Purple, what is it that you really want to say?" A very passionate author, speaker, and spiritual guru asked me this question in front of 300 people at a writing workshop. Actually, she didn't *ask* me; she interrupted a question I was in the middle of stuttering through. She had so much presence, confidence, and power, compared to my crumbling form. I'd wanted to ask about authenticity and what to do when people constructively criticize your writing. How do you listen while remaining true to your work? I even wrote it down, so I could remember what to say and absorb her guidance from the stage. Not that I could read it. My hands were shaking so much the paper vibrated in my hand.

"Um, I, uh, that um, criticism and, um, being yourself . . ."

She interrupted again. "No. That's not it. What do you REALLY want to say?"

I froze in a packed room of watchful eyes and bated breaths. No one moved. I could feel the overwhelm brimming on my bottom eyelids. *Not here—I can't cry here in front of everyone*. It's my own fault, I thought. I should have known having bright purple hair in a room of more natural shades would draw attention. That my choice of equally loud, patterned dungarees was a recipe for "pick me!" The problem wasn't her putting me on the spot in front of everyone; it was the question she asked: *What do you really want to say?*

The truth is, I had no idea. I thought I did, but every time I sat in front of my laptop, I changed my mind. The issue being, I was in crisis about who I really was, what I wanted to say and whether I'd be judged for either. Having completed the first year of an MA in Creative Writing, I was more confused than when I first started. I signed up for the program to help me birth the book I've wanted to write (and been trying to) for years. But my ADHD and autism make it difficult for me. I was determined to write about a special interest despite my paralysis, procrastination, and a constantly changing structure/theme. I was overwhelmed, writing what I thought I should, what would sell, what would be useful, what other people wanted—all of which were end goals and "achievements" drilled into me from my education.

I remember leaving university the first time feeling completely burned out from the demands and pressures saying, "I am *never* doing this again." To this day, I can't read my 10,000-word dissertation that saw me pulling all-nighters in the library, getting lost in unnecessary research, and eating a diet of golden syrup porridge because I was too overwhelmed to make better food choices. I can't bring myself to pull back the pages and glimpse the words of 21-year-old me. Why? Because the archnemesis living in my head won't let me. Allow me to introduce you to rejection sensitive dysphoria (RSD)[1] — where I "anxiously expect, readily perceive, and intensely react to rejection."[2] Now, neurodivergent students and writers may be familiar with this unwelcome head-fellow, but just in case you're not, let me summarize. It's like living in a cupboard-sized apartment with an overly critical parent or grandparent commenting on every mistake, failure, or rejection, seeing less than perfection as a poor effort. As writers, many of us deal with this regularly, but for me, it's amplified. It doesn't help that, despite knowing the due date for the final dissertation, total overwhelm meant that I speed wrote it within two weeks. No time for read-throughs, feedback, or editing. Many waffly sentences and no real conclusion. "It started off strongly with a key theme, but somewhere towards the end, it lost its way," my tutor remarked. Despite sitting down and writing thousands of words, my highly critical head-parent tells me I should be ashamed. It tells me that despite the hyperfocus, getting the assignment in on time, and achieving a pass, it wasn't good enough.

I probably wouldn't have gone back into education except, in lockdown, these things happened:

1 I discovered I'd been misdiagnosed for five years with a mental health condition I didn't have.
2 I was then correctly diagnosed as autistic with ADHD.
3 I got back into creative writing which set me on the path to find my authentic voice.

I realized crippling self-doubt, low self-esteem, and my ability to get distracted stood in the way of my goal. I needed structure to help me with my creative dreams, and it was thanks to a logical suggestion from my husband that I settled on a master's. I think it was the promise of "life or death" deadlines, the need to get my words onto a page, and the promise of improvement that drew me in. As a student with RSD, knowing what you want to say in an authentic way and navigating your critical inner voice can be a challenge, which is why, in this essay, I offer suggestions for creative writing students with RSD and tips for how educators can coax out not just ideas but confidence, too.

---

[1] RSD is a common comorbidity of ADHD, though it presents its own particular struggles.
[2] Kathy R. Berenson et al., "Rejection Sensitivity and Disruption of Attention by Social Threat Cues," *Journal of Research in Personality* 43 (2009): 1064–1072, https://doi.org/10.1016/j.jrp.2009.07.007

I. First and Foremost—RSD Lies to You

It was thanks to RSD that I thought I needed to know everything about creative writing and have work published before I could call myself "a writer." It hit me even harder at the workshop, standing in front of a multiple-times-published success story while being quizzed about my writing intentions. No doubt, hundreds of other people in the room thought publication equaled success. It wasn't until the speaker said the process was the real success story, I realized I was living by my critical head-parent's definition of progress: focusing on achievements and outcomes instead of mastering the process itself.

I chose a part-time, distance-learning master's to do alongside a four-day-a-week job. I knew it would be a challenge considering you need some self-discipline to study, which I struggle with due to my ADHD. The first term, I was enthusiastic and heavily invested in the university experience. However, I then needed guidance on an assignment idea. Immediately, the critical voice was at full volume: *You can't do that— it's awful. You'll never finish it. You'll change your mind before you do it.* A phone conversation with a tutor left me teary after they advised that I couldn't just write about *something I enjoyed* (tarot) because it *had no tangible story* (which it did). My RSD went into overdrive, and I felt deflated by something I'd previously been so excited about. It was only after speaking with a fellow neurodivergent writer and tarot reader that I was encouraged to go with my gut instinct. She said, as an ADHDer and someone who also gets easily distracted, it was important for her to write about something she had a passion for; otherwise, she might procrastinate and never finish it. After all, isn't that what writing was all about? Months later, the flamboyant workshop speaker said something similar: write about something that ignites passion and that you could talk about for the next five years. Luckily for the neurodivergents among us, we're often blessed with hyperfocus. So, despite the doubt, I submitted my out-of-the-box idea, and the feedback was positive. Regardless of my critical head-parent attempting to change my mind, I trusted my gut, and it paid off. I know it's hard sometimes, but students with RSD should try to tune out of the negative noise, as it tends to lie. Instead, look for the positives of an idea because, trust me, there will definitely be some.

II. Creative Writers—Write for You First and Foremost

For students with RSD, it's also good to ask yourself why you're writing in the first place. For me, it was about being a better writer and telling my story in a way others would identify with. I didn't go for marks or validation, and after hearing from published authors at the workshop, none of them mentioned school or college grades. Wannabe authors wanted to know about the process, silencing the inner critic, and the path to publication, as well as sharing their personal writing experiences. Real world stuff. I would've loved to share mine, but as we've established, I'm not a pro with a mic.

The authors told us to go forward and write without the end result in mind. That we must first find our authentic voices. That we should write what we're passionate about, the things that set our hearts alight and that motivate us. Through doing my master's, I've seen higher education put too much focus on guidelines and grades which many of us, rightly or wrongly, associate with being better writers. In the future, educators should strike the right balance between encouraging students to strive for improvement while not diluting their creativity along the way.

III. Write Like Yourself—No One Else

It sounds silly but how many of us have read something by another person and agonized over our own work, getting hit by comparisonitis? I did and still do, but this advice from a tutor stuck in my head, and I want to share it: "write as yourself and no one else." When I said that my writing wasn't as pretty or poetic as the other students', they said "your writing is unique but not in a bad way." They also told me to write what I wanted because that's what mattered. They finished by saying they knew lots of writers who failed creative courses but went on to do big things. I was grateful to them for stepping outside of the tutor role into their writer persona and sharing their words. They saw the cogs in my head whirred differently and, as a student struggling with RSD, I appreciated this authenticity and reassurance. Educators, this goes a long way.

IV. Stepping Back for Perspective Helps

In writing creative non-fiction, it can be difficult not to take constructive criticism personally (which RSD feeds on). At my institution, there was a list of non-permissible topics, those seen as "triggering" for readers. Feedback I once received said that an assignment about my misdiagnosis read as *vindictive, angry* (which would be off-putting for readers) and could trigger someone. Once again, the critical voice took over with unhelpful observations: *You went overboard. See? You're a drama queen. Not good enough.* Sometimes RSD can take over, and we lose perspective. I decided the piece and I needed time apart, like a couple in an argument. On stepping back, leaving the piece for a few days and going back to it, I saw where I could change some of the language while keeping the originality of the piece.

V. Reframing "Successful" Outcomes

As an autistic person, I love rules, structure, and a defined purpose. However, as an ADHDer, I also like to think outside the box, throw the rulebook out the window, and take a chance on a wild idea. Sometimes, what students want to say might not fit into what higher education wants, and this can be a problem. However, all writers should embrace their different creative ideas and take risks on those uncertain, unique ideas. When I first told people about my memoir-through-tarot, there were raised eyebrows, questions about whether it fit the criteria and whether I was allowed to write it. I thought back to the words from my tutor, "write what you want to write," and I went for it. As writers, we know some creative ideas are worth the risk, and those that aren't will definitely teach us something (or give us something to write about). As such, higher education programs in creative writing need to encourage all students, especially neurodivergent students, to take creative risks.

Additionally, we're often told that to be seen as successful, numbers matter because that's how educational achievement is measured. Luckily, some students in my cohort were neurodivergent, and during a WhatsApp chat about grades, one said: *Who's going to ask what grade you got once you have your master's?* As someone who's struggled to "be the best" in education, this message reassured me that it was OK to just pass, that I didn't have to be "the best," which I'd been told throughout my learning life and by my RSD. After all, it's true that I enrolled in the program because I wanted to be better, not the best. Since some of this pressure comes from educational programs, I think educators need to understand and appreciate that everyone's aims and outcomes are different and be mindful of that.

VI. Find your Feedback Friends

For someone who struggles with RSD, I've always had a strong, negative reaction to feedback, taking it to heart instead of seeing it as improvement. However, having group feedback during the course has been such an important part of my qualification, and our connection over writing has helped me to improve my craft.

While in a workshop, I tried to ask the speaker how best to approach feedback and how to process it. As we saw at the beginning of this essay, my question didn't go to plan. What she and a few others did say over the course of the weekend was to take note of feedback but leave what doesn't help you. Feedback can be helpful, but remember that everyone has differing opinions on what they like and don't like. Students with RSD might react negatively at first but as long as the process of feeding back includes positives, improvements, and suggestions, it can really help. It's good to listen to others, but don't let feedback eliminate elements of authenticity or originality from your writing.

VII. Program Faculty: This One's for You

Although I've highlighted some flaws in university programs, which may prevent neurodivergent writers from creating to their fullest, I'm grateful for the structure they provided. For an ADHDer like me, it can be hard to self-study and stay on track. If you have students who are neurodivergent, ask if they'd like any accommodations. For students with RSD, in particular, the following is critical:

1. Having more one-on-one student/faculty time to ask questions, run ideas past, and/or receive encouragement.
2. Being able to specify how we, individually, like to receive feedback.

We've all been conditioned to believe that climbing the success ladder is the most important thing and that being the best at something will get you further. For me, working on a MA in Creative Writing has been much more than the qualification at the end. It's been about the journey, the progress I've made as a neurodivergent writer who's always been told by the critical voice of RSD that her words weren't good enough to share.

The final question posed at my workshop weekend was this:

What did I need to read when I was struggling?

The answer? Something *real*. Nothing meandering or poetic, packed full of adjectives and profound language that triggered my RSD. I wanted to know if life was going to get less difficult. I wanted honesty from the author-lecturers who'd experienced it. I wasn't interested in their achievements or accolades. I wanted to see myself and my experiences reflected back to me through the words on the page. I didn't want to be left drowning in a sea of interpretation or wading through meaning to find that bit of life-changing advice.

Conclusion: So, What Is It You Really Want to Write?

The motivational speaker continued to stare expectantly my way. Her eyes were focused, as mine flitted about the room avoiding all the others fixated on me. The RSD redness of my body crept up my neck, through my sweaty dungarees, up to my face burning with embarrassment as tears rolled from me uncontrollably. No one had ever asked me so directly what I wanted to write: not my university tutor, not the lecturers, not the other students. Whenever someone asked what I was writing about, I would say something about misdiagnosis and sharing my story in "the usual" way. However, I realized I wanted to experiment with form and structure, embrace my ADHD impulsivity, and see in which authentic direction it led my writing. Using my special interest in tarot made it even more "me." Of course, I chase the achievement of my work being published. Who doesn't? However, it's not the "be-all-and-end-all" that creative writing programs tell you it is. All students, not just those with RSD, should consider, "what is it I really want to write about? What is it I want to share?"

For many of us with neurodivergence, higher education tells us what we should be doing or saying so as to fit into society. The better your achievements, the better off you'll be. But, in creative arenas like ours, we should be nurturing authenticity and individuality. Many of us have been told by academia that we can't do what we want, be what we want, or say what we want. By creating space in education to do this, it may bring more stories to the surface and help validate the experiences of those with RSD, ADHD, autism, and other forms of neurodivergence.

On leaving a workshop one day with a head of ideas, someone handed me a Post-it that said "Different is Good." I kept this note on my desk as I continued my studies. Every time I wrote a creative piece or a commentary, or when my RSD piped up to tell me that no one cared about my story, I'd say to myself "Different is Good."

If going back to university as a neurodivergent student taught me anything, it's that "success" is great, but finding your authentic, unique voice is more important than anything else.

Bibliography

Berenson, Kathy R., Anett Gyurak, Özlem Ayduk, et al. "Rejection Sensitivity and Disruption of Attention by Social Threat Cues." *Journal of Research in Personality* 43 (2009): 1064–1072. https://doi.org/10.1016/j.jrp.2009.07.007

Part 3 Dismantling the Traditional Writing Workshop: Interventions, Reckonings, and Inclusive Alternatives

11 Do Away with Writing Workshops: An Anti-Ableist Treatise

SAID SHAIYE

Trigger Warning: this chapter contains a brief mention of suicide as well as a discussion of other sensitive topics, including racism, Islamophobia, and genocide.

I. Lil B Taught Me How to Write in California

The first piece of advice any young writer gets is: if you want to be a *serious* writer, you must take writing workshops. You may be hurt in the process, but the work will grow stronger for it. You must write every day. You can't make excuses. Writing is work. Disabilities, chronic illnesses, raising children? Excuses.

To be a disabled writer is to be excluded from the literary world. My mind/body don't operate how yours do. I have an unreliable energy system. Sometimes I don't write for weeks, months, years. I long believed this was a personal failing, that I wouldn't *make it* if I didn't *try harder*. I wasn't aware of my disabilities at the time, so I internalized the ableist writing advice I'd been taught and pushed my body to a breaking point.

In 2018, I lived in Minneapolis and worked as a Somali medical interpreter while finishing my bachelor's in creative writing at Empire State College (online). I could barely pay rent and lived in a two-bedroom apartment with seven Somali elders in the famous Cedar Towers. The mattress I slept on was sprawled across the living room floor. The elders would step over my sleeping body at 3:00 a.m., fresh off Uber shifts, talking to someone in Africa, as they scratched belly and searched fridge.

I applied for and was accepted to my first writing workshop in California, a short stay program for writers of color. A cross-country trip was beyond my means, but I justified it with little lies, like *this is the price of the ticket for your writing dreams*. I put together a PDF of recent writing, slapped a title and a cover on it, and started selling it on my Facebook. I was raised to be ashamed of asking for help, especially with money. Starting a GoFundMe would bring shame to my family—*how could a grown man capable of work beg for money online?* Selling my writing to pay for a trip seemed like a loophole. I managed to raise $2,000 and packed my suitcase. It felt like a dream come true to be surrounded by other writers. None of them white. I would soon learn that writers can be some of the worst people on this earth.

Two days after I reached California, it was my turn to have my twenty-page writing sample workshopped. I don't remember much after the first few minutes. But I know that they fucking eviscerated me. I now have language for what my body experienced:

ADHD Paralysis.

Selective Mutism.

Autistic Meltdown.

Autistic Shutdown.

Rejection Sensitive Dysphoria.

I became too paralyzed to process what was happening after the first few comments. Then, their questions started, and selective mutism kicked in. Their words kept flying at me like winged daggers, and I dove further into myself—full autistic shutdown. Immediately after the workshop, I found myself running the streets of Berkeley, fueled entirely by anger and hurt.

I ran into the fog, ran to those endless Bay Area foothills that never quite become mountains. I ran until it felt like there were raging fires in my chest instead of lungs. I ran and ran and ran some more. I screamed, I cussed, I cried. I felt myself dying a million times over. There was no way to describe this feeling. I got to the top of a hill and screamed until my throat was hoarse. I am hypervigilant of others' perception of me, but I didn't care how I looked in that moment. If this is what it takes to be a real writer, I thought, then I guess I won't ever be real. I just wanted to go home.

Because I am a verbal autist, people assume my silence is always voluntary. Sometimes I am incapable of speech. At those times, I turn to writing or photography. Now, in a room full of people who are critically destroying my writing, the one safe space I have in the world, how was I to respond? First, they stole the speech from my mouth; then they stole the pages I lived in when mouth-words ran out.

I had only been in Berkeley for two days, barely affording the meals I ate and knowing that I'd go back home unable to pay rent. I did all this for the sake of my writing. Those people tore me down in their attempts to tear down my writing. They made me not want to be alive. Here is where I'm supposed to tell the reader that I was not actually suicidal, that I only wanted to die in a metaphorical sense, but honestly, who gives a fuck? The details are not important. Only the pain.

The pain became a voice in my head: fuck these people, fuck this Bay I once loved, fuck writing, fuck me, fuck everything.

Sometime the next day, I sat with the leader of our workshop. He was an acclaimed author, and I was hoping to soak up game from him, hoping he could help me *make it*. This desire to make something of myself has been the bane of my existence. We sat over Indian food. I was fighting back tears as he talked. He kept telling me how much promise I had, how original my work was. "There aren't very many Black men writing about mental health the way you are," he said. It gave me little comfort. I said I feel like dying. He said workshop can be hard on writers, but it's the cost of the ticket. Months later, after telling him about my sensitivity to rejection, he said I needed tougher skin if I wanted to stay in this game. I didn't think twice about hitting that block button. I would later unblock him, and we agreed that it was water under the bridge. He couldn't have known, just like I didn't know, about the disabilities behind my sensitivity.

Writing has never been a game to me. Writing is all I've ever had. Even now, three years after getting my disability diagnoses which changed my life, writing is all I have. Back when I had no diagnoses, no reason for why I ran screaming through Berkeley or Minneapolis or Seattle streets, writing was my everything.

I couldn't explain why I crumpled into a shuddering pile after stressful days, or why rejection sent me into weeklong spirals that took me to the brink. How no one really taught me to write, yet I always knew how to write. How English ain't even my first language, but I write better than native speakers. Ma ifahamtay saxiib? No? That's okay. Maybe one day you will.

I trust language because language is incapable of lying. As a child, I turned to stories because my world was too painful to survive otherwise. I started writing because it was the most effective salve for a depth of pain, which I still can't express.

I have never thought of writing as a communal act. I don't read with other people—why the hell would I write with them? It's difficult enough to make sense of my own thoughts. It's impossible to walk a stranger through my lived experience. The way my brain learns is unlike most writers. I've learned more about writing through osmosis than direct instruction: reading, writing, repeating, talking with other creatives, watching writers talk about writing, gardening, blocking people on Facebook, taking one semester of beginning Arabic, learning to speak English by watching Cartoon Network, watching films with a writer's eye, reading photos with an accountant's hands, learning to forget every pain which has ever befallen me, and writing some more. You won't find that in a workshop.

II. The Door to Hell Is Marked "MFA PROGRAM"

Many writers of color have spoken about their negative MFA experiences. Junot Díaz's piece in *The New Yorker*, titled "MFA vs POC," came across my feed shortly before I started my own MFA program in Minneapolis. I thought it would prepare me, but it scared me and also turned out to be a foreshadowing of my own experiences. Díaz writes:

> Early that fall (I think) Athena moved home; and I have never heard from her again. Shortly after a second writer of color left our workshop but I didn't know him at all (see how awesomely close we were) so I'm not going to speculate on the reasons. Still. The fact that we lost two writers of color in less than two years should tell you something.
>
> She was tough and she was smart and she'd read loads but in the end, the whiteness of the workshop just wore her out. These people are killing me, she told me repeatedly.[1]

---

[1] Junot Díaz. "MFA VS POC." *The New Yorker*, last modified 2014, https://www.newyorker.com/books/page-turner/mfa-vs-poc

There's no easy way to put it: I felt like I was dying in that MFA program. Three years is a long time to die without actually dying. I won't go into the details, but here's a typical vignette I wrote at this time:

I'm on the floor of my bedroom. Tears stain my eyes. I fight back sobs. On my face: anguish, grief, hopelessness. In my hands: 1 copy of my essay. Littered around me: 11 other copies of said essay. They are all marked up with pen. Comments in the margins. Pure pain. A few hours earlier, my classmates had taken turns annihilating my work with spoken words. Now, I sat with their written words, which were somehow even more painful. As if they hadn't had the courage to tell me what they really felt about me—not my writing, but me—in person. On the page, their real selves shone.

I had never hated writing more. I didn't want to be alive anymore. I didn't try and take my life because faith was holding me back. Thank God I spent 3 years in Somalia before starting this program. Had my faith not been rekindled there, Allah only knows what I may have resorted to. Perhaps relapse. Perhaps an attempt at leaving this earth. Perhaps worse. Something broke inside me that day. Years later, I'm still looking to repair that broken place.

That was one experience. Multiply that by 10 million. It was hell on earth. Besides a few friends and my connection with Allah, I had two professors who held me together during those years. A white woman and a Black man. They know who they are. They were my rafts, my flotation devices. They poured love into me so that I had no choice but to persevere. To believe in myself, despite every attempt my peers made to break me down.

Like Junot, I watched several of my MFA colleagues drop out during my tenure, both of whom were Black. First a brother, then a sister. Back-to-back years, they left, and I was the only Black student the program had left. No one seemed to see this as an issue. No one made an *announcement* about this recurring issue. I showed up for the first day of classes in my second and third years of the program and noticed someone missing.

When you're one of only two Black people in a program, you notice when the other is no longer there. It's like losing one of your lungs. Sure, you can still breathe, but barely. You may be alive, but barely. You may have hope for the future, but it's hard to distinguish hope from abject defeat in that situation.

By the time I graduated, I was the first Black student to do so in four years. Again: two Black students left the program in back-to-back years; both racially traumatized beyond words. The urge to do the same was always on my mind. The pressure, the suffocation, the walls closing in: how the hell was this helping me become a better writer? I had countless conversations with those two students about how hard it was to breathe in this place, on this stolen land. Our pact was to help one another hold on for dear life. We didn't have much in common besides being Black writers in a hostile space, but it was all we needed. Except it wasn't. I wish it was, but it wasn't.

That program, like every MFA program, loves celebrating the success of its students. Celebrate isn't the right word—more like *use* those accomplishments to pit students against one another while attracting new, unsuspecting writers to apply. They squeezed productivity from us like blood from a stone, then used the proceeds to make their house of cards shine like the golden dome atop a pyramid.

The day I graduated was bittersweet. I was a shell of myself. I felt no joy, merely relief. Disbelief. Waiting for them to snatch that degree. They didn't, but it still feels like they took something from me that I'll never get back.

How the hell did I make it? By being pushed into a corner and waiting for graduation. Halfway through the program, a series of events transpired which led to my nearly leaving the program, just as my fellow Black writers had done. First, in a creative non-fiction class (CNF), a white student wrote something I considered racially insensitive. It was an essay about building furniture or something equally mundane. At the end, this white student used George Floyd's death as one would use a garden gnome—an ornament.

I said this is racist at best: what the hell does Brother Floyd have to do with lawn furniture or camping gear? Minneapolis was still burning, and Chauvin was still a free man. White supremacist militias flooded our streets from neighboring states. Reports of Black neighborhoods being targeted, shot at, Black women being snatched off the streets by unmarked vans. Twitter told us to check our alleyways for suspicious buckets, filled with gasoline to be returned to by those white militias in the dead of night. You can guess what their plans were.

After making my objection clear, our professor, a writer of color, decided to play devil's advocate. She challenged me on my stance and gaslit me by asking me to break down *exactly what about this essay was racist*. She humiliated me in front of the class, and no one else had the courage to say a word—either in my defense or to critique the ornamental use of Brother Floyd's murder in an otherwise lackluster essay. I shut my mouth and logged off Zoom.

I wrote an email to program administrators, demanding I be transferred to another class. Poetry (surely, they couldn't hurt me there). There was some back and forth, but they ultimately acquiesced. This wasn't my first time raising concerns with the toxic atmosphere of the program.

In my first week of poetry class, a student shared an Islamophobic poem they had written. Threw my entire faith under the bus. I didn't have words. Immediate trauma response:

ADHD Paralysis.
Selective Mutism.
Autistic Meltdown.
Autistic Shutdown.
Rejection Sensitive Dysphoria.

I leave the Zoom class early. Get on the phone with our white professor. Say "Man, how do you plan to address that inflammatory poem that ridiculed my Faith?" He says, "His hands are tied, freedom of speech, blah blah. What about the poem was Islamophobic, Said?'

I'm losing my fucking mind.

First, they came for my race, then they came for my faith. I pushed back and all I got from faculty was "well, we don't see an issue." That was it. I was done. I sent an email to all the higher ups with a list of demands. Paraphrasing, it went something like this:

> *I can no longer participate in workshops or classes. If you won't protect me, or allow me to defend myself (which, wtf, why should I even have to?), then I will leave this program. I don't care about the pain I endured up to this point or my lack of a degree. I will leave. I will speak ill of your program until my dying day. I will write, because what else can I do in this world? Remember that you had 2 Black students leave your program—due to racial trauma—in back-to-back years. I will make it 3 for 3, this time with Islamophobia added on top. Is that the kind of press you want for this place?*

The path to hell is paved with MFA programs. A few days went by before they accepted my demands. But first, I was to participate in a two-hour Native American healing circle with some (white) higher up in the College. I asked if I could opt out. They told me in no uncertain terms that it was non-negotiable, but I could bring an advocate to support me.

It felt more like a trial than a healing circle. Not to mention the fact that—a fucking Native American Healing Circle done through an institution that literally owns land stolen from Native Tribes? The shit made me sick to my stomach. I would think it was satire if it wasn't so macabre. I clenched my teeth and did it.

For the rest of my tenure, I completed independent studies in place of workshops and seminars. There were only two professors I trusted in that program, so I worked exclusively with them. They gave me reading assignments and I sent them new work. We talked about writing and pain. They taught me things. I felt like I could breathe. But still I felt incomplete. Still waiting for . . . something.

I resented the program, that their solution to my pain was to stuff me in a corner. They could have made substantive changes to their culture, their practices, the framework that allowed so much trauma to fall on Black and Muslim students. White people in positions of power often aren't interested in anything like that. They're interested in causing my pain and then asking where it hurts. They put me in hell and had the nerve to ask me to be on the front of their website for promotion. What if I told you they wanted to host my book launch for my speculative memoir titled, *ARE YOU BORG NOW?*, a book I wrote during the program to *survive the program*. The games these people play. You, the source of my pain, want to *celebrate* the product of that pain? Sometimes I wonder where the studio audience is in this world.

Writing this section of this essay wasn't easy. There's so much I left out, things I can't even think about; things I buried inside. I walk past them in my Hall of Memories.

I avoid eye contact as I look for happier ones. This is the game. What did Omar say in *The Wire*: *the game is the game*. It won't ever change.

III. Jerry Springer's Final Thoughts

This world is not a fair place. I know because I'm sitting in a comfortable library, typing an essay while children are being bombed in Palestine. I won't bother calling them innocent because the idea of needing "innocence" as a qualifier to humanize *children* is asinine. It's genocide. What I'm trying to say is: there is no shortage of ways to become a writer. Traditional writing workshops, to me, are not one of them. They are more performance than substance. A playground for the well-off to talk in abstractions. The revolution will not be found in a fucking writing workshop. No real change can be brought to this world through that modality. It is ego, it is vanity, it is a train of self-serving platitudes.

So, what's the alternative? I'm not sure if I have an answer, but I know that compassion is a starting point.

When I set up my writing courses, I use a combination of Universal Design for Learning, Compassionate Pedagogy, and Trauma Informed Teaching. I operate under the assumption that every one of my students has a disability or chronic illness or neurodivergence or *something* that they're unaware of. I don't penalize late work, and I give alternative assignment options. I use labor-based contract grading and assure them it's nearly impossible to fail my class. We do weekly FLOW (Forever Loving Our Writing) Journals to get them in the habit of writing for the sake of writing. Everything is low stakes by design: I want the focus to be more on writing and learning than on their grade.

The feedback I give to my students is always positive: what I like, what I learned, what I was surprised by. I want the students to home in on the strengths of their writing. The so-called weaknesses will likely take care of themselves over time, with repetition. It's hard to desire writing if someone crushed your spirit with negative feedback. It's hard to *not write* if someone made you believe in your writing with positive affirmations.

I don't force students to get into groups, and I don't do workshop—*ever*. If students want to exchange work, I allow them to do so, but with one caveat: you can't tear this person down. We only build students up. Right now, I have a student who hasn't been able to make it into class for weeks. At first the student was apologetic, but then something changed. I kept responding with assurance and understanding. I kept telling this student I knew exactly how they felt—that I feel the same way myself on most winter days. My small act of affirming this student helped them not be hard on themselves. Based on my experiences in higher ed, I know that many professors wouldn't have been as understanding.

After a certain point, our ability to see students as human beings is obscured by our internalized ableism. I don't believe in grades, in punitive metrics, in rigor for the sake of rigor. I believe teaching is more mentorship than lectureship. That knowledge goes both ways. That compassion goes both ways. Writing saves lives. Writing workshops destroy writers. Ergo: writing workshops take lives. Save a writer's life today: kill your writing workshop right where it stands.

Bibliography

Díaz, Junot. "MFA VS POC." *The New Yorker*, last modified 2014, https://www.newyorker.com/books/page-turner/mfa-vs-poc

12 Perfection of the (Care) Work: A Traditional MFA Workshop Experience vs. A Disability-Centric Workshop Experience

SHANE NEILSON

In this essay, I will contrast my non-inclusive Creative Writing MFA workshop experience at a public university in Guelph, Ontario, from 2011–2013 with that of a disability-centric workshop provided through the D/deaf/HoH, Mad, Non-neurotypical, Disabled, and Sick Poetics Festival, of which I am the director. I will contrast the cohort of my MFA program with the cohort of our disability poetics workshop participants in order to explore the toxic normativity of the standard MFA workshop structure with that of the festival's. Using the lyric essay genre, I will explain how our goal is the creation of "webs of creative care," rather than "pure achievement," and I will show how this looks in practice. Throughout this lyric essay, normative description appears in regular text, and disabled lived experience occurs in italics.

Between 2011 and 2013, I completed a Master of Fine Arts (MFA) in Creative Writing (CW) at the University of Guelph, though the teaching location was actually in Toronto at the Guelph-Humber campus. Am I being too specific? I am specific and organized by details. School colors = red, gold, and black. One of just a handful of MFA programs in CW in Canada. Only one student in the class without at least a bachelor's degree. No one visibly disabled: no wheelchairs, all gaits normal, no visible hearing aids, no signers. No one else who needed to stand up, at random, who stretched and unstretched and stretched, whose hands kept moving and moving. The black and white classic analog clock at the front of the classroom, a clock that was never the wrong time, nor did it ever stall. The headache-inducing fluorescent lights. The distractions in the outdoor hallway—undergraduates with a lack of common space, roughhousing, causing the professor to exit the class at least once per lecture to admonish an ever-refreshing cohort, providing me with a short window to stand.

* * *

Downturned head, loose-fitting clothes, hands that stim unless consciously suppressed; otherwise, thumb down the forefinger forever, overwhelmed in the wrong light, distracted by noises, fluctuating mood and gaze aversion, making interpersonal interaction difficult. One overarching message in my life: go away, you are not wanted. A lifetime of that instruction.

The beginning of the MFA workshops—fiction, poetry, and non-fiction—all followed the same structure. First, the facilitator would explain who they were, including their professional accomplishments and awards.[1] Some would be comprehensive on this score, others brief. Not a single professor failed to mention their most significant award win, which I do not begrudge or judge. All academic programs function according to credentialism, and students were hoping to enter into a profession where credentialism was a regime. As younglings, we were taught the score up front. Then, the workshop process would be explained, always some variant of the Iowa Model. Proscriptions against racism and queerphobia were made by some facilitators; disability was never mentioned, nor were accessibility options. Then the focus turned to students, who were bid to introduce themselves. Places published, provided in a descending hierarchical order. Agent, if any. Current writing project. Who they were—where they came from, their job or profession otherwise, their education—no one offered such information. To one another, we were writers. We were supposed to be writers. The instructor never asked for specific identifiers, of course. We naturally followed the format of their own introduction. Racialized students were not asked to provide identity coordinates, perhaps because their difference was (for the most part) visible, though on occasion specifics were offered: what island they were from or which nation. Some queer and polyamorous students felt comfortable disclosing their identities, though not many, and often much later in workshop when germane writing was shared.

No student during my time at the MFA gave a mad,[2] disabled, HoH,[3] sight-impaired, or non-neurotypical identity.[4] Why would they? The creative writing field

---

[1] One MFA facilitator did disclose a queer identity and periods of mood instability; she also had latterly given herself a new first name, which appealed to the "autie" in me. This facilitator did not run hierarchical workshops and for all these reasons, I asked for her to be my supervisor for my thesis, which would be a book about intergenerational disability (*Saving*, Great Plains Publishing, 2023). This was but one workshop leader of five at any given time. She also no longer teaches at this MFA program.

[2] Identifying as "mad" is a rhetorical choice that comes from the aftermath of the psychiatry consumer/survivor/ex-patient movement of the 1970s. Disability studies emerged as an academic field in the 1980s, in which the focus was upon physical impairment and social relations structured around (and oppressing) that impairment. In the 1990s, Canadian strains of the psychiatry survivor movement created the mad pride movement in Toronto that focused not only upon the reclamation of stigmatized terminology (e.g. "crazy" and "psycho") but also upon the creation and bolstering of community. In the 2000s, the field of mad studies emerged in the academy, integrating all of this pre-existing research, history, and lived experience. Therefore, to use the term "mad" or "madness" is to reclaim non-normative affective and perceptual experiences from the norm, rejecting the concepts of "health," "illness," and "disorder." To be "mad" is to have a positive identity, not a negative one.

[3] The identifying term(s) "D/deaf/Hard of Hearing (HoH)" designates a constellation of people who are culturally deaf (Deaf), who have less interest in identifying as part of Deaf culture, and who, for example, wish to signal that they are physically deaf or have partial deafness (HoH). A related term is hearing impaired (HI).

[4] "Non-neurotypicality" is an identity state that can be distinguished from, but which has tremendous overlap with, both madness and disability. To be non-neurotypical is to be, for example, autistic, to have ADHD, and to be intellectually disabled, recognizing that there are overlaps even within this frame, and many differentiations within the individual entities themselves.

was clearly a system designed to valorize accomplishment over vulnerability and non-normativity, just like all other neoliberal academic systems.

* * *

In 2018, I created the first disability poetics festival in Canada. Every year, we feature a poetry workshop facilitated by a disabled or mad or non-neurotypical writer. The facilitator's identity is part of the promotional material advertising the workshop. He, she, or they share their identity at the beginning of the workshop, and they state that the space is a safe one for participants to disclose their identity, though the participants are not obligated to do so. In our first year, the workshop was conducted in person, but in subsequent years, the workshop has been conducted over Zoom, allowing for participation from disabled people all over the world. For the most part, participants do share their identities. Not all. To me, this means we have created a space of inclusivity, where people are comfortable being themselves in the manner they prefer.

* * *

There was no optional check-in at the beginning of the meeting for MFA workshop members. No one shared how they were feeling, how many spoons[5] they had, if there were particular worries about the material they were about to share: anxiety perceived as the mark of an amateur. Material was to be presented confidently, one had to appear as if there was absolute conviction in "the work," and any hesitation or trepidation was a sign of weakness and inadequacy, of a paltry talent. Most facilitators recommended against "professions of humility," for those would make the work easier to discount.

* * *

In our disability-centric workshop, we provide a template for introductions that people might adopt when sharing: name, general location, number of spoons, any worries or concerns about being in a workshop, or specifically this workshop, and, lastly, their identities, if they are comfortable sharing. Participants are given the option to share work in the chat function or they might read it aloud, depending on preference/ability. One facilitator manages the spoken content, and I moderate the chat, as indirect blank boxes being where I idiosyncratically thrive.

* * *

---

[5]Here, "spoons" refer to "The Spoon Theory," which was conceived by Christine Miserandino and put forth in her 2003 blog entry on her website, titled *But You Don't Look Sick*. As explained in her blog post, Christine Miserandino, a woman with Systemic Lupus Erythematosus (SLE), was asked by a "normie" friend at a diner in 2003 what it was like to live with SLE. Miserandino settled upon a powerful metaphor based on an object right in front of her at the time: a spoon. Likening the substance cupped by the spoon as an aliquot of energy, Miserandino explained that normative bodyminds have close to an infinite number of spoons to expend during a particular day; whereas, the disabled must carefully ration their spoons, allotting a certain number to each activity to not become overwhelmed and unable to complete necessary tasks.

The objective of MFA workshops was craft excellence. Acknowledgment that participants were at different levels of expertise and experience was not done, though this was obvious as introductions cemented the fact. In the distance was perfection, this workshop an instantiation of perfectibility. All should strive to the ineffable, subjective goal. Writing felt to be amateurish generally passed with a minimum of content and engagement; whereas, more polished work received the most careful attention and discussion. This result naturally follows from the stated goals of the workshop—perfection of "the work." I tried to be equitable with responses, but always invested more when a piece represented madness in some way. In the two years of the workshop, I never read of an autistic (named or suspected) person.

* * *

The objective of our disability-centric workshop is to make people feel comfortable practicing the creation of poetry. We aim to provide an experience first, an outcome in which people feel solidarity because the other participants are part of a similar (albeit heterogenous) community. A natural feeling in the workshop is that of immense relief, a warmness, even exhilaration at being able to create and share in friendly and relational conditions, for the opposite was too often the case before. Feedback is, initially, supportive and validating as modeled by the facilitator, who might extemporaneously gloss a contribution or point out particularly arresting lines, images, or metaphors; but gradually over the course of the workshop, some helpful feedback around editing a contribution is given. Because we are not an academic institution that grades students, we weight affirmation over evaluation, but we do not abandon evaluation. There is always a tension between the achievement ethic and the affirmative ethic, but because we are not an MFA, we favor affirmation.

* * *

MFA workshop feedback often followed the direction of the facilitator. If the facilitator praised particular participants, then other participants largely followed that modeling. Care of other participants in the form of recognizing disparities of feedback was not done. Darlings are always darlings in the publishing world: talent, potential, and a marketable face being what they are. Of course, rather than only the lonely, only the social did the best. In this respect, the workshop is merely a microcosm of the wider world.

* * *

In every one of our free-form, one-off disability poetics workshops, some participants inevitably want to share more than others. Good in-camera facilitation manages this issue, but the chat function really becomes important here. The chat facilitator can draw out more silent participants in a trauma-informed way, writing them directly (not shared with the group) and inviting them to share their work directly, if they are not comfortable doing so in the chat. The chat facilitator then provides feedback.

* * *

In many MFA programs, the lack of (visible) disabled people is a natural extension of a lack of direct outreach of MFA programs to encourage applications from the disabled community.

* * *

Some of our disability poetics workshop participants have speech impairments. Others stim on camera. Many have non-normative facial expressions. Still others appear completely normative and identify with chronic physical illnesses. Others are not comfortable with the camera being on, so they remain black boxes with background voice. Mad participants sometimes require assistance with navigation of their participation in terms of maintaining equitable discussion. Judgment of both appearance and content of sharing is not tolerated. This very rarely occurs, because the facilitator models our preferred approach, and because participants share approximate histories of exclusion.

* * *

The MFA workshop feedback I gave was often received as overly critical, for it was detailed, and my affect, which consistently swings from low to mixed states, was perceived as too intense, even aggressive. These years coincided with a tremendous personal crisis: the catastrophic illness of my toddler son, rendering him intellectually disabled. (Sum total of sympathetic, multi-dimensional intellectually disabled character representations in MFA workshops: zero.) My family's difficulty caused imperfect modulation of mood to cycle more rapidly. To boot, there was no safe space to mention personal difficulty with facilitators. As disabled people know, disclosure is a fraught prospect in all but a few contexts. Thus, a community of ostracization formed in the MFA, an outcome which might have been mitigated if the program were more accessible and inclusive. But who can ask an institution to care, to even be part of a care network? That is not the purpose of the craft excellence mission.

* * *

A stated condition of participation in the disability poetics workshop is living with a disability/disabled identity (for reasons of inclusivity, we use both person-first and identity-first language). We do not authenticate the identity, but simply ask that participants be comfortable that we assume a non-normative group when providing workshops.

* * *

In my MFA program, feedback was rigidly systematized. Two participants would take the lead and offer formal feedback; the remainder of the group was expected to provide briefer, more extemporaneous commentary that responded to the formal commentary just given.

* * *

In our disability poetics workshops, people offer feedback as they are comfortable. Creating the conditions of this comfort at the outset is paramount. Only as a last resort are individuals assigned to give a first response, for a successful workshop requires some level of participation, and usually this is necessary just at the beginning of a workshop. People become comfortable when they witness that the first material shared is welcomed and appreciated on its merits.

* * *

Should madness be depicted in characters or poems, MFA workshop participants only alluded to periods of personal difficulty that cohered symptomatically as depression or anxiety. Suicidality too, albeit very occasionally. These representations tended to primarily be truncated, hidden, skipped past, reallocated to events and facts occurring outside the main narrative.

* * *

In our disability workshops, representations mainly—although not exclusively—concern lived experience. Part of the reason is that our facilitators give participants some disability-centric prompts or share favorite poems that represent disabled lived experience; however, the other part is that participants finally feel comfortable sharing their reality, something they routinely say aloud and in the chat function. Workshops also feature more open-ended prompts.

* * *

The MFA offered instruction in composing query letters for publishers. Professionality was emphasized, and a general rubric was given for the composition of query letters. Normality in this situation was suffocating and oppressive: "There is only one way to do this. There is only one way to do this. If you do not do it this way, you will not even be read. Agents and acquisitions editors will scan the paragraphs and know if the letter has been done properly. There is only one way to do this."

* * *

In the latter half of our disability poetics workshop, we open a space for discussion of submission protocols. We explain that we recognize that some of the participants may not be interested in publishing their work but that some might, and no one need declare so. Our facilitator leads off with some anecdotes about stigmatizing experiences in the publishing world (we all have them) and asks if anyone else would like to share some of their own. Once a few of these are offered—providing a shared sense of oppression for the purposes of identification but also to organize the basis of future resistance—we begin our submissions mini-clinic by emphasizing that the publishing world is full-on ableist and that the disabled community, and in particular the mad/autistic community, face unique challenges. Not only might the content of their work be rejected because of stigma, their work might be rejected because of certain common affronts to normativity in the query letter. By acknowledging the oppressive terrain, we empower our participants through knowledge. We explain the system they face so that they might take rejection on the basis of identity less personally. We provide a template they might use for submission, encouraging them to adapt it to their needs. We express our discomfiture with this capitulation to normativity, but we also point out certain publishers and magazines with a reputation for more inclusive submissions processes, thereby suggesting a more liberatory future.

* * *

At the end of an MFA, one received a degree. This credential could be used to secure a position teaching creative writing, and it also signified membership amongst the MFA community, opening certain doors in publishing. Students might get a book deal out of the association, having met powerful people in publishing while completing the degree.

* * *

At the end of one of our workshops, participants are encouraged to direct message each other, as they are comfortable, particularly those whom they have identified with, so as to create longitudinal relationships and possible webs of creative care. They attest to being seen, which affirms our effort. They tell us that they didn't expect to create, let alone share; they tell us they wish the workshop was offered more often throughout the year. They tell us that it is good to make things amongst those who understand.

* * *

This cliché: bedecked with awards, performativity high, gestures grand, much sighing and harrumphing and interrupting of others, a scarf and a big bedraggled red dress, thick glasses, saying this at the close of our MFA training: "You must sacrifice your life for your work. If you have to starve, starve. You will not regret taking the chance. Does a writer work a day job when the muse calls?"

* * *

Famously, Yeats wrote the following in "The Choice":

> The intellect of man is forced to choose
> perfection of the life, or of the work,
> and if it take the second must refuse
> a heavenly mansion, raging in the dark.[6]

Too often, normativity says: be all in. Normativity says: sacrifice. Normativity says, perfection of the life means lusting for lucre, being material. Normativity does not

---

[6]William Butler Yeats, *W. B. Yeats: Selected Poetry*, ed. A. Norman Jeffares (Macmillan, 1968), 250.

recognize that life is not perfectible, nor is the work; normativity does not understand that before perfection, some disabled people are merely trying to survive. Is it not sacrifice for the disabled person on their terms? Is the disabled person not all in when considering their impairment? Disabled people understand that normativity's perfection never wanted them, eugenics being normativity's wet dream. What is perfection for the non-neurotypical? Yeats offers a false choice:

> The intellect of they is forced to find
> daily bread and shelter. Not "or of"
> but both, and if it chooses one kind
> then it will die either starved or cold.[7]

The neurotypical romance cannot conceive of itself as a romance. It prefers the genre descriptor of "realism." Similarly, the MFA is a romantic credential predicated on a fallacy of perfectibility as viable work aspiration and process. The reality is that it is an academic marker of exclusion based on its predicate. What crosses the aesthetic gap between normates and non-neurotypicals? The MFA cannot know, because such aesthetics are not recognized within the larger writing industries that it serves. "Conform," commands normativity. "You mean, pass?" ask the non-neurotypicals. "We decide who passes," says the program.

Bibliography

Miserandino, Christine. "The Spoon Theory." *But You Don't Look Sick?* MitoAction.org, June 27, 2025. https://www.mitoaction.org/wp-content/uploads/2023/03/BYDLS-TheSpoonTheory.pdf

Yeats, William Butler. *W. B. Yeats: Selected Poetry*. Edited by A. Norman Jeffares. Macmillan, 1968.

[7]Ibid.

13 Poem Brut: What the Writing Workshop Can Learn from the Outside World

JULIA ROSE LEWIS

I would like to explore the exclusionary attitudes, beliefs, and practices within creative writing classrooms by contrasting them with the Poem Brut event series. Poem Brut embraces our broad and complex relationship with language through experiment. I suspect that teaching experimental writing in introductory courses can improve the success of neurodivergent students by allowing them to explore the ways in which their brains process language.

Poem Brut takes neurodiversity as a starting point for its experiments with writing. The founder, SJ Fowler, is quite explicit about his desire to encourage the multiple ways in which the human mind can understand language. He writes:

> Rooted in an exploration of cognitive difference, of everything from autism, dyslexia, aphasia and dyspraxia to mental health conditions, Poem Brut seeks to ask whether it is in service to original and powerful writing for writers and poets with these experiences to try and "escape" them into sense and order, rather than embracing how their brains understand language.[1]

Here, Fowler offers a space for writers to embrace their brains' different ways of understanding language as a site for potential experiment in writing.

Poem Brut is cultivating a sympathy for neurodiversity that can be translated into a more inclusive approach to the writing workshop. It is important to note that Poem Brut is less a reading series and more a performance series where people may read, paint themselves, collaborate with a violin player, make collages, and assemble sculptures. In this sense, it is the epitome of experimental poetry in that it is always asking *is this poetry?* I think that we should be allowing students to ask *is this poetry?* at the same time they are asking themselves if they might be poets. We should be encouraging introductory creative writing students to experiment with language as a way to learn about poetry and themselves.

Poem Brut is interested in appealing to all the senses and observing how writing is processed through all the senses. This is opposite to academic institutions, because it does not divide writers into the categories *abled* and *disabled*; it is a

---

[1] SJ Fowler, "About Poem Brut," *Poem Brut*, accessed August 10, 2023, https.//www.poembrut.com/

radical rejection of the deficit model of teaching. Instead, Poem Brut takes diagnoses as opportunities to learn about our neurobiology. The result will be a more rigorous and inclusive pedagogy.

Poem Brut is a radically inclusive event, and participating as an audience member and performer has given me permission to make my internal experience of language external. For example, I recently found myself reading the CIN III acronym as sin and kin simultaneously. For me, dyslexia makes it difficult to remember acronyms, so I might say that we take acronyms for granted. It means cervical intraepithelial neoplasia.[2] It is the result of being exposed to the human papilloma virus, which means that I have a sexually transmitted disease that might kill me. It is a lot of information to process; it is the beginning of a poem for me. There is sin and kin and a sinking feeling in the pit of my stomach, and that is enough for me to start writing.

I begin writing with a feeling or question or something I need to think through or a desire to linger. The finished piece of writing is a reflection of my thought process. My writing follows the ways in which my neurodivergent mind naturally moves, and has therefore been labeled as experimental, original, and surreal. We take mainstream and traditional writing for granted as the natural starting place for teaching writing, and this is wrong. The dominant creative writing pedagogy is to insist that students master traditional and mainstream poetry before they are allowed to experiment. Here is where we are failing neurodivergent students. We allow them to write about their lived experience of neurodivergence, but we begin by divorcing the content and form of their writing. Instead, I think we should begin with allowing students to experiment in introductory courses. We should encourage thoughtful experimentation.

I want my introductory students to learn through experiment, meaning experience, research, and self-reflection on what poetry can do. This is best tested by learning what poetry cannot do through exploring works of art, literature, and performance that ask the question *is this poetry?* Let us let students test the limits for themselves. Let us offer courses introducing creative writing to students as some serious play with the ways in which poetry can reflect their lived experience. Let us teach creative writing students first and foremost not to take writing for granted. Poem Brut reminds us with its tag line that "we take writing for granted."[3] The dyslexic inside me is already singing, sighing out relief, insisting that I belong here, and that my mind deserves this intellectually loving home.

Fowler has opened a space for poets to reflect on the many unique ways in which their brains work to make language into poetry. He has simultaneously made for himself and funded an environment that neither requests nor requires the disclosure on the part of its participants being audience or performers themselves. To be clear, there is no need to identify oneself as neurodivergent or other in order to consider accommodations

---

[2] "Cervical Dysplasia," *Diseases and Conditions*, Cleveland Clinic, accessed October 9, 2023, https://my.clevelandclinic.org/health/diseases/15678-cervical-intraepithelial-neoplasia-cin
[3] SJ Fowler, "About Poem Brut," *Poem Brut*, accessed August 10, 2023, https.//www.poembrut.com/

for making the experience of poetry more meaningful. In this environment, it is enough for poets, and by poets, I mean everyone involved, to self-identify. I want to highlight the importance of taking poets at their word, to quite simply trust that they know their own minds and needs. What a gift it would be, if we teachers could treat our students with the same respect! What might accommodations look like if we asked students to tell us what they need to succeed and rewarded this self-insight?

It might take the simple form of asking students to write a paragraph at the start of the semester on what they know or imagine might help them succeed and then allowing them to reflect on this experience at the end of the semester. We would be allowing students to experiment, to learn for themselves, and to teach us in the role reversal of expert and learner. I believe that all learning is the process of gaining self-insight in order to move through the world.

In the UK, Poem Brut has become a dynamic movement in contemporary literature through events, exhibits, publications, workshops, and partnerships with other organizations. It has grown with the audience at events becoming performers at later events. The events are structured to promote multiple interactions between performers and audience members, to solicit engagement, to make new responses to previous work. In this way, every event is also a workshop and an opportunity for poets to receive feedback and learn from their peers. Here is a space that values everyone's presence and contribution. The excitement of these events is that one never knows when an audience member will be performing and when a performer will be in the audience. This switching is reminiscent of the ways in which writing is presented in workshop and has the same pedagogical effect on participants. However, rather than fearing a mark or a grading rubric, the poet can devote themselves wholly to feedback. It is a deeply educational environment without ever charging a fee, granting a degree, or entering into the ableist habits of academia. Poem Brut has been building ideas and extending itself since 2017. It has blurred the lines between poet and audience, poet and artist, poet and teacher, in order to create a more rigorously inclusive environment.

These events serve as a workshop-like space, embracing all the same excitement and performative aspects. The Poem Brut movement gives writers self-reflection and practice as a way to progress in their work outside the academic workshop. Fowler writes:

> *Poem Brut* celebrates artistic creative writing and its relationship with neurobiology—embracing text and colour, space and time, handwriting, composition, abstraction, illustration, sound, mess and motion. It affirms the possibilities of the page, the pen, the process and the performance in a computer age and celebrates authentic originality in poetry, without overt recourse to biographical context, resisting a literature of control, neatness, poise and direct, didactic meaning.[4]

---

[4] SJ Fowler, "About Poem Brut," *Poem Brut*, accessed August 10, 2023, https.//www.poembrut.com/

Here is an exploration of process as performance and performance as process. It offers a refusal of finishing. When there are commissions, anthologies, publications, and book launches, there is a sense of *ongoingness*. Poem Brut aims to make progress from process and process from progress. It is growing forward.

A word on the work of Paul Hawkins as a key participant whose exquisite work in performance, publication, and teaching has helped define Poem Brut. He explains his work exploring the relationship between thoughts and sounds, and he writes about his collaboration with Patrick Cosgrove:

> Patrick and I are both fascinated with sound(s), verbal and non-verbal, scratches, scrapes, booms, etc. and this software really lends itself to experimentation, a sound-mapping of thoughts, electrical impulses and mulched brain-mechanics. When it's finished, our commission will take the form of a live, improvised soundtrack to an abstract short film.[5]

This work is for a commission funded by Serendip Studio for a limited series of Poem Brut projects. In his self-reflection, it is clear to see the role for process informing progress and for the sake of progressive meaning making. Cosgrove and Hawkins wanted to investigate the ways in which sounds relate to the impulse to make emotion and thought external in order to develop a meaningful, bidirectional exchange.

I believe that these events offer an opportunity to explore the world the poem has created with the audience as opposed to simply explaining the poem to the audience. For example, what is afoot as the audience member asks what Fowler's selected collaborations are about? In the performance "Q&A with a Mole," a mole bites him on the back, but it is important to note that it is a mole puppet present to be revealing and concealing himself. His motivations serve as moles are known for concealing themselves. What does it mean to speak to a mole? What does it mean when a mole bites someone on the back to demand to speak? Is this the unconscious, the cognitive unconscious seen as read? The mole is a blemish on meaning or about beds aboutness is a blemish on the back of a poem. Here is the skin of a poem. The mark hiding behind the poem, behind the face of the poem, ultimately asks the question: is dialogue a way to find the deeper meaning of a poem? Is interviewing the poet themselves the only way to be certain of the meaning of a poem? Is the poem about the poet being in dialogue with himself? The mole as the shadow poem? What makes the poet tick? The mole gets to be the voice for things the poet is thinking and not saying, according to the very conventions of the poetry reading. Criticizing the audience establishment and poet, asking what kind of animal doesn't bring money to buy the books at a book launch? Fowler, together with the mole, laughs at himself and invites the audience to do so. Here is an opportunity for infusing humor into criticism and self-reflection to turn the process into product.

---

[5]Paul Hawkins, "A Word on Poem Brut," *Poem Brut*, Serendip Studio, 11 August 11, 2023, https://serendipstudio.org/oneworld/poem-brut/paul-hawkins

It is important to note that Poem Brut is not simply for introducing poetry to a broader range of potential writers and readers; it is simultaneously pushing limits of experimental literature. The movement is so named, with "brut" being pronounced as "brew" as a nod to the French language, especially the phrase *avant garde*. Fowler is interested in observing what inclusivity can learn from the the avant garde and what the avant garde can learn from inclusive practice. I want to underline how each is seen as an important tradition that can contribute to a larger conversation about poetry.

Poem Brut is approaching the neurobiology of the avant garde tradition. Here is an interdisciplinary take on the evolution of poetry that is grounded in the human mind and the poetry tradition. Poem Brut is simultaneously challenging contemporary established poets, and welcoming emerging poets and interdisciplinary practitioners. Let us consider the study and understanding of neurodivergence as a discipline that can become interdisciplinary with poetry. This is an opportunity to take neurobiology and poetry seriously in the service of self-reflection. What might it look like to take experiment with interdisciplinarity? Fowler writes that "for live events, it is a chance for writers to expand what is possible, or instinctual, in time and space, playing with concepts, sound and motion."[6] Here is more than the traditional poetry reading. Poem Brut makes a space for self-insight in the moment as well as the planning and reflection afterwards. It allows for the poet to make themselves the subject of the experiment or experimental literature; it is some serious play with tradition and neurobiology.

Two decades ago, neurobiologist and philosopher of science Paul Grobstein identified a need for a broader engagement with science. He singled out the power of stories for telling and reflecting on narratives meant to summarize our lived experiences as a natural partner for scientific inquiry. He writes:

> There is a need, both within science and in culture in general, for a less divisive and more widely engaging story of science. And it is a practical need, one that must be met not only in the classroom but in each of the many arenas where science is impacting on culture. It requires not only deliberate thinking about science but also acting deliberately in ways that reflect those thoughts.[7]

I see no reason why Poem Brut, with its emphasis on the role of language processing in the creation and appreciation of literature, cannot contribute to a deeper understanding of neurobiology and psychology. All this is to say that poetry has something to offer science, and science has something to offer poetry perfectly selfishly. Poem Brut takes a meaningful bidirectional exchange between science and

---

[6]SJ Fowler. "Event #55: Poem Brut," *Writers' Kingston*, Writers' Kingston, accessed 11 August 11, 2023, https://www.writerskingston.com/poembrut22
[7]Paul Grobstein, "Revisiting Science in Culture: Science as Story Telling and Story Revising," *Journal of Research Practice* 1, no. 1 (2005): 4, https://www.researchgate.net/publication/26408265_Revisiting_Science_in_Culture_Science_as_Story_Telling_and_Story_Revising

culture as its foundational principle for encouraging poets to experiment in this double sense of the word, and therefore satisfies Grobstein's call for greater engagement.

Poem Brut is no more or less than applied neurobiology, where it explores the relationship between the brain and language. Let me be clear, it is located at the intersection between applied neurobiology and experimental poetry. It is interdisciplinary because it is focused on a meaningful bidirectional exchange between applied neurobiology and experimental poetry. For me, Poem Brut is a moment in time to talk about almonds and neuroanatomy. There is a sonic echoing between almond and amygdala, that hints at the historical relationship between the words: amygdala is the Latin for almond. For my performance on fear responses, I used this echoing to make the neuroanatomy more palatable to the poets.[8] The almonds in the pillowcase allowed me to show what it feels like to balance on a mountain of fear, to speak with fear inside my cheeks, to place my fear inside their ears. SJ Fowler was generous enough to let me place an almond into each of his ears. It is important to note that he consented in advance. My performance was a translation of the definition of the amygdala into the lived experience of motivation, fear, and aggression. According to the *Oxford English Dictionary*, the amygdala is "one of the basal ganglia in each cerebral hemisphere, situated towards the front of the temporal lobe and concerned with the control of motivation and aggression."[9] I like to think the almonds served as earbuds for humans or sponges for overstimulated horses by taking up space and deadening outside sounds. It is an open question of the line between stimulating and overstimulating an audience.

I have been extraordinarily fortunate to learn and grow from Poem Brut. It has impacted my writing and teaching. I find myself trying to recreate Fowler's rigorous insistence on inclusion and self-insight. Oftentimes, I tell my students what I am working on, where I am stuck, how frustrated I feel, and I hope that modeling my neurodivergent process inside the classroom is meaningful for them. It is expressing the confusing experience of writing as process and progress intertwined. Poem Brut has made me a more ambitious writer and teacher in that it reminds me to continue to seek connections with my students outside the bounds of the traditional workshop.

There are infinitely many ways to get involved in Poem Brut after reading this essay. It lends itself to the nature of the interested party. The movement is very much welcoming to newcomers inside and outside of the mainstream poetry scene. I personally would recommend beginning with watching recordings of the events over the years; they are available on YouTube with closed captions. These recordings can be accessed on the "fowlerpoetry" YouTube channel or the Poem Brut website: https://www.poembrut.com/. The website itself details the underlying philosophy, contact information, commissions, exhibitions, publications, past events, and

---

[8] Julia Rose Lewis, "Julia Rose Lewis: Poem Brut at Writers Kingston," Writers' Kingston, *YouTube* October 18, 2022, accessed August 10, 2023, https://www.youtube.com/watch?v=tp52CiCDoyU
[9] "Amygdala," *Oxford English Dictionary*, Oxford University Press, accessed August 11, 2023, https://www.oed.com/dictionary/amygdala_n?tab=meaning_and_use#12745835

upcoming events. It is ideal to attend one or more live events in order to fully understand the community of practitioners; however, it is not necessary. For example, an artist or visual poet might get started by reading *3:AM Magazine*, which is available online.

It is important to note that Poem Brut is simultaneously more than I have written here and open to outgrowing itself. If anyone reading this essay thinks they might have something to contribute, then they should reach out to Fowler. What is here is only my lived experience and its interpretation. I feel confident after many years involved in the movement, that if readers were to ask another three practitioners, you would receive different answers. I truly deeply hope that Poem Brut will grow beyond what I have written here in the coming years with the contribution of a reader of this essay.

Bibliography

Fowler, SJ. "About Poem Brut." *Poem Brut*. Accessed August 10, 2023. www.poembrut.com/

Fowler, SJ. "Event #55: Poem Brut." *Writers' Kingston*. Writers' Kingston. Accessed August 11, 2023. https://www.writerskingston.com/poembrut22.

Grobstein, Paul. "Revisiting Science in Culture: Science as Story Telling and Story Revising." *Journal of Research Practice* 1, no. 1 (2005): Article M1, 1–18, https://www.researchgate.net/publication/26408265_Revisiting_Science_in_Culture_Scince_as_Story_Telling_and_Story_Revising

Hawkins, Paul. "A Word on Poem Brut." *Poem Brut*, Serendip Studio. Accessed August 1, 2023. https://serendipstudio.org/oneworld/poem-brut/paul-hawkins

Lewis, Julia Rose. "Julia Rose Lewis: Poem Brut at Writers Kingston." *Writers' Kingston YouTube*, October 18, 2022. Accessed August 10, 2023. https://www.youtube.com/watch?v=tp52CiCDoyU

Oxford English Dictionary. "Amygdala," *Oxford English Dictionary*, Oxford University Press, accessed August 11, 2023, https://www.oed.com/dictionary/amygdala_n?tab=meaning_and_use#12745835

14 Spinning Words: Poetry Creation by Autistic People from Brazil

GUSTAVO HENRIQUE RÜCKERT

Introduction: Poetry and Autism

From the pioneering research of Kanner, Asperger, and Sukhareva to the present day and within the *Diagnostic and Statistical Manual of Mental Disorder* (DSM) and the *International Classification of Diseases* (ICD), autistic language has been classified in terms such as absent, evasive, empty, imprisoned, difficult, incapable, incomprehensible, unintelligible, arbitrary, circular, rigid, mechanical, tense, automated, impertinent, inconstant, without meaning, without feeling, without metaphor, without naturalness, without notion, without context, without intentionality, without logical progression, without theory of mind, without unconsciousness, without subjectivity, without self, without other. Forgive me, this author is autistic and likes extensive lists. In short, these classifications reveal a vast repertoire of what I defined in another text as a "taxonomy of absence."[1] Among the absences exhaustively enumerated by the biomedical model of autism, I highlight "without metaphor." This supposed inability to use figurative language would therefore be responsible for understanding "autism" and "poetry" as diametrically opposed terms. How would someone who doesn't understand metaphors write this genre traditionally characterized by the use of figurative language?

On the one hand, it turns out that the philosophy of language has already deconstructed the myth of an objective language. After all, the nature of language is to name a referent that is not there, therefore, a figuration.[2] On the other hand, the written work of autistic people, in both poetry and prose, has already shown that there is no inability to use figurative language, but rather a specific path of attributing meanings that passes first through the visual imagination.[3] In this way, wouldn't poetry be a suitable space to freely expose this visual imagination?

In a provocative essay, autistic activist Amanda Baggs defines neurotypical language as a mountain that is difficult to access. In this metaphor, the valley would

---

[1] Gustav H. Rückert, "In Our Language: Um Manifesto Poético e Político de Amanda Baggs," *Linguagem e Autismo: Conversas Transdisciplinares* (Bordô-Grená, 2021), 14–29.
[2] Jacques Derrida, "White Mythology: Metaphor in the Text of Philosophy," *Margins of Philosophy* (The University of Chicago Press, 1982), 207–272.
[3] Oliver Sacks, "An Anthropologist on Mars," *An Anthropologist on Mars: Seven Paradoxical Tales* (Alfred Knopf, 1995), 244–296.

be autistic language, with all its corporeality and sensoriality: repetitive movements, echolalia, stims, engagement with beings, objects, colors, aromas, textures. In the following excerpt, Baggs describes in a powerfully metaphorical way her relationship with autistic language, seen as the absence of language by the mountain inhabitants:

> I know, of course, that the valley I live in is anything but desolate, anything but a mountain minus the mountain itself. There are all kinds of trees, many of which can't grow on the mountain. I splash in the creeks, and the smell of the rocks is vivid. I roll on the ground and the smell of the soil is dark and satisfying. Each experience is like a new rainbow for every sense.[4]

In this excerpt, the importance of metaphors for Baggs' thinking becomes evident, and this is not an isolated case. There are countless autistic authors who use metaphorical images, in their own way, to express themselves.

The relationship between autism and poetry may seem strange to some people, but not to me. I have been writing poetry since I was a child. As an adult, I became a literature professor. So I have always resorted to metaphors. I am not a paradoxical or meritocratic case either: I do not live on Mars to be ethnographically portrayed, I have not surpassed myself to express myself, I simply express who I am in my rhythms and images.

In this sense, finding Ralph Savarese's research was fundamental, as it allowed what I already knew through empirical means to gain references in literary criticism. Savarese, who, not surprisingly, is the father of an autistic boy, noticed the relationship between the autistic body and poetry, finding that the autistic body manifests itself through patterns of repetition and rupture, such as circular movements, pendulums, inclinations, sounds, and echolalia. Poetry, in turn, is nothing more than the search for pleasure and self-regulation through repetition and rupture of sounds and/or images. Ultimately, poetry is about engaging in stimming with language. In "What Some Autistics Can Teach Us About Poetry: A Neurocosmopolitan Approach," Savarese defends poetry as a neurocosmopolitan space, a zone of confluences, of translation, of multiple experiences with language.[5] Observing his experiences in poetry reading classes with the participation of the autistic poet Tito Mukhopadhyay, he points out that there is a greater aptitude in autistic readers for musicality, for synesthesia, and for specific details of the text, while in neurotypical readers there is a greater aptitude for the semantic issue and the overall meaning of the text.[6]

Literary critic Julia Rodas also offers important arguments for the defense of poetry and literature as possible spaces for autistic language. She, however, uses the

---

[4]Amanda Melissa Baggs, "Up in the Clouds and Down in the Valley: My Richness and Yours," *Disability Studies Quarterly* 30, no. 1 (2010): n.p., https://dsq-sds.org/index.php/dsq/article/view/1052/1238

[5]Ralph J. Savarese, "What Some Autistics Can Teach Us About Poetry: A Neurocosmopolitan Approach," *Oxford Handbook of Cognitive Literary Studies*, edited by Lisa Zunshine (Oxford University Press, 2015), 393–417.

[6]Ibid.

opposite route from Savarese in her work *Autistic Disturbances: Theorizing Autism Poetics from the DSM to Robinson Crusoe*. Instead of analyzing literary texts by autistic people, Rodas studies classics of English Literature. Her conclusion is that there are many similarities in the language used by the literary canon and in autistic language. The compulsive resumption of a theme, lists and enumerations, encyclopedic explanations, the breaking of semantic expectations, and speech that overflows in peaks of euphoria are some of the characteristics of this autistic and literary poetics, according to Rodas.[7] While these characteristics are valued in literature, they are the target of prejudice in everyday speech.

The poem "Misfit" by Tito Rajarshi Mukhopadyay highlights the aspects mentioned above, as it claims in the writing itself the freedom to rotate freely: "Why stop turning and turning?"[8] The movement of the lyrical subject's body is in line with the body of the Earth: "There was the earth, turning and turning."[9] At the same time, the body of the lyrical subject is in dissonance with the body of a society who classify divergent bodies as "misfits" and who reduce their language to the absence of language: "Men and women stared at my nodding; / They labeled me a Misfit / (A Misfit turning and turning)."[10] Rather than an absence of language, Mukhopadyay's language is full of meanings and metaphors. He expresses the circularity that his body demands through rhymes, reiterations, personification, and stanzas. It is precisely because of the sensory pleasure caused by the use of patterns of repetition and rupture of language, by circularity and synesthesia, that poetry becomes a propitious and safe space for the expression of autistic people as well as for a possible neurocosmopolitan encounter.[11]

I. Spinning Words: Autistic Poetry in Motion

My diagnosis as an autistic person took a while: I was diagnosed as an adult at the age of thirty-two. Unfortunately, in Brazil, access to qualified medical staff and information about autism is still privileged. Most of the Brazilian autistic population does not know they are autistic and live under the label of strange, weird, bizarre, crazy, disturbed, inconvenient, lazy, disinterested, aggressive. Excuse me for venting, but this autistic writer has already found another escape for his lists.

Before my diagnosis, literature was my salvation to deal with all these social labels. A collection of damned and extravagant authors (misfits like me) was my support network. Writing poetry, in turn, was the only way to be myself, without masks, without social appearances, just letting the language flow my way. After my diagnosis,

---

[7]Julia M. Rodas, *Autistic Disturbances: Theorizing Autism Poetics from the DSM to Robinson Crusoe* (University of Michigan Press, 2018).
[8]Tito Rajarshi Mukhopadhyay, "Misfit," *I'm Not a Poet but I Write Poetry: Poems from My Autistic Mind* (Xlibris, 2012), 44.
[9]Ibid.
[10]Ibid.
[11]Mukhopadhyay, "Misfit."

autistic literature was my salvation. Reading other autistic writers was the best way for me to understand neurodiversity (and ultimately myself). In fact, reading the poetry of people like Tito Mukhopadhyay, Birger Sellin, Callum Brazzo, or the prose of Donna Williams, Amanda Baggs, Amy Sequenzia, Naoki Higashida, Ido Kedar, was one of the most wonderful things that happened to me. Although each of these authors has their own style and they are different from each other, I was able to recognize traces of my poetry in each of them. It was the greatest sense of belonging I could have: seeing how the language of autistic people from different parts of the world can reverberate in a kind of collective echolalia.

However, something was still missing. Who were my compatriots who write with their autistic bodies? What do they say? This is how, in 2022, the project "Spinning Words: Autistic Poetry in Motion" emerged, which I coordinated at the Federal University of Pelotas. The objective of this project is to discover, highlight, and publish Brazilian autistic poets currently writing. The search for autistic poets has meant looking through research in printed and virtual publications, in the traditional but also alternative publishing market, with blogs, social networks, fanzines, video poems, and others. The final product of the project will be the publication of an anthology of contemporary autistic poetry in Brazil, scheduled for 2025. This anthology aims to introduce autistic poets to the publishing market and readers. Poetry may be open to neurodiversities, but the publishing market is not and often still selects authors based on their personal relationships, socialization, and popularity.

Additionally, this project promotes a series of extension actions, such as poetry writing workshops. These meetings take place in both virtual and face-to face formats. Virtual meetings allow greater participation of non-oral people, people with mobility barriers, and people from different parts of the country. However, face-to-face meetings are also important because a significant portion of the Brazilian population does not have access to quality Internet, especially the poorest population and residents of rural areas. If Judy Singer stated that the Internet was the resource for mobilizing and socializing the autistic community, it is necessary to remember that, in the Third World, this is a resource in the hands of few.[12]

The goal of these meetings was not exactly to teach poetry but to create a community of autistic writers and readers, in accordance with bell hooks' idea of an "open learning community."[13] Thus, the purpose of sharing experiences was to bring together autistic people with common interests, encourage those who would like to write, qualify those who already write, and expand support and intertextuality networks. These experiences managed to bring together autistic people who already publish and others who would like to start writing, people with higher education and others without school training, oral and non-oralized, people from different regions of Brazil, with different genders and sexual orientations, different racial identities, and

---

[12] Judy Singer, "Why Can't You be Normal for Once in Your Life?" *Disability Discourse* (Open University Press, 1999), 59–67.
[13] bell hooks, *Teaching to Transgress: Education as the Practice of Freedom* (Routledge, 1994), 8.

different ages. First of all, we learn how heterogeneous autism can exist in postcolonial contexts. This diversity was reflected, of course, in texts with multiple languages and experiences shared throughout the workshops.

The poem "Something Is Missing"[14] by Milena Martins Moura, mapped in the research, explains the importance of sharing experiences in a community of autistic people who write and read each other's work.[15] The poem appears as an autobiographical space so that autistic people can vent about the violence they have experienced and recognize themselves in order to support each other. Echolalia, in the following excerpt, appears as a resource for denunciation, as its polyphonic character allows the voices of social prejudice to appear in the poem:

> something is missing
>
> a face
>
> she was born it's an angel
>
> what a shame
>
> knowing how to exist
>
> fitting where one should fit
>
> the last to laugh is a fool
>
> in the old photo
>
> the sad girl looks back at me
>
> glasses
>
> curly hair
>
> laughter
>
> so forgotten
>
> abused
>
> laugh first at yourself
>
> a joke
>
> the teacher the classmate
>
> the old aunt the grandparents
>
> this girl will be left behind in life
>
> hide hide
>
> stop blinking too much
>
> moving your neck and feet at night
>
> rubbing against one another
>
> it's wrong

---

[14] This is an English translation of the title.
[15] Milena Moura, "Something Is Missing," *A Orquestra dos Inocentes Condenados* (Primata, 2021), 89–90.

shaking the hands

it's wrong

only babies can clap hands

you need to cancel yourself

what will they think what will they think

you need to hide yourself

what will they say what will they say[16]

II. From Poems Toward Autistic Poetics

The poems discovered in the research surveys and the poems developed in the workshops demonstrate the aesthetic elaboration of common elements of autistic language. Jonathan Culler argues that every contemporary poem is, first of all, an inscription in poetics.[17] In this sense, amidst the diversity of autistic poems, it is possible to think about autistic poetics and how it erases the contours of genre and expectations when reading a poem. To elucidate these questions and share some of the autistic poetry currently written in Brazil, I will divide the following poems into characteristics of autistic language that were encouraged in the workshops. Thus, the same characteristics of autistic language that are the target of prejudice become poetic singularity and potentiality.

i. Stims

Stims are traditionally seen as repetitive, mechanical, or senseless movements. However, among the autistic community, there is a consensus that they serve for sensory self-regulation and are important means of organization, ritualization, and engagement of the autistic body with its surroundings. In Flavia Neves' concrete poetry, stims also become a source of aesthetic pleasure for the lyrical subject:

sometimes I don't stop

i speak speak speak speak

i jump jump jump jump

i recite recite recite recite

i spin spin spin spin

i palpitate palpitate palpitate palpitate

---

[16] Moura, "Something Is Missing," 89–90.
[17] Jonathan Culler, "Rhetoric, Poetics, and Poetry," *Literary Theory: A Very Short Introduction* (Oxford University Press, 2022), 69–81.

you get irritated

call me a weird animal

asks me to be quiet

and you don't understand anything I say

i'll try to be very succinct:

have you ever thought about how to shake up the creative

when the imagination

tickles the dendrites?[18]

ii. Echolalia

Considered as a repetition of sounds, words, or phrases, echolalia is generally understood by biomedical communities as lacking meanings or communicative intentions. Researchers Laura Sterponi and Jennifer Shankey show us the opposite: echolalia can be full of meaning and communicability.[19] The poet Luiz Henrique Magnani has a vast body of unpublished work that is based on the expression of a lyrical subject who captures the sounds around him: a kind of songbook with auditory hypersensitivity. In this context, the metropolis of São Paulo is a source of a poetics of noise and its consequent disturbance, such as this fragment from his poem "what the neighborhoods tell":

partly muffled by thin walls

also in the surprise of crossed lines

ricocheting through echoes between rooftops

some

what's the problem with me staying on my own?

what's the problem?

sometimes I want to stay on my own for minutes

sometimes hours

sometimes I want to stay on my own for days

sometimes months

years centuries millennia

---

[18]Flavia Neves (@flavianeves.art), "sometimes I don't stop," trans. G. H. Rückert, Instagram, March 15, 2023, https://www.instagram.com/flavianeves.art/
[19]Laura Sterponi and Jennifer Shankey, "Rethinking Echolalia: Repetition as Interactional Resource in the Communication of a Child with Autism," *Journal of Child Language* 41, no. 2 (2014): 275–304, https://doi:10.1017/S0305000912000682

what's the problem with me staying on my own?
tell me what's the problem
and others may be screaming
or the almost secret whispers
in farewell letters, notes that anticipate
who knows, maybe some calamity
we are an age of the damned
wrapped up in ourselves
loose, in shoals, scared, furious!
and some still
in soirees and also elegies
on radios that play in grocery stores
humming laments
before any visible future
nothing new in what we are
cancerous silly little creatures
bumping into each other in limbo
and others
these human beings
these skeptics these devotees
wild natives, these immigrants
miserable young old men these insurgents
oh these are all of them
and some
how they say
good time was in the time of barabbas
of pyramids of rock'n'roll
of sputnik of neolithic
i'm not the best with dates[20]

iii. Synesthesia

Synesthesia is linked to sensory disorder. For biomedical communities, it is a neurological condition in which sensory stimulation in one modality causes a reaction

---

[20] Luiz Henrique Magnani, "What the Neighborhoods Tell," trans. G. H. Rückert, unpublished poem.

in another modality. For Ana Freitas, "synesthesia can be understood as a defect that appears during development, but recent studies demonstrate that it can also be acquired."[21] For poetry, smelling the aroma of colors, seeing sounds, hearing textures, among other synesthetic effects, is not a defect, but an increase in sensoriality. Since Mallarmé and Rimbaud, synesthesia has been highly valued by poets and readers. If, in the everyday context, synesthesia is the target of criticism in autistic language, in poetry it is valued. For autistic writers, writing synaesthetically can become a demand for respect for their ways of thinking. For example, the poem "[you]" by Diego Callazans (now known as Diana Meira) approaches the traditional form of the Latin sonnet to modulate the disorder of sensations:

> i wanted to feel your idea
> like an expensive perfume
> or a desired narcotic
> that cripples my soul.
>
> and when i arrive in your form
> i wanted to say the words
> like a frayed rosary
> on the floor of a mass.
>
> i wanted docked to your taste
> like a steady sailboat
> growing old in port.
>
> i wanted to embrace your absence
> like a pilgrim
> at the gates of faith.[22]

iv. Hyperfocus

The *DSM-5* characterizes autism, among other characteristics, with repetitive interests. The ICD-10 classification system speaks of a restricted repertoire of interests. Among the autistic community, the term hyperfocus is preferably used to describe this characteristic of brain functioning, which suggests a deepening of concentration on a certain topic, not an "incapacity" or a "lack of flexibility." Furthermore, the media greatly explores the fascination of autistic children with dinosaurs, insects, trains, characters, etc. One of the frequent hyperfocuses in autistic people is fictional universes, such as *Star Wars* or *The Wizard of Oz*.

---

[21] Ana Freitas, *Sinestesia Espelho-Toque* (Universidade da Beira Interior, 2018), 2.
[22] Diana Meira (formally Diego Callazans), "[you]," *Ensejo* (7 Letras, 2022), 33.

Writer and artist Patricia Eugênio (now known as Ilus) wrote *Hair and Bodies: A Dramaturgy of Fluctuations* (title translated), a work in a hybrid genre that appropriates the imagery of *Alice in Wonderland* by Lewis Carroll. In Eugênio's work, Alice becomes a signifier for all women and their experiences, so fantastic and so real, in a patriarchal society. Thus, the mirror metaphor presents the experience of different women in Alice. In the poem "Note about Alice," Alice is a woman with a case of divorce. Did she go through an abusive relationship? Has she been attacked? Her fight is for freedom (marriage, gender, race). A black Alice who embodies entities from Afro-Brazilian religions, entities that were demonized by Christianity, such as *Iemanjá* (orisha of the seas), the *Exus* (male messenger spirits, like *Exu of the Seven Crossroads*, *Exu of the Seven Cauldrons*), and the *Pombagiras* (female messenger spirits, like *Pombagira of the Seven Skirts*). Here is an excerpt from this poem:

Alice, after 7 years, got divorced.

They say that 7 is a Kabbalistic number.

7 crossroads

7 pombagiras

7 skirts

7 cauldrons

Jump the 7 waves in honor of Iemanjá

Which, it's worth remembering, is black.

Alice was separated.

She had that manumission letter.

But freedom was something else.[23]

v. Engagement with Objects

Historically, autism has been understood as a condition of isolation. The origin of the term, from the idea of auto-eroticism in Freud, is an example of this. The classic *The Empty Fortress* by Bettelheim contributed decisively to this conception. It was argued that autistic people were incapable of deep interactions, as they were incapable of recognizing otherness. Once again, absence is the conception that underpins this view of autistic people. However, it is possible to think from another conception. Contrary to what was imagined, autistic people seek interaction and are capable of "double empathy."[24] In the video titled "In My Language," Baggs interacts with water,

---

[23] Patricia Eugênio, "Note about Alice," *Hair and Bodies: A Dramaturgy of Fluctuations*, trans. G. H. Ruckert (Cândida Editora, 2020), 35.
[24] Damien Milton, "On the Ontological Status of Autism: The 'Double Empathy Problem,'" *Disability & Society* 27, no. 6 (2012): 883–887, https://doi.org/10.1080/09687599.2012.710008

wind, a doorknob, a book, a flag.[25] Contrary to utilitarian logic that reduces non-human bodies to mere objects, Baggs takes them as subjects of interaction. For this reason, Elizabeth Fein defines autistic language as a "mode of engagement."[26] The poem "Anima" by the poet Mô Ribeiro says: "Things have life / if we give them life."[27] A kind of perspectivism or animism runs through the lyrical subject, which reflects that what animates the bodies around us is the interaction we have with them. In another poem titled "I'm Stone" by Sarah Munck Vieira, "objects" like stones, water, and time become subjects of interaction. They have voice and are agents of transformation. Thus, the figure of speech called personification transcends from simple textual rhetoric to an autistic way of occupying space:

> I heard a sound
> near the gravel
> thrown on the ground:
>
> *I'm stone*
> *I poured out the poison*
> *of tasteless rawness*
>
> time inscribes the mud
> in the cracks of the rock
> with mythical fingerprints
> smoothing the terrain.
>
> I'm water
> *I deceived the destiny*
> of the ledge[28]

vi. Visuality

With the increase in publications of autistic autobiographies since the 1990s, it has become common to associate the autistic brain with visuality. The argument was made, above all, by Grandin, who defended that autistic people think in pictures. The words (whether mental, oral, or written) would then emerge later, through a translation

---

[25] Amanda Melissa Baggs, "In My Language," January 14, 2007, YouTube video, 8:36, https://youtu.be/JnyIM1hI2jc?si=94xsbxBF4bJgL_Jb

[26] Elizabeth Fein, "Autism as a Mode of Engagement," *Autism in Translation: An Intercultural Conversation on Autism Spectrum Conditions* (Palgrave Macmillan, 2018), 129–154.

[27] Mô Ribeiro, "Anima," *Paganíssima trindade*, trans. G. H. Rückert (Editora Penalux, 2020), 17.

[28] Sarah Munck Vieira, "I'm Stone", *O Diagnóstico do Espelho*, trans. G. H. Rückert (Mondru, 2023), 133.

exercise. Today, we know that this is not a rule. Even Grandin admits this in "Rethinking in Pictures," a chapter in Grandin and Panek's 2013 book, *The Autistic Brain*.[29] In any case, the argument was important for decentralizing verbal language as the only form of thought. In addition to visuality, any sense can be structuring of thought and mediations with the world. This requires us to admit a multiplicity of languages based on corporeality.

In the workshops, the need for a multiplicity of languages soon emerged. An online platform was created where everyone could post their poems. The platform accepted the sending of text files as well as audio, image, and video files. This is how writer and visual artist Ana Cândida Carvalho shared her bilingual creations. Carvalho is a multi-artist, photographer, installation artist, actress, filmmaker, and writer. Visuality is fundamental in any of her work, which finds greater expression in photographs. Challenged to write, she created poetic prose texts related to her visual creations. More specifically, the order always included the image first and, later, the text. The untitled fragment of text below deals with the process of self-translation: bringing the internal flow into a more or less organized form (which is also related to alexithymia). The supposed withdrawal expressed at the end, however, does not invalidate the route. In this journey of writing a thought becoming, we follow the voice that expresses itself and are taken on an inner journey through the paths of expression:

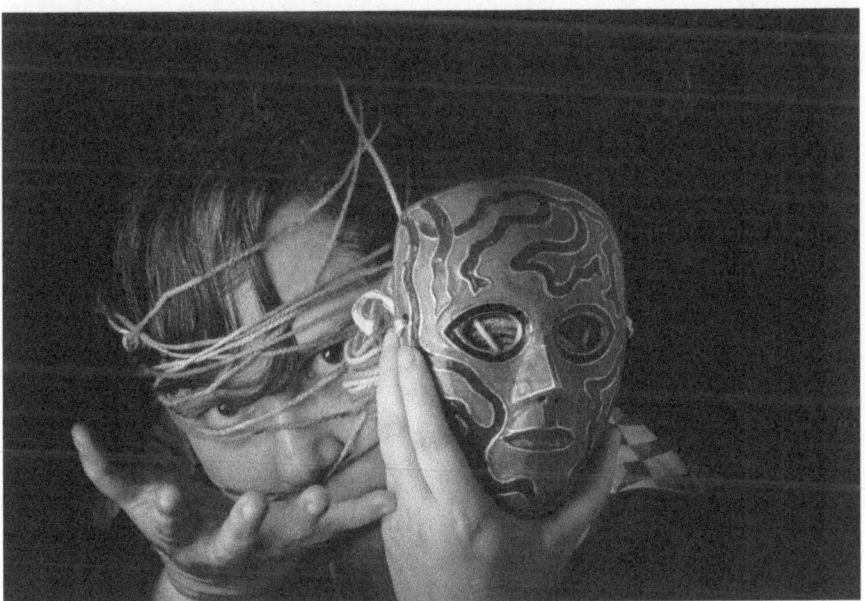

Fig. 14.1 "Self-Portrait" by Ana Cândida Carvalho.

---

[29]Temple Grandin and Richard Panek, *The Autistic Brain: Thinking Across the Spectrum* (Houghton Mifflin Harcourt, 2013).

3 P.M. I tried to write some poetic lines, without grandiose intentions. Lie! I really wanted to find words that would translate exactly that exhausting thought that has been throbbing in my mind for hours. The dawn always plays these tricks. I see my reflection in the new mirror I bought, also without pretensions . . . Lie, lie! I wanted to capture my face, in a precise connection of teary eyes, close to nothingness, full of solid abysses. The abysses that I collect without any pretensions . . . Ah, lies! The lies that I try to divert, between two thoughts, are bound to increase the creases embedded in the details of the brow. I'm not young anymore . . . Echo! The frown became perpetual: I repeat. I will raise accurate weapons against specular reflections, I say once again. I intend to break that new mirror that I bought, into particles that perfectly fit into the promises I make, thinking, precisely, about those times when I try to write some poetic lines, without pretensions. I will speak no more lies, however. I won't speak. The poetic lines will not be recited either, obviously! There was never any pretension![30]

vii. Movement

Another fantastic case that taught me about the multiple languages in workshops was the creation of Josiane Correa. She is an autistic woman who teaches dance at university level. Therefore, movement is fundamental to her communication with the world. Faced with the challenge of writing about patterns of repetition in a Spinning Words workshop in 2023, Correa did not hesitate and expressed herself through movements in a disturbing dance that she called poetry, a dance in which she performs a series of circular and repeated movements to conceptual music. She turns around, turns her torso, turns her arms, swings. Video editing effects work by blurring her body and duplicating images. Thus, the body loses contours, mixing with light, shadow, sounds, and movement itself. When a position is grasped, the body is no longer there. I thought it was important to consider her poetic bodily expression, since the autistic body blurs the boundaries of genres.

This image/poem hybrid is a surprising reflection on repetition and movement, suggesting that the autistic person cannot be grasped or defined in some concept or image. We are complex, plural, and always in motion. Like anyone, we are always provisional and ongoing.

Cases like those of Correa and Carvalho reminded me of some of Baggs' videos and made me rethink the concepts of poetry. If an autistic person's language does not need to be exclusively verbal, why should their poems? Autistic expression strains the boundaries of gender. We thus move from autistic poems to an autistic poetics. An autistic poetics would, therefore, be found in the poems of Mukhopadyay, Sellin, Moura, Neves, Ribeiro, and others, but also in the prose of Williams and Higashida, in the photographs of Carvalho, in the videos of Baggs, in the dance of Correa.

---

[30] Cândida Carvalho (@ana.candi), "Untitled," trans. G. H. Rückert, Instagram, October 10, 2023, https://www.instagram.com/ana.candi/

Fig. 14.2 Frame from "Echolalia" by Joseane Correa.

Conclusion: The Last Spin

Reading, writing, and sharing poetry with the autistic community proved to be an important form of knowledge and recognition. Basically, the diagnosis of autism is constituted by the biomedical belief in a linguistic insufficiency. A "taxonomy of absences" defines our language as non-existent, excessive, exhaustive, meaningless, contextless, clueless, ultimately without rationality. The poems produced or read in the Spinning Words workshops revealed that elements, such as stims, echolalia, synesthesia, hyperfocus, engagement with objects, visuality, and movement, are full of meaning, intentionality, or rationality. More than that, they are also full of beauty and can be aesthetic pieces. The existence of spaces for poetic experiences through autistic language, therefore, is a powerful instrument for expression, self-esteem, formation of networks, and combating ableism.

One of my goals with the workshops was to discover characteristics of autistic poetry in Brazil. In a historically complex country, autism proved to be crossed by intersectionalities, such as gender, race, and class, which mark bodies here. This is revealed in patriarchal violence against autistic women, very present in poems by Moura and Neves. Elements of Afro-Brazilian religions and the soundscape of São Paulo singularize the autistic experience written by Eugênio and Magnani. At the same time, intertexts, such as Lewis Carroll, Patti Smith, and French symbolism, connect autistic poems to global references in poems by Eugênio, Ribeiro, and Meira. This demonstrates how heterogeneous and unique the Brazilian autistic community (and its poems, by extension) can be.

The main discovery of this experience, however, is how much the idea of poetry can be confronted and renewed through free autistic expression. Carvalho's photographs and Correa's dance challenge bodily and linguistic limits. How can we say, however, that the symbolism of its images, that the repetition and rupture of its movements, are not poetry? And wouldn't poetry be precisely the most radical manifestation of linguistic freedom? Perhaps the act of blurring the boundaries of categories is the most important element of an autistic poetics. After all, claiming the right for our bodies to express themselves freely is our history. It would be no different with our poetics. We write, draw, paint, photograph, dance, swing, spin . . . all of this to be ourselves, to be free bodies in expression.

Bibliography

Baggs, Amanda Melissa. "In My Language." January 14, 2007. YouTube video, 8:36. https://youtu.be/JnylM1hl2jc?si=94xsbxBF4bJgL_Jb

Baggs, Amanda Melissa. "Up in the Clouds and Down in the Valley: My Richness and Yours." *Disability Studies Quarterly* 30, no. 1 (2010): n.p. https://dsq-sds.org/index.php/dsq/article/view/1052/1238

Culler, Jonathan. "Rhetoric, Poetics, and Poetry." *Literary Theory: A Very Short Introduction*. Oxford University Press, 2022.

Derrida, Jacques. "White Mythology: Metaphor in the Text of Philosophy." *Margins of Philosophy*. Translated by Alan Bass. The University of Chicago Press, 1982.

Eugênio, Patricia. *Cabelos e Corpos: Uma Dramaturgia das Flutuações*. Cândida Editora, 2020.

Fein, Elizabeth. "Autism as a Mode of Engagement." *Autism in Translation: An Intercultural Conversation on Autism Spectrum Conditions*. Edited by Elizabeth Fein and Clarice Rios. Palgrave Macmillan, 2018.

Freitas, Ana Francisca Goncalves. *Sinestesia Espelho-Toque*. Universidade da Beira Interior, 2018.

Grandin, Temple, and Richard Panek. *The Autistic Brain: Thinking Across the Spectrum*. Houghton Mifflin Harcourt, 2013.

hooks, bell. *Teaching to Transgress: Education as the Practice of Freedom*. Routledge, 1994.

Meira, Diana (Formerly Diego Callazans). *Ensejo*. 7 Letras, 2022.

Milton, Damien. "On the Ontological Status of Autism: The 'Double Empathy Problem.'" *Disability & Society* 27, no. 6 (2012): 883–887. https://doi.org/10.1080/09687599.2012.710008

Moura, Milena. *A Orquestra dos Inocentes Condenados*. Primata, 2021.

Mukhopadhyay, Tito Rajarshi. *I'm Not a Poet but I Write Poetry: Poems from My Autistic Mind*. Xlibris, 2012.

Mukhopadhyay, Tito Rajarshi. "Misfit." *The Troubles of the World: Poetry Collection*. Wordpress, 2010. https://fromtroublesofthisworld.wordpress.com/2018/08/30/misfit-by-tito-rajarshi-mukhopadhyay/

Ribeiro, Mô. "Amina." *Paganíssima Trindade*. Editora Penalux, 2020.

Rodas, Julia Miele. *Autistic Disturbances: Theorizing Autism Poetics from the DSM to Robinson Crusoe*. University of Michigan Press, 2012.

Rückert, Gustavo Henrique. "In Our Language: Um Manifesto Poético e Político de Amanda Baggs." *Linguagem e Autismo: Conversas Transdisciplinares*. Edited by L. H. Magnani and G. H. Rückert. Bordô-Grená, 2021.

Sacks, Oliver. *An Anthropologist on Mars: Seven Paradoxical Tales*. Alfred Knopf, 1995.
Savarese, Ralph James. "What Some Autistics Can Teach Us About Poetry: A Neurocosmopolitan Approach." *Oxford Handbook of Cognitive Literary Studies*. Edited by Lisa Zunshine. Oxford University Press, 2015.
Singer, Judy. "Why Can't You be Normal for Once in Your Life?" *Disability Discourse*. Open University Press, 1999.
Sterponi, Laura and Jennifer Shankey. "Rethinking Echolalia: Repetition as Interactional Resource in the Communication of a Child with Autism." *Journal of Child Language* 41, no. 2 (2014): 275–304. https://doi.org/10.1017/S0305000912000682
Vieira, Sarah Munck. *O Diagnóstico do Espelho*. Mondru, 2023.

Part 4 Ableism in Higher Education, Writing Programs, and Academia: Insights, Pedagogy, and Visibility

15 "Reduced to Depraved Animals":[1] The Need for Faculty and Administrators to Consider Disabled, Neurodivergent, and Chronically Ill Students in Graduate Creative Writing Programs

CHRISTIE COLLINS

In his memoir, *Planet of the Blind*, poet and professor Stephen Kuusisto recounts his lived experience as a blind student at the Iowa Writer's Workshop, a highly regarded creative writing MFA program in the United States, during the late 1970s/early 1980s. Kuusisto shares the following of his experience in classes at Iowa: "I can't read the worksheets, I sit in the fog . . . What else can I do? I listen with care, but the fluorescent lights produce a vitreous squinting . . . I am again the boy in the first grade listening hard to make sense of something on the blackboard."[2] When Kuusisto later asks a professor for extra time writing an essay, a reasonable request given that he is a student who is legally blind, the professor tells him that such accommodations are not acceptable and that he does not belong in the course.[3] Decades have passed since Kuusisto's MFA experience, but anyone who has been a disabled, neurodivergent, and/or chronically ill student in the academy since knows all too well that, despite technology upgrades and enhanced campus disability resources, little has actually changed in terms of academic physical spaces and institutional biases.

It's no secret that academia is largely elitist, prizing efficiency and productivity above all else. Nicole Brown argues that "rather than embracing difference as a reflection of wider society, academic ecosystems seek to normalise and homogenise ways of working,"[4] and this is true for many graduate creative writing programs as it is for other fields within academia; writing programs can be equally guilty of ableism, exclusionary practices, and fostering overall competitive, toxic environments. In fact, Felicia Rose Chavez argues that since its origin, "the traditional writing workshop

---

[1] The first part of the title comes from a quote in Stephen Kuusisto's *Planet of the Blind* (Dial Press, 1999), 103.
[2] Kuusisto, *Planet of the Blind*, 102–103.
[3] Ibid., 104.
[4] Nicole Brown, "Disclosure Dances in Doctoral Education," *Social Sciences* 13, no. 12 (2024): 5, https://doi.org/10.3390/socsci13120689

model" has been "silencing writers,"[5] and this is true not just of racial minorities but of any student-writer that doesn't fit the mold.

The aim of this essay is to provide current and future creative writing faculty, where needed, with practical advice and hands-on suggestions for making their teaching and mentoring practices more inclusive for students who face disabilities, chronic illnesses, and/or neurodivergence.[6] To do so, I discuss relevant data and research and draw on 1) my lived experience as a creative writing student who struggled through graduate programs with forms of neurodivergence (dyslexia, ADHD, and broad autism phenotype (BAP)) and 2) my insights from my almost twenty years as a college writing educator. It's important to note that, at present, little research exists that focuses on neurodivergence and ableism within creative writing classrooms and programs, though these topics have started to pick up traction. I hope that this essay will help to fill this gap. I have chosen to focus on creative writing programs at the graduate level (MA, MFA, and PhD) because these programs operate differently from undergraduate programs, in which students usually have a wider network of professors, peers, and resources across campus. However, much of what is discussed here is applicable and useful to creative writing faculty at any level and to courses in other disciplines that are writing and reading intensive, for example, literature and journalism courses. Finally, this essay is mostly geared toward faculty in the United States, where there is no mandated universal design to guide university educators on matters of inclusivity; however, studies suggest that even universities in countries governed by universal design struggle to implement and embrace inclusive policies; therefore, this essay is relevant to creative writing classrooms, workshops, and programs across the world.

I. Disabled Students by the Numbers and the Role of Faculty

The National Center for Education Statistics (NCES) found that in 2019–2020, 21 percent of undergraduates in the United States reported having a disability. For graduate students, however, only 11 percent reported disabilities. Furthermore, the percentages of disabled students were higher, at both undergraduate and graduate levels, for student veterans, for several racial minority groups, including Native American, Pacific Islander, and Hispanic, and for non-binary students.[7] The discrepancy in the number of undergraduate (21 percent) compared with the number of graduate students (11 percent) reporting disabilities can be explained, in part, by Nicole Brown, who found that the rate of disclosure drops at "transition points," such as moving from undergraduate into graduate programs,[8] a reality that college

---

[5]Felicia Rose Chavez, *The Anti-Racist Writing Workshop* (Haymarket Books, 2021), 2.
[6]Occasionally, I will shorten this list to just "disabilities" because most chronic illnesses and forms of neurodivergence can be classified as types of disabilities.
[7]"Students with Disabilities," *NCES*, accessed January 25, 2025, https://nces.ed.gov/fastfacts/display.asp?id=60
[8]Brown, "Disclosure Dances," 1.

administrators and department heads should carefully consider. Furthermore, there is, perhaps unsurprisingly, a discrepancy between the number of students who have disabilities and the number who report/disclose their disabilities to their universities. In fact, NCES found that "only about one-third of students [with disabilities] informed their college."[9] Why is this? In her study on disclosure rates in doctoral education, Brown offers one explanation; she says that doctoral students as well as other members of academia are always weighing "the cost of disclosing a condition or impairment, such as stigmatization and the resulting additional emotional labor"[10] against the potential support or accommodations they may receive but are not guaranteed. When this study is updated, it will be interesting to see if the numbers of students who disclose their disabilities will have increased, given that much has changed culturally in the last six years in the way of combating stigmas and embracing diversity and inclusion. However, how much has really changed in the academy in those six years? Has it benefitted from attitude changes in the wider world?

In their 2024 study on the impact of higher education on students with disabilities, Goodall et al. interview faculty to get a sense of their attitude toward inclusive education and students with special needs. Even though the study is based at a university in Norway, where colleges and universities are mandated to follow the principles of universal design, the results reveal that faculty are still reluctant toward disabled students and overall reproduce institutional "ableist expectations and ideas."[11] Goodall et al. concede that faculty are in a tough position: "Educators are expected to promote inclusion while adhering to the rigidity of institutional policies and procedures, all with very little to no support from the university. Thus, understandings of what inclusion entails and how to promote inclusion are mixed and often misinformed."[12] The following can be gleaned from this study regarding the ongoing problem of ableist treatment of students in higher education: first, just because a country, state, or region mandates certain inclusive standards of education does not mean that, for any number of reasons, these standards will always be put into action or that faculty members will have individually internalized anti-ableist principles and practices. Second, it is unfair, however, to put the blame solely on faculty when the problem is often a systemic one.

However, individual faculty members must shoulder at least part of the blame. In Goodall et al.'s study, some faculty members share that rather than providing individualized accommodations to students, they'd rather their students "test their limits" and "confront their problem," showing that these faculty members' commitment

---

[9]"A Majority of College Students with Disabilities," *NCES*, accessed January 25, 2025, https://nces.ed.gov/whatsnew/press_releases/4_26_2022.asp

[10]Brown, "Disclosure Dances," 1.

[11]Gemma Goodall et al. "'Breaking a Vicious Cycle': The Reproduction of Ableism in Higher Education and Its Impact on Students with Disabilities," *Frontiers in Education* 9 (2024), https://doi.org/10.3389/feduc.2024.150483213

[12]Ibid.

is to the academy's elitist and ableist grind culture rather than to their students' wellbeing or success.[13] Additionally, the Postsecondary National Policy Institute reports that when students with disabilities were asked to identify "barriers to access and participation on campus," one of the key barriers they name is the actions and attitudes of their faculty, including "faculty unaware of disability accommodations, faculty who push back against accommodations, and instructors who do not respond to requests for accommodations."[14] In short, we, as faculty members, need to do better.

At present, there is little to no research that looks at disability, chronic illnesses, and/or neurodivergence within academic creative writing programs, though countless writers across the world have started sharing their experiences with institutional ableism. As such, what follows is a discussion of five key aspects of the creative writing graduate experience[15] that faculty and administrators need to (re)consider, ensuring that their practices and policies are inclusive to the world's largest minority group: those with disabilities.

II. Reconsidering Physical Spaces, Asking Students What They Need, and Confidentiality

Considerations for students with disabilities, chronic illnesses, and/or neurodivergence should start before a new academic year/new semester begins. In fact, regarding the physical space of writing classrooms, lecture halls, and other learning environments, administrators should constantly be reassessing to ensure that these spaces are up to date and in compliance with The Americans with Disabilities Act (ADA) requirements and recommendations and similar guidelines in other countries. This is vital because of the high number of students facing disabilities who do not disclose their disability and/or their particular needs, a reality I discussed in the previous section of this essay. For this reason, I suggest department heads send out a list to all incoming graduate students, highlighting available disability resources and mental health resources on campus. Doing so works to break down the stigma of disability in academia and would allow students to receive support from their new programs and universities before they even arrive on campus. Additionally, when students disclose disabilities to their new programs, administrators and/or faculty should offer to coordinate with campus disability services to offer pre-semester campus tours and overviews of support services, for instance, to students with visual impairments, students with

---

[13] Ibid.
[14] "Students with Disabilities in Higher Education," *Postsecondary National Policy Institute*, accessed January 25, 2025, https://pnpi.org/wp-content/uploads/2023/11/StudentswithDisabilities-Nov-2023.pdf
[15] As previously mentioned, while this essay focuses on graduate writing programs (MA, MFA, and PhD), much of what is discussed throughout is applicable to creative writing workshops and courses at any level.

hearing impairments, and students who use wheelchairs. It's vital, however, that such services be offered, though not required, as forcing students who are differently abled to accept help can shame and victimize them.

Individual professors and lecturers may feel at a loss for how to help when it comes to physical learning environments, but professors can be a powerful force for good. At the start of a new semester, they should ask students to let them know if they have any needs or requirements and make a point to articulate to the class that they value and want to assist students with disabilities. Additionally, professors and lecturers should ask students about the physical space of the classroom that has been assigned to the course. Is it a comfortable and conducive space for their learning? Is it easily accessible for everyone? Students may well have invisible disabilities that makes certain classrooms challenging. For example, if the classroom is on a higher floor, is there a working, reliable elevator? Is there a bathroom nearby with useable handicap facilities? It may not be easy to switch rooms, but professors can always request a room change and/or request that the student be otherwise accommodated.

Additionally, a faculty member's use of color in course content as well as the classroom's lighting can have major impacts on students' course experiences and outcomes. Keep in mind that some students may be colorblind and unable to differentiate colors, such as color-coded assignment schedules, an important reason to ask students if they have any requests or special needs. Also, does the classroom or workshop space have fluorescent lighting?[16] If so, it is vital to ask students if the lights are likely to cause anyone in the class to develop a migraine, nausea, and/or seizures. As someone with migraines and light sensitivity, I suffered for decades in classrooms lighted by fluorescents. Those spaces are no easier for me now as an educator, though I was a thirty-year-old PhD student before I ever told a program administrator about this. In my own work as a college educator, if the room has ample natural lighting, I always ask if anyone would mind if we turned off the fluorescent lighting. My students always seem to prefer natural lighting to harsh fluorescents, regardless of medical necessity, though this may not always be the case. Another consideration is noises inside and outside of the classroom during class instruction, for example, music, loud talking, and repetitive sounds from HVAC or other mechanical systems. Students with hearing impairments, sensory sensitivities, and forms of neurodivergence may struggle to cope in environments where multiple, conflicting, and/or repetitive sounds are present. Finally, be sure to consider all places and spaces used by the program, including those off-campus. A highlight of many writing programs is attending readings and events. Before such event spaces are booked, however, be sure that they are accessible and inclusive for all students.

---

[16] I encourage all readers to explore the research on the harmful effects of fluorescent lights in classrooms. The impacts of fluorescent bulbs can be detrimental to all students and faculty, though students and faculty with disabilities may feel the effects more acutely.

Beyond matters of physical space, professors should be willing and open to engage with requests from students regarding different learning styles and regarding mental health, such as social anxiety and bipolar disorder. It's also vitally important that any concerns disclosed to admins and/or professors be kept absolutely private. At present, disability is still highly stigmatized in academic spaces. For this reason, many students do not disclose their disabilities and do not ask for help or accommodations, even when such help is desperately needed. Furthermore, students who disclose their disabilities are often treated differently. Never discuss another person's private health-related information, not even with spouses and close friends/colleagues, unless you have express consent. Even if shared with the best of intentions, it could harm and other the individual.

For too long, students were expected to keep silent, yielding personal need to the benefit of the class as a whole. While it's certainly not possible that each professor can meet every conceivable need of each student, faculty need to make reasonable changes to physical learning spaces and course content; they need to be flexible, accommodating, allowing their students to have a voice.

III. Perpetuating Fixed, Ableist Ideas About Writing Habits, Publishing, and "Success"

Professors and mentors in graduate writing programs commonly offer students guidance on writing habits, on publishing, and on how to achieve "success." Practically every student welcomes such advice with open arms. After all, publishing and "making it" as a writer can be a tricky, elusive business, so receiving advice from practitioners who have successfully navigated the field seems like a boon to students. However, writing educators and mentors need to carefully reconsider the guidance they put forth, making sure that what they say isn't ableist or exclusionary, lest they harm the very students they are meant to help and guide.

The reality is that publishing in elite journals and magazines as well as securing agents and book deals with top presses is, for almost everyone, hard, stressful, demoralizing, and can take years, if it happens at all. Students should absolutely be made aware of this. However, an already challenging and competitive field is even trickier to navigate when you're never guaranteed good days. When your mind won't focus or can't see written or typed language accurately or at all, when fatigue, pain, or other health concerns are either present or imminently forthcoming, you cannot always accomplish writing tasks and submit work for publication in the same ways or on the same timelines as writers who are neurotypical and non-disabled. Yet, these mindbody realities faced by millions of writers are rarely, if ever, considered in workshops; rather, many student-writers facing these concerns are told they're just lazy, lacking drive, or just not up to the task. In short, this field, including creative writing graduate programs, is often unkind and overly competitive for all, yet it particularly does not see, acknowledge, or value disabled writers or their realities, and it certainly does not make allowances for them.

The following is a list of problematic, ableist writing beliefs I've heard over the years from writing professors, mentors, and colleagues. While ostensibly shared with good intentions in mind, the following writing beliefs leave many disabled writers feeling othered, less than, and deflated. Because we often hear these fixed ideas in classrooms and workshops when we're vulnerable, either young or new to the field, the words stick to us from then on. When you're othered, directly or indirectly, even once by those you admire and respect, it's hard to forget. Beneath each commonly held writing belief, I include an explanation of the problem with the wording and possible ways to reframe the advice. This list is not exhaustive, and I encourage readers to apply the insight I share here to other ableist writing beliefs, as well:

- **Writers Write Every Day. If You Don't, You Are Deficient, Uncommitted, and/or Lazy:** This archaic writing belief desperately needs to be tweaked. Establishing a writing routine is certainly helpful, as it really can keep writers on track and producing work. However, not all writers write every day or are even physically or mentally able to do so. Some write sporadically; some write once per week. Some write on a project-by-project basis, taking lengthy breaks in between. Despite what we're made to believe, it's the quality of the work that matters and that will lead to publication, not how many words we type in a day or how many days in a row we write. Writers need days (or weeks, months, years) for revising, for resting, for thinking through the work, and for finding inspiration. Encourage students to develop a writing schedule/routine/habit/pace that works for them and keeps them energized and producing work.

- **Writing Is Easy. If It's Not Easy, You Shouldn't Do It. You Should Instead Move On To Something That Comes More Naturally:** This is grossly ableist (particularly to neurodivergent populations that struggle with writing, reading, and concentrating), but it's also just not true. Writing well is challenging. It can be rewarding, even fun. It can be meaningful and a source of real joy in an otherwise stressful, uncertain world. But writing well is hard work. It often requires sustained focus, long-term commitment, and putting a tremendous amount of pressure on oneself. To make the case that writing should be "easy" sounds like someone who's never pushed themselves far enough in their work to reach any real complexity; this can't be a good sign for the quality of their creative work. It also seems like a deliberate attempt to discourage and deflate the spirit of other writers, thereby making the field smaller and less competitive for themselves. While I've heard variations on this belief more than once, one time in particular involved a young student at a reading who asked the featured writer, in front of a large audience, for advice on writer's block. He definitively told her that she needed to find another hobby, that this published book of his only took three weeks to write. If she had any real talent, she should be able to follow suit. The student looked so deflated when she sat back down in her seat. The field may have lost a promising writer that night.

Similarly, don't tell students that "there's no such thing as writer's block." If someone tells you that they feel "blocked," believe them. Don't tell them that they're not. Also, the term "writer's block" can mean many different things. In fact, it could mean a period of time in which, for reasons of disability or health concerns, a person is unable to produce creative work.

Instead, students need real insight and encouragement, as they work through writer's block and difficult stages of their writing projects. Share your own experiences with writing struggles, delays, and setbacks. And emphasize that breaks are human and that sometimes a new tactic is needed, but that other times when writing feels hard it can be a sign that you're onto something good, maybe even great.

- **Writing Is Hard, But It's Hard for Everyone, Equally:** Writing *is* hard. But there's a difference between the normal immense pressure writers place on themselves to produce work and confronting that same pressure with the many, additional hardships faced by those with disabilities. In other words, writing is much, much harder for some. Many professors seem to find a kind of democratic beauty to the belief that writing is equally hard for everyone. Yet not only is this not true, it also conveniently releases them from having to do the hard work of creating and implementing equitable, diverse lesson plans and teaching strategies. In truth, effective, moving writing is hard for everyone in completely different ways. Ask your students what they each struggle with in particular. Offer kind suggestions, not absolutes or value judgments.

- **Writers Need to Be Naturally Effective Public Speakers and Engaging Public Readers if They Want a Writing Career:** It's true that being an effective public speaker and an engaging reader can help sell books and promote one's work. However, writing, public speaking, and public reading are completely different skill sets. Writers who are equally gifted at all three are certainly quite lucky, though are almost certainly the minority. It's also okay, however, to struggle with public speaking and/or public reading. In fact, many students with autism and other forms of neurodivergence find these tasks challenging or even impossible. Those realities do not make these students less valuable as writers or as people. Avoid setting unfair standards for students with disabilities, and help students, when asked, brainstorm alternatives to traditional public readings and speaking events, for example, creating pre-recorded content.

To conclude this section, negative outcomes can arise when those in positions of authority perpetuate one-size-fits-all advice to a classroom full of completely different humans, with different learning styles, different bodies and minds, and different strengths. Advice like this, that is ableist in nature, does not allow for otherness and difference, suggesting that the writing field is not open to everyone. In truth, however, success is never guaranteed, even for neurotypical and non-disabled writers who bend over backwards to perfectly follow traditional writing advice. To avoid proffering advice that is ableist and exclusionary, it's important that writing professors and mentors consider and embrace diversity and inclusion in all forms and encourage students to build on their individual strengths. Reconsider the writing advice you provide your students: is it kind, actually true 100 percent of the time, and necessary for students to hear? Does it need to be tweaked so as to be helpful, encouraging, and inclusive to everyone?

IV. Reconsidering Program, Classroom, and Workshop Policies and Practices

For years now, changes have been proposed to the creative writing classroom and the traditional Iowa Model Workshop. For instance, Felicia Rose Chavez's seminal work *The Anti-Racist Workshop: How to Decolonize the Creative Writing Classroom* stresses the need for workshop facilitators to be more mindful, knowledgeable, and inclusive with regards to race. In a similar vein, this section focuses on considerations needed to address ableist policies and practices in creative writing classrooms and workshops and ways that faculty can be advocates for students with disabilities rather than obstacles.

- **Representation:** To be a catalyst for social justice and real change, educators need to consider if the readings assigned in classes and workshops depict a wide range of human identities and experiences. In recent years, there's been much positive change on this front, including professors de-colonizing their syllabi. Such change is needed regarding other forms of diversity, as well. For example, professors and lecturers need to make efforts to assign works by writers with different disabilities. Also, it would be useful to assign work that shows complex poetic speakers and round characters in fiction and non-fiction who contend with forms of neurodivergence, mental illness, and other types of disabilities. Such additions to reading lists will help to destigmatize people, including currents students, who live with forms of disability, bring awareness to their conditions, and show them as real people, living full, complex human lives.

- **Eliminating Exclusionary Course Policies:** Professors should regularly review their syllabi and course materials, looking for exclusionary policies and requirements. Also, consider asking colleagues to peer review your course syllabi in case they see something that you missed. For instance, an overly strict attendance policy may be unmanageable for someone with health concerns; this is a form of ableism. Additionally, it is tremendously important that educators do not require assignments and/or activities, graded or non-graded, that leave students feeling exposed or othered. An example of this is requiring students to read aloud (an embarrassingly near impossibility for dyslexics and others) or requiring that they perform extemporaneous speaking (which can be challenging or unmanageable for those, for instance, who have forms of autism and mental illness). Instead, always ask for volunteers. Even though reading aloud and public speaking are part of many writers' careers, that does not mean that these tasks should ever be forced on anyone, as it can be shaming, distressing, and can have long-term repercussions.

- **Inclusive Lesson Plans and Workshop Strategies:** Creative writing faculty should continuously strive to make lesson plans, assignments, and workshopping approaches more inclusive. The efficacy of the Iowa Model Workshop has long been questioned; educators should seize the opportunity to be innovative and reconfigure the creative writing workshop. According to Kiljunen et al., one approach that could benefit a diverse student group is called the Flipped Classroom (FC), in which "students learn basic elements on their own, before face-to-face meetings, and then deepen their understanding with the help of an expert instructor."[17] Of particular importance, FC offers advantages for teachers when it comes to working with students with visible and invisible disabilities because "it may help teachers to know their students better, interact with them more, and differentiate learning content based on individual need."[18] This method also de-emphasizes class meetings as overly formal and hierarchical in which the teacher reigns supreme. To apply FC to a writing workshop, perhaps workshopping between class peers could take place online via discussion boards, freeing class time for generative writing prompts and activities as well as discussions of students' writing processes.

- **Eliminating Penalties and Shaming for Typos:** I want to first make the distinction between occasional typos and work that's riddled with errors. In either case, choose kindness in your response to the work, even if the grade is ultimately lowered for work that was hastily or poorly completed. However, in my experience as a student, even occasional typos were never accepted as normal, "to be expected" human error. They were almost always interpreted by educators as a sign that the person who perpetrated the offense was just not committed enough or was too lazy/incompetent to effectively review their work. Sadly, I watched many peers be publicly ridiculed in workshops for typos, and I have experienced similar shaming myself. Educators need to make peace with the fact that students make mistakes. Typos should not be seen as a sign of someone's lack of commitment to a course or an assignment; they're merely common slips that can often be missed by even seasoned editors.

    Furthermore, typos can be windows into hidden disabilities: small moments when the invisible becomes visible. The truth is, students with forms of neurodivergence, like dyslexia, can often not see these mistakes at all, no matter how much time they spend on the work. The same is true for those with

---

[17] Juho Kiljunen et al., "Higher Education and the Flipped Classroom Approach: Efficacy for Students with a History of Learning Disabilities." *Higher Education* 88, no. 3 (September 2024): 1129. https://doi.org/10.1007/s10734-023-01162-1
[18] Ibid.

vision impairments. Because of my neurodivergence, I must review my work much more thoroughly than most of my colleagues. In fact, I listen to everything I write, from emails to long essays, read back to me via my computer's accessibility features, which takes extra time and effort.

If you make the choice to cruelly chide a student for a typo, you may well be shaming someone whose brain sees and processes language differently, thereby marginalizing a student who may already be working harder than everyone else. Instead, let it go. Typos do not make or break good writing; they're common, and they're easily fixed. Furthermore, deducting points for typos is far from equitable teaching behavior. You might say *well, students will face the same criticism from future editors and agents*. I have news for you: those agents and editors also need to reconsider how they interact with possibly disabled writers.

- **When a Student Struggles, Don't Assume Deficiency:** Don't assume that students are deficient or lazy if they are struggling to complete assignments or to meet expectations. First and foremost, graduate writing programs—by and large—handpick their students. They have access to students' writing samples, letters of recommendations, and previous transcripts. While they may not tell the full story, these records provide insight into the student's capabilities and strengths before the student is even accepted into a graduate program. If a program accepts a student, they should embrace and stand by that student in both times of success and in times of struggle. Professors and advisors should offer assistance and understanding, not ridicule. They should also not impose "tough love" coaching techniques, which do not appeal to or work for everyone.

Rather, if a student is struggling academically, for instance, failing to complete assignments or meet deadlines, ask them what could help. However, keep in mind that a student, regardless of their age, could have yet to be diagnosed with, for instance, a learning disability or a mental illness. In other words, they may not yet have the insight or tools needed to understand why they are struggling or what they need. In these situations, encourage the student to attend campus counseling centers and/or disability centers, which should have resources to help the student find answers, support, and coping strategies.

Finally, graduate programs should not assume that students already possess all writing and researching skills needed to complete projects and dissertations/theses. As students, they are there to *learn* such skills. Also, the knowledge and skills they possess when they enter into a program are tightly bound to their socioeconomic background; don't judge or demean them. Take the opportunity to work in favor of equity.

- **Reconsidering Graduate Comprehensive Examinations:** In many graduate programs, comprehensive examinations are designed to test the students' reading and writing skills, their "academic rigor," as I've heard it called. Only, in many cases, these exams do not *actually* test a student's ability to write academically as they would in a real-world setting: in their own environment, at their own pace, and with all materials they need at hand. In my PhD program in the United States, we were tested in four broad fields of study: tasked with passing four written exams and one oral exam. Most of the possible exam areas did not provide a reading list, and no exam area provided the questions beforehand. Each of the four written exams had to be completed in a computer lab in a five-hour period under fluorescent lighting. You could not use the books and articles you'd spent months reading and annotating. You could not use your own device. You were allowed breaks for food and drinks and to use the restroom, but you couldn't leave to go home and rest. And, for most of the exams, students were required to write four substantial essays in the five-hour period. Academic rigor in this case was code for academic hazing.

The unfortunate truth is that most of the content produced was often unusable, even in the passing exams; they read after the fact like mad, frantic ramblings, like data dumps of information from the frazzled brains of students desperately trying to prove they had done their reading. Prior to exams, I excelled: I finished coursework with a 4.0, and I was publishing my work. But, in this pressurized two-year period of examinations, I struggled. The ambiguity of facing exams with no reading lists left me in a constant state of ADHD paralysis, not knowing how to best prepare or what to focus on. Without the books I'd read and my thorough notes, it was unbearably hard to focus during the exams and to recall all the material I'd attempted to retain. My eyes dried out during each exam. I developed headaches and nausea. All of this was worsened by the knowledge that my whole academic future, and the stability of my personal life, depended on passing these exams, an anxiety that recurred over and over during each test.

Comprehensive examinations at the PhD level were the single most egregiously ableist experience of my educational journey, even for those of us who were granted meager "accommodations." Ten years later, I still think about the ways these exams damaged my love of learning, impaired my mental and physical health, broke my confidence and self-worth, and all but ended my trust in university programs. While many programs have made productive changes to exams in the year since, it is still vitally important that this problem be discussed and that programs continually reevaluate their examination practices. In fact, I question the necessity of examinations in master's and PhD humanities-based programs. A much kinder, more inclusive practice, not to mention a practice more rooted in *actually teaching* academic research and writing, is to require students to complete, with mentoring and guidance, a creative and/or critical research practicum: for example, an extensive annotated bibliography or literature review that will serve as a precursor to students' thesis/dissertation, followed by a discussion with professors. There's no justifiable reason for an exam format in this field or even for using the term "exam," which can itself induce anxiety.

Overall, programs need to seriously consider if they value the pretense and elitism of academia over the flesh-and-blood students who trust and rely on them. Instead of perpetuating systemic ableism and academic hazing, we need to break out of *this is how it's always been done* and *I did it so you should too* mentalities. We also need to become particularly considerate and mindful of students who are neurodivergent, chronically ill, and/or disabled and implement parameters that are doable and meaningful for everyone. Enforcing in-person, timed exams and other problematic test formats of this magnitude is not just ableist; it's also a waste of time for all students, who could instead be reading and learning to produce quality research and writing.

- **Eliminating Ambiguous Expectations and Feedback:** In my seventeen years as a university student (at the BA, MA, and PhD levels), I witnessed a wide variety of communication styles when it comes to professors mentoring students and conveying their expectations, be that for a class assignment or the structure and content of a thesis/dissertation. Some professors meticulously define expectations to the point of leaving students little room for individuality and creativity. Some barely offer any guidelines, leaving students to completely create the parameters for themselves. Many approaches fall somewhere in the middle. The efficacy of a mentoring/feedback approach is largely dependent, however, on the individual students and their needs and preferences, and professors need to be aware of this; they also need to be willing to modify their methods, when necessary, for the sake of the student's success. For example, students with certain forms of neurodivergence, like autism and ADHD, can have a low tolerance for ambiguity and uncertainty. Henderson, Wayland, and White explain that these students often desperately need *explicit context* because it makes it easier for them "to interpret and integrate details into a unified whole."[19] For me, as a diagnosed neurodivergent, this means that I have to be able to clearly see the whole picture and thoroughly understand all moving parts and all feedback, particularly with research-based endeavors, before I can effectively start the writing process, a reality that made writing my PhD dissertation[20] very challenging. In part, this was because at the time I didn't understand my own neurodivergence, in part because there's not a defined dissertation/thesis structure in the creative writing field as there is in others, and in part because of ambiguous and unclear feedback that did not suit my learning style or my needs. I urge readers to hear me here: ambiguous/unclear feedback, particularly in high stakes projects, can be much more than just nor preferable or ineffective; for some students, it can be harmful and can have devastating effects. In my experience, merely switching to a supervisor with a

---

[19]Donna Henderson, Sarah Wayland, and Jamell White. *Is This Autism?* (Routledge, 2023), 193.
[20]I completed my PhD in the UK, where the term is PhD thesis. However, because I'm from the United States and work here currently, I use the American term: PhD dissertation.

more direct and clear feedback style completely changed my thesis writing experience for the better. I went from being unable to make forward progress to passing my defense with no corrections.

In terms of faculty guidance and feedback at any level and on any kind of student work, it's imperative that an appropriate style of feedback and communication be offered to students based on their individual needs and preferences, even if that means the students working with a different professor or advisor/supervisor. Furthermore, this is not the only possible problem that could arise in student–faculty mentorship pairings, particularly when working with neurodivergent students, which is why faculty and program administrators need to be knowledgeable about different learning styles and about forms of neurodivergence more broadly. The larger point is to be curious about a student's needs/process, to be a resource, an ally, a champion. The larger point is that you can both tell a student they need to make changes while also being kind, clear, and specific or otherwise working to meet the student's particular learning needs.

Conclusion

Looking back on his MFA experience at Iowa, Steve Kuusisto argues that "higher education is a race. Semesters are timed contests. The speed of absorption is all that counts. In this race the visually impaired are reduced to depraved animals."[21] While Kuusisto's experience involved navigating a highly competitive MFA program as a blind student decades ago, many other students since have also been made to feel "reduced to depraved animals" by the ableist expectations of graduate writing programs. I still grapple with the times I was told I wasn't good enough merely because I was a different learner, a different writer with different needs, that I was told just "test your limits" and "confront your problem," that I was looked at and talked to like I was less than human and certainly not deserving of higher education. Despite all the support I received during my PhD experience, all my publications from those years, and all the compliments, praise, and accolades I received in both my PhD programs, it's the times I was put down and othered that come to mind first; I can't imagine that will ever change. In the years since I finished my PhD, I have heard countless similar experiences from writers around the world. This is because the longstanding fear of being seen by the academy as "different" in body and in mind is finally starting to dissolve, and so many impacted former students now have stories to share.

The purpose of this essay has been to highlight disabled, chronically ill, and neurodivergent student needs in creative writing graduate programs at both the master's and PhD levels. In doing so, I have combined research, my own lived experiences as a neurodivergent student, and my insights from my almost twenty

---

[21]Kuusisto, *Planet of the Blind*, 103.

years as a university writing lecturer. At present, creative writing faculty have a lot to contend with regarding the new reality of generative artificial intelligence (AI) systems and their impact on student originality and creativity as well as the uncertainty facing humanities-based programs. It's also easy to become overwhelmed amid all the new concerns and specific needs of so many student demographics. However, I feel strongly that implementing inclusive policies and practices to better serve disabled students will benefit *all students* and need not feel overwhelming; rather, it can quickly become intuitive, standard practice. It is my hope that this essay has provided clear guidance and useful suggestions that will help faculty members easily implement meaningful changes. Paradigm shifts can be slow, but they start with individuals. An important first step is just embracing physical and mental otherness in colleagues and students and choosing to value humans over the pretenses of the academy and the writing field at large. Ultimately, to increase visibility and awareness, more research and firsthand accounts are needed, involving disabled students in creative writing programs and their individual needs and experiences.

Bibliography

Brown, Nicole. "Disclosure Dances in Doctoral Education." *Social Sciences* 13, no. 12 (2024): 689. https://doi.org/10.3390/socsci13120689

Chavez, Felicia Rose. *The Anti-Racist Writing Workshop: How to Decolonize the Creative Classroom*. Haymarket Books, 2021.

Goodall, Gemma, Odd Morten Mjøen, Odd Morten Witsø, Sissel Horghagen, and Lisbeth Kvam. "'Breaking a Vicious Cycle': The Reproduction of Ableism in Higher Education and Its Impact on Students with Disabilities." *Frontiers in Education* 9 (2024). https://doi.org/10.3389/feduc.2024.1504832

Henderson, Donna, Sarah Wayland, and Jamell White. *Is This Autism?: A Guide for Clinicians and Everyone Else*. Routledge, 2023.

Kiljunen, Juho, Erkko Sointu, Aino Äikäs, Teemu Valtonen, and Laura Hirsto. "Higher Education and the Flipped Classroom Approach: Efficacy for Students with a History of Learning Disabilities." *Higher Education* 88, no. 3 (2024): 1127–1143. https://doi.org/10.1007/s10734-023-01162-1

Kuusisto, Stephen. *Planet of the Blind*. The Dial Press, 1998.

NCES. "A Majority of College Students with Disabilities." NCES. Accessed January 25, 2025. https://nces.ed.gov/whatsnew/press_releases/4_26_2022.asp

NCES. "Students with Disabilities." NCES. Accessed January 25, 2025. https://nces.ed.gov/fastfacts/display.asp?id=60

PNPI. "Students with Disabilities in Higher Education." Postsecondary National Policy Institute. Accessed January 25, 2025. https://pnpi.org/wpcontent/uploads/2023/11/StudentswithDisabilities-Nov-2023.pdf

16 Teaching Creative Writing to Neurodivergent Students: A Fairly Friendly FAQ

LEIGH CAMACHO ROURKS

This essay is a hermit crab: a memoir tucked inside pedagogy tucked safely inside an FAQ (frequently asked question). It is an attempt to speak authentically and simultaneously as a neurodivergent writer and professor of exclusively "neurospicy" students, the term my students prefer. I also train our new faculty at Beacon College, America's first accredited college for neurodivergent students. These are the questions I face about neurodivergence in all my roles: creative writing professor, student advisor, faculty mentor, and writer struggling with my own neurodivergence. Below each question is my answer.

I. Are You Neurodivergent, and Do You Work with Neurodiverse Students?

Yes, I have ADHD and what is now called Specific Learning Disorder (SLD) with an emphasis on reading and writing. When I was diagnosed, the *DSM* utilized more (inaccurately) discrete categories, and my diagnosis was Disorder of Written Expression. I also have chronic diseases that impact memory, language, and energy levels, effectively impacting my ability to think, speak, and write. And yes, I'm a professor at Beacon College in Leesburg, Florida, where every student is neurodivergent. I also run our sixteen-week new hire training, which teaches new faculty and staff about learning differences, how they manifest, how they affect and even derail our students, and how we can best serve our community.

II. What Is the Most Difficult Thing About Being a Neurodivergent Creative Writer?

I think it must be exhaustion.

Before we can consider the potential negative impacts of failing to meet the expectations of those in our field (or our own expectations), we must consider how the act of writing itself butts up against the realities of neurodivergence. Here is an incomplete list of commonly disordered cognitive skills/systems[1] in neurodivergent people (to different degrees and in different ways):

- **Executive Function(s):** Executive function(s) can be defined as a "family of top-down mental processes needed when you have to concentrate and pay attention,"[2] such as when writing. The main categories of executive functions involve self and cognitive control (for example, being able to begin a task or choose what to concentrate on), working memory, and flexible thinking (including creativity).[3] Executive functions are the drivers of our mental bus when we turn off our autopilot and are utilized for every aspect of writing.

- **Working Memory:** Working memory is the "cognitive system that allows for the manipulation of temporarily stored information . . . Because of its role in reasoning, decision-making and many cognitive functions central to literacy and numeracy, working memory is considered crucial for learning and academic attainment" and writing.[4]

- **Encoding, Decoding, and/or Processing Language and/or Sound:** These incredibly complicated cognitive skills include spelling, reading, and handwriting. They also include organizing language, organizing writing, language retrieval, language processing speed, comprehension of complicated organizations of language, and even identifying speech as different from background sounds.

For everyone, writing creates an intense cognitive load, which can be defined as "the amount of working memory resources used when engaged in a cognitive task."[5] For neurodivergent writers, thanks to different deficiencies in these systems and others, the cognitive load can be overwhelming. In "The Parkour of Writing with Dysgraphia," Elvira Kalenjuk likens writing tasks to parkour, because writers must "navigate a path from Point A (the assigned writing task) to Point B (the completion of the task) while negotiating the obstacles on route."[6] Those obstacles come from both their neuro-differences and a lack of understanding from those around them, especially teachers, peers, and mentors. While Kelenjuk is speaking specifically about students with

---

[1] The term "skill" feels like a misnomer, as skills are gained and improved with effort, while "cognitive skills/systems" are neurologically wired. A neurodivergent person cannot simply improve their brain the way one might improve cooking skills, for example.
[2] Adele Diamond, "Executive Functions," *Annual Review of Psychology* 64 (2013): 136, https://doi.org/10.1146/annurev-psych-113011-143750
[3] Diamond, "Executive Functions," 136.
[4] Anne-Laure Le Cunff, Eleanor Dommett, and Vincent Giampietro, "Neurophysiological Measures and Correlates of Cognitive Load in Attention-Deficit/Hyperactivity Disorder (ADHD), Autism Spectrum Disorder (ASD) and Dyslexia: A Scoping Review and Research Recommendations," *European Journal of Neuroscience* 59, no. 2 (2024): 257, https://doi.org/10.1111/ejn.16201
[5] Ibid.
[6] Elvira Kalenjuk, "The Parkour of Writing with Dysgraphia," *English in Australia* 57, no. 2 (January 2022), 27, https://doi.org/10.3316/informit.017689968941473

dysgraphia, the metaphor works for all neurodivergent writers. It is an effective way to better understand how exhausting this cognitive load can be. Simply imagine a group of neurodiverse writers "jumping, ducking, and weaving their way through" the writing process, every time they engage in it.[7]

Cognitive load can be physically measured in a variety of ways, including EEGs, MRIs, and eye-tracking,[8] but we don't have the ability to quantify or even recognize our own cognitive load. Neurodivergent writers don't know how much harder we are working, as it is masked from both us and everyone else. The cognitive load itself is tiring, but so is the fact that it is invisible labor. Added to this is the stigma not only of being different, but of the mistakes we make. It is all so very exhausting.

III. What Are Some of the Main Struggles Neurodivergent Writers Face in Classrooms and Workshops?

- Producing a "clean" manuscript, fully devoid of spelling, transcription, and layout errors, especially in early drafts, where cognitive resources are devoted to other aspects of the process.
- Reading manuscripts and texts that are not available in forms accessible through text-to-speech programs/screen readers.
- Reading and writing and processing at the same speed as others.
- Speaking more or less than is expected, or being unable to speak quickly enough due to delayed processing.
- Emotional regulation, especially in the fraught workshop environment.
- Meeting deadlines.
- Maintaining motivation.

The result is that neurodivergent learners are often called out for being sloppy or lazy writers and/or participants, though they generally work harder than their neurotypical counterparts out of necessity. This is often compounded in workshop, where the whole period can be spent discussing editing flaws in a single manuscript instead of content or craft. Moreover, those flaws are often seen as moral failings, deliberate choices, and a waste of everyone's time. It is demoralizing and embarrassing, and it robs neurodivergent writers of the quality of feedback their counterparts receive, making growth difficult, if not impossible.

Additionally, the workload to time ratio can feel overwhelming. For example, neurotypical students who have effective executive functions can decide to begin writing and then simply begin. Without issues with working memory, they are able to

---

[7]Kalenjuk, "The Parkour of Writing with Dysgraphia," 24.
[8]Le Cunff, Dommett, and Giampietro, "Neurophysiological Measures and Correlates of Cognitive Load," 259.

multi-task, find the desired words quickly, and generally remember what they've just written. Without language encoding, decoding, or processing issues, their first draft has few errors. They often have time to revise, focusing on exploring their craft. They can do all this while reading, considering, and responding to manuscripts and sample texts. However, as pieces of the writing process hit obstacles for the neurodivergent writer, the delays become cumulative. It is as if they, no matter how talented, capable, or hard working, simply have less time.

IV. Should Neurodivergent Students Not Have to Meet Deadlines or Use Proper Spelling, Etc.?

It is important to remember in the United States, all policies that are part of any business or educational endeavor, public or private, traditional (for example, a university course) or non-traditional (for example, a writing workshop offered by a literary journal or an individual) must comply with the Americans with Disabilities Act (ADA), which states that "reasonable modifications in policies, practices, or procedures shall be required, unless an entity can demonstrate that making such modifications in policies, practices, or procedures, including academic requirements in postsecondary education, would fundamentally alter the nature of the goods, services, facilities, privileges, advantages, or accommodations involved."[9] Many other countries have similar laws. This means that if a learner identifies themselves as having a disability and makes a request for a reasonable accommodation, then you must offer that accommodation. Asking for no rules—no deadlines or requirements—is probably not reasonable, but asking for modifications to those rules can be. Assuming we are adhering to both the letter and the intent of the ADA and similar laws elsewhere, the answer to the question posed in this section has two parts, neither of which should be taken on its own.

To return to the question above, should neurodivergent students not have to meet deadlines or use proper spelling, etc.? First, no. Neurodivergent students can and should be required to meet basic (appropriately accommodated) policies, such as adhering to deadlines or producing edited copies of their work. Unless (or until) all of publishing—no, all of the world—decides that these things no longer hold weight (and unless a class or workshop can go on indefinitely), it would be both impractical and, I believe, actively damaging to ambitious creative writers who are neurodivergent to ask them to never have to adhere to deadlines or editing expectations. I realize this is a controversial view in the neurodivergent space (even in this book, perhaps). Nonetheless, we can do more harm than good by creating false expectations and not preparing students for real-world success. Many (if not most) people who expend the heavy cost (financial, temporal, and personal) of pursuing creative writing in any

---

[9]"Americans with Disabilities Act of 1990, As Amended," ADA.gov, accessed February 2025, https://www.ada.gov/law-and-regs/ada/

educational setting do so (at least in part) because they wish to write for an audience. It's our duty to help them pursue that goal, a goal which is a practical, real-world endeavor. We must remember—it will not only be traditional gate-keepers who value these things.

Second, yes. Sometimes these policies should be voided—for everyone participating, not just neurodivergent students. Any accommodation that serves one can serve all. As the writing community has acknowledged that traditional ideas about creative writing pedagogy come from an educational model that purposely lacked diversity and thus produced writers and writings of only one sort,[10] our conversations have tended to focus on the workshop model and its rules of conduct. However, serving a diverse set of learners means recognizing that they will have a diverse set of goals, needs, and obstacles. Simultaneously, we will not know the true scope of diversity in front of us. There may be writers with both visible and invisible disabilities, socioeconomic stressors, visible and invisible language barriers, lack of resources, differences in cultural or technological literacies, temporary setbacks due to issues outside the scope of a course, and more. We should take for granted that every human we work with may invisibly struggle, may at any point—despite neurotypicality—have effectively less time or physical or cognitive resources than expected. Doing so encourages each of us to first reevaluate why, when, and how to implement policies, in order to best serve the whole diverse class.

For example, we can assume we will have students that, for one reason or another, will struggle with deadlines. This encourages us to evaluate why, when, and how deadlines are set up and implemented. An inflexible deadline may better serve some learning goals and course realities, while flexibility will have little to no effect on others. Similarly, the consequences of a missed deadline can be different for different activities, depending on the goals and timelines of those activities. This is all true in the real world (as best enshrined by Douglas Adams and his infamous joke: "I love deadlines. I love the whooshing noise they make as they go by").[11] Therefore, there is no reason for it not to be true in our learning environment.

V. That Was A LOT. Can You Give Another Example?

Many of us with SLDs have horror stories of turning a new manuscript into a workshop and, instead of receiving useful feedback on our work, we spend the workshop being derided for not having a "clean manuscript." I have several of these stories I could tell. While this is clearly problematic, so is the idea that a clean manuscript is unimportant, which is objectively untrue. It is also objectively untrue that what we bring to workshop is not a draft or that a draft must be "clean." Otherwise, why receive input, why draft?

---

[10] Disturbingly, the latter has been a larger concern than the former for too many for far too long.
[11] Douglas Adams. *The Salmon of Doubt: Hitchhiking the Galaxy One Last Time* (Random House, 2005), 26.

Despite its problems, I use the general workshop model. When I do, it may not function exactly the same as those I took as a student, but it is similar. When designing my workshops, I first outline my objectives. I start with an audience of one: me. What are my goals in utilizing a workshop? These differ, depending on who I am working with and the greater objectives of the course, but here are some examples:

- I want students to build and comfortably use the vocabulary of the larger writing community, so they can confidently engage and easily understand everyone else. I want them to be so comfortable using writer jargon "correctly" that members of the community who may be gate keepers, especially rigid gate keepers, don't form incorrect assumptions and box them out.
- I want my writers to continue to build and understand their own aesthetic, by examining and articulating their likes and dislikes. This way they can become cognizant of the choices they are making in their own writing and work to build toward their goals.
- I want students to become aware of different styles, approaches, genres, aesthetics, and ways to solve problems, to learn to recognize, appreciate, and help serve other writers' goals regardless of their own tastes. That way they will be better readers and editors, and hopefully become more open to possibilities in their own writing.
- I want students to help each other take risks and work together to make those risks pay off, while learning to enjoy the journey when they don't.

A "clean" manuscript isn't important to any of these goals, so I now know I don't need to require one. Instead, I explain that we won't be discussing basic typos or editing mistakes in workshop, but that we are free to help each other out by offering non-judgmental, non-intrusive fixes directly on manuscripts, if we so choose. I point out that a reader can be wrong in these edits, and ultimately, it is the author's responsibility to make corrections. On the other hand, when appropriate for the audience and purpose of a course, I do include activities or assignments that require clean manuscripts. However, that's the last step, saving a lot of time for everyone and allowing those who struggle to concentrate their efforts appropriately at each stage.

VI. If You Had One Piece of Advice for Teaching Creative Writing to Neurodiverse Students, What Would It Be?

There is nothing so important in what writers do that it is worth denying a fellow human their dignity. To assume the worst of a learner: that they are sloppy, lazy, uncaring; that they are choosing to vex—instead of assuming the best of a learner—that they are *trying*, especially when the stakes are so very low (this isn't hate speech or threats, after all) is terribly unkind. It is—excuse the language but this is the most precise wording I have—shitty pedagogy. To share these low opinions of students, especially in front of others, is actively cruel.

Unfortunately, even the best of us can fall for the trap of bad assumptions, especially when over-worked, over-tired, and over-stressed. Luckily, a well-considered set of policies, assignments, and exercises that are built by taking for granted that we will be faced with diverse learners can help us avoid this trap. It starts by ensuring every part of our educational plan is grounded in well-considered objectives that we clearly communicate (first and foremost, to ourselves), instead of being based on tradition. Knowing your goals for your students at each step will help you remove unnecessary requirements, thus ensuring both you and the students focus on what is most important.

VII. Any Advice for Neurodivergent Writers?

I have been suffering from terrible, crippling burnout for several years. In writing this FAQ, I finally began to understand why: I had masked my struggle from myself. Not my struggle against a community that stigmatized my learning disabilities (which I have been very open and loud about), but my struggle every single time I come to the page. For decades, I have masked the toll it takes on me just to write at all. I was bearing a cognitive load I couldn't acknowledge, and it made me hate what I had once loved (and myself).

So here is my advice to neurodivergent writers, my advice to myself: big breath. It's okay to be slow, to be tired, to find writing hard, even as you find it exciting and fun and invigorating. It is even okay to dislike writing, just as much as you love having written (or vice versa). Many things can be true at once. It's okay to rest, to take time off, to even quit. I quit writing regularly, and here the world sits, fairly intact. But don't hide. Acknowledging your struggle does not negate your desire and it does not mean you are admitting defeat. Neither does needing rest. In fact, you are at your best when you rest. So, rest. Let the others write every single day, rain or shine, burnout or not. Learn the value of rest and find the schedule(s) that work for you.

Finally, know this: you can be a writer even if writing is harder for you, because that effort you are putting in, that is *love*. And I will never be convinced that anyone loves writing more than those who do it despite the fact that their brains fight them every step of the way.

VIII. Is There Any Benefit at All to Being a Neurodivergent Writer?

I hate when someone refers to someone else's disability as "a superpower" (which is very different from calling your own a superpower—more "power" to you!). Not only does this sound condescending and toxically chipper, but if I could, I would give up my SLD and ADHD in a heartbeat. They have never been very "super" for me. However, if a writer's true job is to show us the world in unexpected ways that force us to see it anew, then every time a neurodivergent person writes the world they see, through a language they inevitably encode and decode differently, they are doing the writer's true job simply by being themselves.

Or, perhaps, all we need to do to understand what neurodivergent writers bring to the page is to remember just how magical and beautiful parkour really is.

Bibliography

ADA.gov. "Americans with Disabilities Act of 1990, As Amended." Accessed January 9, 2025. https://www.ada.gov/law-and-regs/ada/

Adams, Douglas. *The Salmon of Doubt: Hitchhiking the Galaxy One Last Time*. Random House, 2005.

Diamond, Adele. "Executive Functions." *Annual Review of Psychology* 64 (2013): 135–168. https://doi.org/10.1146/annurev-psych-113011-143750

Kalenjuk, Elvira. "The Parkour of Writing with Dysgraphia." *English in Australia* 57, no. 2 (January 2022): 23–35. https://doi.org/10.3316/informit.017689968941473

Le Cunff, Anne-Laure, Eleanor Dommett, and Vincent Giampietro. "Neurophysiological Measures and Correlates of Cognitive Load in Attention-Deficit/Hyperactivity Disorder (ADHD), Autism Spectrum Disorder (ASD) and Dyslexia: A Scoping Review and Research Recommendations." *European Journal of Neuroscience* 59, no. 2 (2024): 256–282. https://doi.org/10.1111/ejn.16201

17 The Power of Words: Neurodiversity, Authenticity, and Inclusion in the Creative Writing Classroom

RACHEL CARNEY

A few years ago, I attended a creative writing workshop where we discussed "Poem Beginning with a Retweet," by Maggie Smith.[1] Her poem begins with the following quotation from a tweet that went viral: "*If you drive past horses and don't say horses / you're a psychopath.*" After reading this line, I was so enraged by that quotation that I found it almost impossible to focus on the poem itself. In fact, my emotional response was so strong that I could barely speak.

What was it about that simple—and, let's be honest, fairly ridiculous—tweet that incensed me? Why did it raise the hackles on the back of my neck? It was not the derogatory use of the term "psychopath," even though there is much that could be said about how we use mental health terminology with no regard for the feelings of those for whom these terms are an uncomfortable reality. No, it went deeper than that, back to my childhood.

I was a shy child. I struggled to cope with many of the social aspects of life, always anxious of saying or doing the wrong thing, desperate to conform, without ever understanding why I could not. Things changed, as I grew older, but I dragged that weight of social expectation, humiliation, and exhaustion behind me, into my adult life. It wasn't until I was in my mid-thirties, when I sought and received a diagnosis of dyspraxia, that I finally began to understand why I had struggled with so many things. That was when the weight began to lift. Dyspraxia explained, at last, my difficulties with co-ordination and balance, and why, despite having excellent hearing, I always struggle to catch what people say in pubs and restaurants, because of the background noise. It explained why I take longer than others to remove my shoes, or put them on, why I find it difficult to write by hand, and why I struggle to read my own handwriting. But dyspraxia has benefits, too. It may be the reason why I have far more empathy than the average person. It may be the source of my skills in problem solving, teaching, creative writing, and strategic planning, and the reason behind my ability to spot typos everywhere I look.

Since the diagnosis, I have begun to understand myself more clearly, to realize why I have often struggled with things that others find easy, but also to see just how

---

[1] Maggie Smith, "Poem Beginning with a Retweet," *Colorado Review* 46, no. 2 (2019): 150.

ridiculous it is that the society in which we live is entirely geared toward one way of seeing. That was why I was so enraged by that tweet, quoted in Smith's poem. It epitomized, for me, the notion of conformity that is entrenched in our society. It doesn't even matter what the words are, the power of that simple formula is acute: *If you don't X, then you are Y*. If you don't follow the crowd, if you don't say this, or do that, then you will be excluded, no matter what.

It is this conformity mindset, or "pathology paradigm," which shapes our understanding of the society in which we live, based on two key assumptions:

1 There is one "right," "normal," or "healthy" way for human brains and human minds to be configured and to function (or one relatively "normal" range into which the configuration and functioning of human brains and minds ought to fall).

2 If your neurological configuration and functioning (and, as a result, your ways of thinking and behaving) diverge substantially from the dominant standard of "normal," then there is Something Wrong With You.[2]

The alternative, Walker argues, is a shift toward the "neurodiversity paradigm," where a diversity of minds is perceived to be "a natural, healthy, and valuable form of human diversity," and there is "no 'normal' or 'right' style of human mind, any more than there is one 'normal' or 'right' ethnicity, gender, or culture."[3] It is ironic, therefore, that Maggie Smith's poem undermines this sense of conformity-as-sacrosanct. Those first two lines, borrowed from a viral tweet, may be designed to startle the reader, but the following lines take something positive from that initial shock. They focus, not—as I did—on the notion of conformity and social shame, but on our relationship with the world around us, and the inbuilt human desire to share this simple enjoyment of life with others. Throughout, the poem lists other natural wonders: "A rainbow, / a cardinal, a butterfly," celebrating our ability to share such encounters with others and to appreciate these encounters fully: "If you hear a woodpecker / and don't shush everyone around you / into silence."[4] Therefore, Smith's poem borrows that initial startling line, and twists it in on itself so that the emphasis is not on conformity but on the horses and our delight in them. The quotation becomes a celebration of life, our ability to appreciate it, and our desire to communicate that appreciation to others in a way that is genuine. Smith's use of colloquial language in the line *"oh my god look at the moon"*[5] emphasizes this sense of genuine wonder. And there is deep irony in the fact that those who are more likely to conform are probably less likely to notice natural wonders such as these, and less likely to draw attention to them in front of others, without embarrassment.

---

[2]Nick Walker, *Neuroqueer Heresies: Notes on the Neurodiversity Paradigm, Autistic Empowerment, and Postnormal Possibilities* (Autonomous Press, 2021), 14–15.
[3]Ibid., 16.
[4]Smith, "Poem Beginning with a Retweet," 150.
[5]Ibid.

As a neurodivergent person, this poem speaks for me when it takes the concept of conformity and turns it into a celebration of responding to the world in an immediate, authentic, and unaffected way. Kirsty Oehlers interprets the poem as a "demand" that "we live life fully . . . and not be afraid to express it,"[6] but the poem does not stop there. The final couplet returns us to that initial focus on social connection and communication: "If you feel yourself receding, receding, / and don't tell anyone until you're gone."[7] It asks us how much value we place on honesty. Are we always authentic with ourselves and with those around us? What might happen to us if we are too afraid of social norms to communicate the realities of our experience to others? If we do not reach out and seek help when we need it?

When I encountered that strange little poem, I was too incensed by that quotation and its silly, but equally hurtful message, to appreciate what followed. Smith's poem takes what is effectively a divisive and derogatory—but also extremely popular—comment from social media, and turns it into a thought-provoking, and potentially empowering question. The poem both acknowledges our reliance on the pathology paradigm and implodes it at the same time, emphasizing our desire for genuine social connection alongside what is often an equally strong desire to conform. But it also encourages all of us to connect with others—and with the world around us—in a way that is authentic, unaffected by societal pressures.

So, what relevance does Maggie Smith's poem—and my encounter with it—have in an essay about the teaching of creative writing? You don't need to be an expert in neurodiversity to realize that many people still labor beneath that weight of social expectation, struggling to communicate and connect in a world where normalcy is valued above all else. Around 1 in 7 people in the UK are neurodivergent in some form or other, meaning that their brain "functions, learns and processes information differently."[8] The neurodiversity movement uses the social model of disability to argue that neurological difference is a natural form of variation that results in strengths as well as challenges.[9] Although the stereotypes imply that neurodivergent individuals must always be perceived as "that socially awkward uncle writing code in a dark corner of the basement,"[10] research by Chrysochoou et al.[11] as well as Grant and Kara[12] indicates

---

[6]Kirsty Oehlers, "Honouring the Artistry in Qualitative Social Work Research." *Qualitative Social Work* 22, no. 5 (2023): 813–818, https://doi.org/10.1177/14733250231197715.
[7]Smith, "Poem Beginning with a Retweet," 150.
[8]"Neurodiversity in the Workplace: Bridging Research, Practice and Policy." Advisory, Conciliation and Arbitration Service (ACAS), effective July 6, 2025, https://www.acas.org.uk/research-and-commentary/neurodiversity-at-work-research-practice-and-policy
[9]Judy Singer, *NeuroDiversity: The Birth of an Idea* (Judy Singer, 2017).
[10]Daniel Bowman Jr., *On the Spectrum: Autism, Faith, & the Gifts of Neurodiversity* (Brazos Press, 2021), 42.
[11]Maria Chrysochoou et al., "Reframing Neurodiversity in Engineering Education." *Frontiers in Education* 7 (2022), https://www.frontiersin.org/articles/10.3389/feduc.2022.995865
[12]Aimee Grant and Helen Kara. "Considering the Autistic Advantage in Qualitative Research: The Strengths of Autistic Researchers." *Contemporary Social Science* 16, no. 5 (2021): 589–603, https://doi.org/10.1080/21582041.2021.1998589

that neurodivergent strengths often include creativity. Indeed, Daniel Bowman Jr., an autistic author, poet, and academic, states: "Poetry was a natural fit for my neurodivergent brain wiring,"[13] while neurodivergent poet and educator Chris Martin describes the moment he began writing as a college student: "I had discovered a multiverse where my racing, discursive, associative intellect was channeled into buzzing focus,"[14] and there are numerous examples of neurodivergent creative celebrities.[15] It is, therefore, highly likely that many of those individuals who elect to study creative writing will be neurodivergent, even if they have not yet sought or received a diagnosis.

The creative writing workshop is a space where thinking differently can be perceived as a positive attribute, and approaching a text from an unusual angle can be helpful. Therefore, diverse perspectives should be valued in creative writing. In fact, they are essential if we want to teach our students to avoid cliché and to produce work that is original and engaging. The setting for my encounter with Maggie Smith's poem was ironically the very place where I ought to have felt free from that weight of social expectation. Perhaps those of us who teach and facilitate creative writing workshops can take away a little of that weight and remove some of that exhaustion. The following sections of this essay outline three different ways in which we can equip our creative writing students—including those who are, or who might be, neurodivergent—with the skills they need to celebrate the positive aspects of diversity and the courage to do so.

I. Cultivating a Safe Space

Deryn Rees-Jones compares the role of the creative writing tutor with the role of the therapist, drawing on the history of creative writing teaching and psychoanalytic theory to argue that the creative writing class will always be more "intense" than a literature seminar:

> Due to the inherently personal aspect of creative writing, even though the teacher-writer may be using some literary critical terms, the classroom dynamic often feels very different because of an awareness of the bodily presence of the "author," coupled with a strong sense of a connection between author and text—however complex that relationship might be. For this reason, the writer [tutor] has to work hard to create a space that will hold the movements between subjective experience and objective analysis.[16]

---

[13]Bowman, *On the Spectrum*, 140.
[14]Chris Martin, *May Tomorrow Be Awake: On Poetry, Autism, and Our Neurodiverse Future* (Harper Collins, 2022), 12.
[15]"Posters," Neurodiversity Celebration Week, last modified January 12, 2019, https://www.neurodiversityweek.com/posters
[16]Deryn Rees-Jones, "Jump to the Skies: Critical and Creative Responses to Creative Writing—Theory and Practice," *The Writer in the Academy: Creative Interfrictions*, edited by Richard Marggraf Turley (D.S. Brewer, 2011), 167–168.

Rees-Jones concludes that, as a result of this need to negotiate between emotional support and objective criticism, the creative writing classroom should become a "nurturing . . . space" where students feel "sufficiently relaxed" enough to play.[17] Inspired by the work of Elliott Spaeth and Amy Pearson,[18] I have found the Universal Design for Learning (UDL) to be a particularly helpful pedagogical approach for cultivating the kind of "safe place" that Rees-Jones describes,[19] one that will foster a sense of freedom that will enable and empower students to experiment and be creative, without fear of stigmatization or discrimination.

The existing education system in many parts of the world is based on "differentiation," where those who are neurodivergent are provided with additional help to overcome the barriers they face. This additional support can be extremely beneficial for many students, but such a system cannot help everyone, as Sheila R. Ross explains:

> Some students who have a diagnosis receive support through a disability services office. These students typically receive support that is adjunctive to instruction, such as tutoring, technology, and exam accommodations. However, this support is not generally available to students who do not already have a diagnosis or have not been able to meet the college's documentation requirements.[20]

The existing system, which is prevalent in the majority of higher education institutions, means that those without a formal diagnosis do not receive any help at all. This is problematic because so many of us are not diagnosed until later in life. Rebecca Twinley,[21] who reflects on her own diagnosis of autism at the age of forty, acknowledges the fact that such diagnoses are overly dependent on "luck" and "privilege" in many parts of the world.[22] The existing system also focuses on segregation, which inevitably reinforces the stigmatization and exclusion of some learners. Furthermore, Gill Porter's research indicates how this can place "additional demands" on neurodivergent and disabled students, "perpetuating an 'othering' of such students, who are forced to continually 'self-advocate' in a way that is both physically and emotionally exhausting."[23]

---

[17] Rees-Jones, "Jump to the Skies," 169–170.
[18] Elliott Spaeth and Amy Pearson. "A Reflective Analysis on Neurodiversity and Student Wellbeing: Conceptualising Practical Strategies for Inclusive Practice." *Journal of Perspectives in Applied Academic Practice* 11, no. 2 (2023): 109–120, https://doi.org/10.56433/jpaap.v11i2.517
[19] Rees-Jones, "Jump to the Skies," 169.
[20] Sheila R. Ross. "Supporting Your Neurodiverse Student Population with the Universal Design for Learning (UDL) Framework," paper presented at the 2019 *IEEE Frontiers in Education Conference*, Covington, KY, USA, https://doi.org/10.1109/FIE43999.2019.9028693
[21] Rebecca Twinley, "Actually Autistic at 40: A Source of My Auto/Biographical Troubles." *Auto/Biography Review* 3, no. 1 (2022): 62–76, https://doi.org/10.56740/abrev.v3i1.3
[22] In the UK at this present time, a diagnosis of dyspraxia must be sought privately at significant cost, unless the individual concerned is able to receive a free means-tested diagnosis though their school or higher education institution. Autism and ADHD diagnoses are organized through the NHS, but these come with waiting lists of many months.
[23] Gill Porter. "Neurodiverse Students, Ableism and HE as Sites of Exclusion." *Dyslexia Review* 33, no. 1 (2023): 19–22.

In contrast, UDL is based on the simple premise that every student is different and will learn in different ways.[24] It was developed by David H. Rose and Anne Meyer, aiming to create a "barrier-free educational environment that answers the individual needs of all learners" and is based around the provision of flexibility and options.[25] The principles of UDL can be applied to the creative writing classroom in many different ways, but I have found two methods to be particularly effective in fostering the kind of safe space that Rees-Jones describes—that is, to regularly invite and normalize feedback and adaptation and to provide options.

In practice, the first of these is simply an invitation for honest communication. I invite feedback from my students on a regular basis, making adjustments in response to their feedback where possible, and passing on suggestions to others where such adjustments are outside of my control. Feedback can be sought through a formal, anonymized system such as Mentimeter, or more informal questions designed to continually acknowledge and reinforce the diversity of the learning experience. The adaptations required might be as simple as closing a door to prevent distraction for those students who find it more difficult to focus, introducing a five-minute comfort break, or moving furniture around so that everyone can see and hear each other during class discussion. Options for participation might be as simple as setting a group task, and allowing those students who find group work difficult to complete the task on their own if they prefer.[26] It is impossible to predict the needs of every single student, so feedback and adaptation, and the provision of options, are the only way in which we can cultivate a learning environment that is as inclusive as possible. The aim is to ensure that no individual student is left to suffer in silence, to enable every student—including those who lack the confidence to speak out loud—to feel comfortable enough to develop at their own pace in an environment where diversity is valued as a natural and integral aspect of the learning experience.

II. Attention to Language

Anyone studying or teaching creative writing should be interested in the nuances of language. In our classrooms, we need to stress "attention to language" to our writing and literature students. We also need to be sure that we pay attention to how we label forms of neurodivergence and forms of disability, both inside and outside of our classrooms. Kate Simpson recently published an article in *Mslexia* magazine arguing that the language we use can "subtly influence our behaviour."[27] She discusses recent changes to the terms we use when referring to our impact on the planet:

---

[24]Whitney H. Rapp. *Universal Design for Learning in Action: 100 Ways to Teach all Learners* (Brookes Publishing, 2014).
[25]Anne Meyer et al., *Universal Design for Learning: Theory and Practice* (CAST, 2014).
[26]Spaeth and Pearson, "A Reflective Analysis."
[27]Kate Simpson, "Agenda: A Brighter Shade of Green," *Mslexia* 86 (2020): 6.

In October 2019, the *Guardian* officially updated its Style Guide to reflect and illustrate the severity of the climate emergency. In an online announcement, the organisation outlined six new journalistic principles, such as using "global heating" instead of "global warming" and "climate denier" rather than "climate sceptic." This also extended to referring to "climate emergency" or "climate crisis" as opposed to "climate change."[28]

As I write this, three years later, it is clear that that small change to the vocabulary we use to describe what is happening to our planet—used not just by *Guardian* journalists but by many people in different parts of the world—has altered our perception in a way that may well have a lasting impact. Simpson argues that, in the context of the climate crisis "we can use language to re-establish a positive and intimate connection to the environment, strengthening our capability to discuss it in all its complexity."[29]

In a similar sense, Walker argues that a shift from the pathology paradigm to the neurodiversity paradigm calls for "a radical shift in language, because the appropriate language for discussing medical problems is quite different from the appropriate language for discussing diversity."[30] We can stop using words associated with disease, such as "condition," "syndrome," or "disorder." Instead, more positive terms such as "neurotypes" (different forms of neurological difference), "neurominorities,"[31] and "neurological differences" will be understood by more and more people, as we begin to use them in our conversation and in our writing. Even the term "diagnosis" is synonymous with the concept of sickness or disease, and it is difficult to find a suitable alternative, but talking of "traits" rather than "symptoms" may be a good place to begin.

Labels such as *dyspraxia* can be empowering for those of us who have spent our lives confused as to why we often fail to meet the expectations of those around us. But such terms can also lead to confusion and stigmatization. Many people have never heard of the term *dyspraxia* before. Others may have heard of it, but do they really know what it means? Even among dyspraxic people there is much debate about what dyspraxia actually is, and whether or not it should be classed as a disability. If someone searches online for a definition, there are many competing sources of information, with explanations that cannot hope to shed sufficient light on the complex, multi-faceted experience of every single dyspraxic individual. In the United States, it is often known by a different term altogether: DCD.[32]

Both the *Oxford English Dictionary*[33] and the NHS website[34] use the word "clumsy" in their definition of dyspraxia. That word, *clumsy* is inaccurate. It suggests

---

[28]Ibid., 7.
[29]Ibid., 9.
[30]Walker, *Neuroqueer Heresies*, 21.
[31]Ibid., 41–42.
[32]"Developmental Co-Ordination Disorder (Dyspraxia) in Children." National Health Service (NHS), effective July 6, 2025, https://www.nhs.uk/conditions/developmental-coordination-disorder-dyspraxia/
[33]"Dyspraxia," *Oxford English Dictionary—Online*, effective July 6, 2025, https://www.oed.com/dictionary/dyspraxia_n?tab=meaning_and_use
[34]See NHS website listed above.

carelessness, but many dyspraxic people are incredibly careful. They have to be. If you are dyspraxic, then ordinary everyday tasks are fraught with risk, and must always be completed with far more concentration, care, and forward planning than a neurotypical person can possibly imagine. The NHS definition doesn't say that we *are* clumsy, just that we may "appear to move clumsily" to an observer, but it still uses that word, with all its connotations of carelessness.[35] Definitions such as these are clearly embedded in the pathology paradigm and are often far too simplistic. If I—an intelligent, dyspraxic, open-minded academic—only began to realize that dyspraxia means more than just *clumsy* in the last few years, then surely the majority of people are unlikely to understand how complex it can be, how it relates, or does not relate, to other neurotypes such as dyslexia or autism, and how every dyspraxic person can experience different challenges to different degrees. The fact that Microsoft Word is underlining every instance of the term "dyspraxic" in red, as I type this, indicates that there is a long way to go before such terminology is commonly understood.

The umbrella term *neurodiversity*, on the other hand, is one which I am beginning to accept as a positive alternative that can be easier for many people to understand. To begin, there is no negative prefix of *dys* or *dis*. There is, instead, a focus on *diversity*: the clear sense that difference is good, that it should be celebrated and valued. The prefix *neuro* indicates that this difference is something fundamental in how people understand and interact with the world. It is not a terrible mistake, something that we need to change or mend. It is the world itself that needs to change, in line with the social model of disability,[36] to accept that diversity can be positive and that fresh perspectives and new ideas are essential to the workings of society and for the effective functioning of any organization. Indeed, Judy Singer, an influential figure in the development of the Neurodiversity Movement, states that neurodiversity echoes the same principles as the term biodiversity, where difference is seen as not only positive, but essential.[37]

The term neurodiversity is also inclusive, referring to all types of neurological difference, and acknowledging that we do not, and may never, fully understand how, or why, such traits exist in the human race, or exactly how they interconnect. It also acknowledges the vast differences across the globe in how we understand and diagnose neurological difference. A recent article in *Dyslexia Review* examines the fact that "different countries, different cultures, and different assessment bodies, cannot agree on what dyslexia is or how to measure it."[38] Even within a single country, such as the UK or Germany, there are different approaches in different regional areas.[39] It is unlikely that we will ever fully agree on the definitions of each neurotype, so the term neurodiversity is particularly helpful as a means of including every form of difference.

---

[35] See NHS website listed above.
[36] Victoria Honeybourne, *The Neurodiverse Workplace: An Employer's Guide to Managing and Working with Neurodivergent Employees, Clients and Customers* (Jessica Kingsley, 2019).
[37] Judy Singer, *NeuroDiversity*, 87.
[38] Martin Bloomfield. "The Dyslexia Compass." *Dyslexia Review* 33, no. 1 (2023): 6–9.
[39] Ibid.

That change of terminology from "climate change" to "climate crisis" proves that we can "actively change the way we write—and think—for the positive."[40] If we want to celebrate diversity, we must carefully consider all of the language that is used in our classrooms. Just because a word or phrase is accurate—in a grammatical or a medical sense—that does not automatically make it free from prejudice. Our teaching should be self-critical, as well as critical, always inviting students to consider the impact of words on those who read or hear them. We can reclaim the language used by neurotypical individuals to describe our lack of conformity. It will take time, but that time will not be wasted.

III. Assigning Diverse Texts and Diverse Authors

Poetry can affect us deeply, as my encounter with Maggie Smith's poem demonstrates. Literary texts can foster empathy, connect directly with a reader's emotions, and use the complexities of language to represent the world from a particular perspective. I propose that, as we encounter more and more texts that represent or evoke the lives of those we perceive to be different from us, or those who seem to *diverge* from the norm, we will gradually begin to feel a greater sense of freedom to express and articulate our own feelings of divergence. There is evidence to suggest that stigma around certain health conditions can be reduced through "contact" with a stigmatized individual, and that even if this contact is indirect, via a literary text, it can "demystify and dispel misinformation and generate empathy."[41] The texts that we present to creative writing students, as examples to criticize and emulate, should be those that present diverse perspectives. Our example texts should indicate that no subject matter is off limits and that difference can be valued and celebrated. Such texts may be overt in their desire to communicate lived experience, such as Esther Ottaway's poetry collection *She Doesn't Seem Autistic*,[42] or they may be more subtle in their presentation of difference, such as the depiction of a character with Ehlers-Danlos Syndrome (EDS) in Rebecca Yarros' *Fourth Wing*.[43]

However, we are not limited to contemporary texts. Although Daniel Bowman Jr. acknowledges that the practice of "retrodiagnoses" is far from problematic, as a newly diagnosed autistic writer he describes feeling "nourished" by his encounter with texts that dig into our literary canon to unearth examples of neurodivergent writers from the past:

---

[40]Simpson, "Agenda," 7.
[41]Miriam Heijnders and Suzanne van der Meij. "The Fight Against Stigma: An Overview of Stigma-Reduction Strategies and Interventions." *Psychology, Health & Medicine* 11, no. 3 (2006): 359, https://doi.org/10.1080/13548500600595327
[42]Esther Ottaway, *She Doesn't Seem Autistic* (Puncher and Wattmann, 2023).
[43]Rebecca Yarros, *Fourth Wing: The Empyrean Series, Book 1* (Entangled: Red Tower Books, 2024).

Within a few short months of understanding autism as the underlying operating system that ran my brain, I was also thrilled to put myself in the probable company of Emily Dickinson, Herman Melville, William Butler Yeats, and others. I was like them, in neurotype if not talent. They were weird, to be sure, but *literary* weird, my favourite kind.[44]

Not long after receiving my own diagnosis, I encountered Victoria Biggs' book *Caged in Chaos*,[45] in which she argues that the character of Helen Burns from Charlotte Brontë's *Jane Eyre* may have been dyspraxic. In the novel, Helen Burns tends to forget things. She struggles with bad posture and handwriting, and she is punished for daydreaming and "carelessness."[46] It is thought that Charlotte Brontë based the character on her sister, Maria, who was highly intelligent, but struggled with sewing and handwriting.[47] We have no proof that this interpretation of Helen Burns is correct. Even so, such characters may be helpful in eliciting empathy for those who struggle to conform. They can also encourage and inspire those of us who experience similar struggles, reaching out from the literary past to reassure us that we are not alone.

There is no doubt that such texts should be critically discussed in every creative writing classroom. But it is also crucial to consider the perspective of the writer behind the text. Bowman argues that bestsellers, such as *The Curious Incident of the Dog in the Night-Time*, and popular TV shows, such as *The Big Bang Theory*, tend to be "written by and for neurotypicals . . . in ways that often play to simplistic clichés," which can lead to "a skewed and sometimes even grotesque understanding" of neurodivergent experiences.[48] Texts written by neurodivergent writers can offer a counterbalance to this problematic trend, presenting the nuance and complexity of neurodiversity from a perspective that moves away from potentially harmful stereotypes and misconceptions.

An example text that I have found particularly helpful when teaching the art of memoir, or non-fiction, is *Just So You Know: Essays of Experience*,[49] in which several writers discuss their experiences of marginalization and difference. In particular, Josh Weeks' essay "Dear O,"[50] written in the form of a series of letters addressed to his OCD, inspired engaging and well-written texts from a group of students who had previously been struggling with attendance and workload. We can inspire and empower our students simply by introducing them to a variety of contemporary texts that do not shy away from such topics.

---

[44] Bowman, *On the Spectrum*, 20–21.
[45] Victoria Biggs, *Caged in Chaos: A Dyspraxic Guide to Breaking Free* (Jessica Kingsley, 2005), 19–20.
[46] Ibid.
[47] Ibid.
[48] Bowman, *On the Spectrum*, 219.
[49] Hanan Issa et al., eds., *Just So You Know: Essays of Experience* (Parthian, 2020).
[50] Josh Weeks, "Dear O," *Just So You Know: Essays of Experience*, eds. Hanan Issa et al. (Parthian, 2020), 42–55.

Conclusion: Joining Up the Threads

The written word, as illustrated by my encounter with Smith's poem, can have a powerful, profound, sometimes visceral impact. As creative writing educators, we are in a unique position of influence. The students we teach will not all end up as prize-winning poets or novelists. But their skill with words will remain with them throughout their lives. Perhaps some of them will write advertising copy. Others may write for local media or news stations. Others may become teachers or parents. Whatever our role in life, as writers, we will always have an affinity for words and an ability to utilize their power. Therefore, of all the different academic disciplines, the teaching of creative writing should strive to be the most inclusive, and the most accepting of difference. Here are the reflections of one autistic poet, author and academic, on the definition of autism:

> The name "autism" comes from the Greek *autos*, which means "self". The "ism" means "a state of being". So autism connotes "the isolated self"—apropos of the alienation I have spoken of. In many ways, I wholly identify with that connotation. Yet I would like to claim the literal meaning as a new name for what I was and am: the word "autism," in its purest form, actually means "the state of being one's self." There's a larger issue of authenticity here, one that I would need, and still need, to keep living into.[51]

Bowman's claim that autism denotes "authenticity" asserts a kind of agency over such language that, for many years, has remained out of reach, for those of us who are affected by such terms. He continues:

> With my autism diagnosis, I came to learn much more about what made me tick, what lay beneath the surface. I came to know that my way of being in the world, which made me deeply ashamed throughout my childhood, was not my fault. I came to know that the constellation of traits I displayed had a name: autism—and that taking on the name autistic, while scary, could also be redemptive. In the end, it's about being my true self.[52]

The language that we use, or fail to use, can be complex. It can also be implicitly prejudiced, as I have demonstrated. But, just as Maggie Smith's poem turns something problematic and extremely painful into a challenging celebration of authenticity, our use of language can also be redemptive. That was Daniel Bowman Jr.'s experience. It has also been my own experience, explored in many of my own poems.[53] As those who seek to inspire and equip a new generation of creative writers, we can acknowledge the evolving nuances of language. We can recognize the capacity of language to confuse, to mis-inform, or to be laden with prejudice or shame. We can cultivate an environment of inclusion and acceptance, where

---

[51] Bowman, *On the Spectrum*, 171.
[52] Bowman, *On the Spectrum*, 180.
[53] Rachel Carney, *Octopus Mind* (Seren Books, 2023).

feedback and adaptation become the norm, following the principles of UDL. We can select example texts that are thought-provoking, written by diverse authors, and featuring diverse characters. And we can encourage our students to write their own texts from a place of authenticity, to challenge, provoke, engage, and inform a new generation of readers.

Bibliography

ACAS. "Neurodiversity in the Workplace: Bridging Research, Practice and Policy." Effective July 6, 2025. https://www.acas.org.uk/research-and-commentary/neurodiversity-at-work-research-practice-and-policy

Biggs, Victoria. *Caged in Chaos: A Dyspraxic Guide to Breaking Free*. Jessica Kingsley, 2005.

Bloomfield, Martin. "The Dyslexia Compass." *Dyslexia Review* 33, no. 1 (2023): 6–9.

Bowman Jr., Daniel. *On The Spectrum: Autism, Faith, & the Gifts of Neurodiversity*. Brazos Press, 2021.

Chrysochoou, Maria, Arash E. Zaghi, and Connie Mosher Syharat. "Reframing Neurodiversity in Engineering Education." *Frontiers in Education* 7 (2022): https://www.frontiersin.org/articles/10.3389/feduc.2022.995865

Grant, Aimee, and Helen Kara. "Considering the Autistic Advantage in Qualitative Research: The Strengths of Autistic Researchers." *Contemporary Social Science* 16 no. 5 (2021): 589–603. https://doi.org/10.1080/21582041.2021.1998589

Heijnders, Miriam, and Suzanne van der Meij. "The Fight Against Stigma: An Overview of Stigma-Reduction Strategies and Interventions." *Psychology, Health & Medicine* 11, no. 3 (2006): 353–363. https://doi.org/10.1080/13548500600595327

Honeybourne, Victoria. *The Neurodiverse Workplace: An Employer's Guide to Managing and Working with Neurodivergent Employees, Clients and Customers*. Jessica Kingsley, 2019.

Martin, Chris. *May Tomorrow Be Awake: On Poetry, Autism, and Our Neurodiverse Future*. Harper Collins, 2022.

Meyer, Anne, David H. Rose, and David Gordon. *Universal Design for Learning: Theory and Practice*. CAST, 2014.

Neurodiversity Celebration Week. "Posters." Last modified January 12, 2019. https://www.neurodiversityweek.com/posters

Oehlers, Kirsty. "Honouring the Artistry in Qualitative Social Work Research." *Qualitative Social Work* 22, no. 5 (2023): 813–818. https://doi.org/10.1177/14733250231197715

Porter, Gill. "Neurodiverse Students, Ableism and HE as Sites of Exclusion." *Dyslexia Review* 33, no. 1 (2023): 19–22.

Rapp, Whitney H. *Universal Design for Learning in Action: 100 Ways to Teach All Learners*. Paul Brookes, 2014.

Rees-Jones, Deryn. "Jump to the Skies: Critical and Creative Responses to Creative Writing—Theory and Practice." *The Writer in the Academy: Creative Interfrictions*. Edited by Richard Marggraf Turley. D. S. Brewer, 2011.

Ross, Sheila R. "Supporting Your Neurodiverse Student Population with the Universal Design Learning (UDL) Framework." Paper presented at the 2019 IEEE Frontiers in Education Conference, Covington, KY, USA. https://doi.org/10.1109/FIE43999.2019.9028693

Simpson, Kate. "Agenda: A Brighter Shade of Green." *Mslexia* 86 (2020): 6–9.
Singer, Judy. *NeuroDiversity: The Birth of an Idea*. Judy Singer, 2017.
Smith, Maggie. "Poem Beginning with a Retweet." *Colorado Review* 46, no. 2 (2019): 150.
Spaeth, Elliott, and Amy Pearson. "A Reflective Analysis on Neurodiversity and Student Wellbeing: Conceptualising Practical Strategies for Inclusive Practice." *Journal of Perspectives in Applied Academic Practice* 11, no. 2 (2023): 109–120. https://doi.org/10.56433/jpaap.v11i2.517
Twinley, Rebecca. "Actually Autistic at 40: A Source of My Auto/Biographical Troubles." *Auto/Biography Review* 3, no. 1 (2022): 62–76. https://doi.org/10.56740/abrev.v3i1.3
Walker, Nick. *Neuroqueer Heresies: Notes on the Neurodiversity Paradigm, Autistic Empowerment, and Postnormal Possibilities*. Autonomous Press, 2021.
Weeks, Josh. "Dear O." In *Just So You Know: Essays of Experience*, edited by Hanan Issa, Durre Shahwar, and Özgür Uyanik. Parthian, 2020: 42–55.

18 Embodiment and the Body in Pain: Observations from a Poet in Academia

MIRANDA L. BARNES

In Nicole Brown's introduction to *Ableism in Academia*, she is critical of the ableist machine that is the present-day academy, calling it a "rigid regime of productivity, effectiveness and excellence," entirely engineered toward "tangible outcomes and outputs," operating fully in support of "the prestige economy."[1] Within this machine, the standard is "normative, fully able and abled being."[2] Because the construct of the ideal scholar within academia is bound up in perfectionism, excellence, performativity, and productivity, which is often internalized,[3] this framing is not always accessible to academics with disabilities and chronic illnesses. Additionally, when discussing the focus of Claudia Gillberg's chapter in her introduction to *Ableism in Academia*, Brown highlights how those who are disabled are often seen as "non-academic or intellectually weaker"[4] than their able-bodied counterparts, reflecting their less-than-fully human, diminished status. Not only are these outliers seen as diminished, they are also assigned the additional burden of "the extra workload required for anyone with a disability to participate on the same terms as able-bodied colleagues."[5] This dynamic is inherently inequitable and not limited solely to any one field within academia.

However, the academy is not the only writing space that is ableist; the wider writing community has also unfortunately shown chronically ill and disabled writers they do not belong in a fully-human, undiminished capacity, often inadvertently. As Karl Knights concedes in *Poetry London*: "people say 'I didn't realize' or 'I simply didn't think about it.'"[6] But this acknowledging after the fact does not prevent the

---

[1] Nicole Brown, "Introduction: Theorising Ableism in Academia," *Ableism in Academia*, eds. Nicole Brown and Jennifer Leigh (University College London Press, 2020), 3.
[2] Ibid.
[3] Ibid., 4.
[4] Ibid., 6–7.
[5] Claudia Gillberg, "The Significance of Crashing Past Gatekeepers of Knowledge: Towards Full Participation of Disabled Scholars in Ableist Academic Structures," *Ableism in Academia*, eds. Nicole Brown and Jennifer Leigh (University College London Press, 2020), 13–14.
[6] Karl Knights, "No Disabled People Wanted Here: Accessing The Estate of Poetry," *Poetry London* no. 102 (2022), https://poetrylondon.co.uk/no-disabled-people-wanted-here-accessing-the-estate-of-poetry/

erasure of disabled writers who cannot attend events due to accessibility limitations. Knights cites the Covid pandemic as evidence that accessibility is possible, despite disability activists being told for years there was no way to make widespread change: "For the first time, I could easily attend launch readings, festivals, Q&As, panel discussions. Poetry events were liberated from physical locations."[7] Yet, this was to be short lived, as Knights suspected it would be, post-pandemic: "Watching remote accessibility options vanish in real time is as heartbreaking as it is infuriating. I am not sure which is worse: never experiencing accessibility, or experiencing it, and then watching it being taken away."[8]

While I do not have the limits of mobility many do, I have had to miss many events due to chronic pain. Sometimes, this is due to the level of pain I am in; sometimes, this is due to knowing I cannot sit several hours in a hard chair or hide the suffering from my face during interactions (which makes people uncomfortable). There is a weariness that comes from having to mask your suffering in social circumstances for the comfort of people. Other times, the fatigue is so overwhelming that no matter how much I want to be present, my body requires rest over anything else. When writers and academics have chronic illness and chronic pain, their limits present themselves over and over until they respect them. What I wish others understood about living with chronic illness and chronic pain is the grieving we do over this lack of choice. We cannot just power through and "make the effort," at least not without consequences that will remove our agency in some other capacity. This is why accessibility and inclusive practices need to be considered and enacted in writing communities as much as in the academy.

I am a poet, writer, and academic with multiple health conditions, two of which cause chronic pain: endometriosis and fibromyalgia. Chronic pain has, quite plainly, diminished my quality of life and limited the fulfilment of my abilities. The current landscape of professional expectation, whether in the academic world or the writing world, is saturated with similar ableism. If you cannot "keep up" with what is expected of you, you are simply left behind. In this essay, I will discuss my experience as a writer and academic with chronic illness and my experiences with institutional and communal ableism. I hope this chapter will be helpful not only to similarly impacted writers but to their institutions and colleagues. But I hope it will particularly be useful also to those who may feel they are suffering alone, giving them strength to advocate for themselves.

I. The Thief Within the Body

An often-unspoken challenge of forms of neurodivergence as well as chronic pain conditions is the reality you may suddenly not be able to perform at expected levels

---

[7] Ibid.
[8] Ibid.

or be able to perform with any kind of consistency. While our abilities may be exceptional during "good" periods, there are agonizing hours when executive dysfunction and mental paralysis make impossible what you might be able to smash out at light-speed on another day. Some days, I can complete a super-human amount of intensely focused work incredibly quickly. Other days, I sit paralyzed, unable to make progress on a task, as my brain and body refuse to cooperate.

In my lived experience, I have found that deep and widespread misunderstandings persist about what endometriosis is and how it impacts the body and mind. Many people think this condition is equivalent to just a "bad period," meaning a particularly painful case of cramps, with pain only occurring cyclically. In fact, endometriosis is a condition where endometrial tissue, similar to that which grows in the uterus lining normally shed during menstruation, grows in extra-uterine locations throughout the body. This can be anywhere within the pelvis but can also occur in the areas as extraordinary as the diaphragm, lungs,[9] and the sciatic and sacral nerves.[10] The reality of endometriosis can be nearly constant pain, not limited to pelvic and abdominal pain. For me, 80 percent of the time I was in substantial pain, and the other 20 percent of the time, the pain intensified to excruciating and unbearable. I spent multiple days each month in bed. I had no choice. The pain encompassed my entire body, with shooting, burning, sharp and stabbing pains, deep throbbing aches, and overall musculoskeletal myalgia. Often, I felt as if I was on fire on the inside or being flayed alive, which I wish was hyperbole. Sometimes the pain could rapidly spike without warning, rendering me nearly incapacitated. As an ambitious, creative person, I never once wanted to lose days, weeks, and, cumulatively, months and years, preventing me from my goals.

After my second surgery in 2023, I was shown the surgical images and a full list of eleven excision cites within my pelvis where endometriosis lesions and scar tissue were removed, along with my uterus (due to adenomyosis). Organs in multiple locations were adhered together with endometriosis and scar tissue, including my bowels. My appendix was medically declared "obliterated" and removed. Deep infiltrating endometriosis was embedded into both of my ureters, which in time would have obstructed them and destroyed my kidneys, potentially killing me. I was told by the first surgeon in 2019 that I had a "mild case" of endometriosis and my urinary tract and bowel were uninvolved. Chronic illness is expensive, not least in time and money, but also in the effort of having to keep searching for answers when "experts" dismiss your pain as "minimal." The additional psychological impact of medical gaslighting for people experiencing endometriosis cannot be overstated.

---

[9]Camran Nezhat et al., "Thoracic Endometriosis Syndrome: A Review of Diagnosis and Management," *JSLS: Journal of the Society of Laparoendoscopic Surgeons* 23, no. 3 (2019), https://doi.org/10.4293/JSLS.2019.00029

[10]Ahmet Kale et al., "Comparison of Isolated Sciatic Nerve and Sacral Nerve Root Endometriosis: A Review of the Literature," *Journal of Minimally Invasive Gynecology* 29, no. 8 (2022): 943–951, https://doi.org/10.1016/j.jmig.2022.05.017

I did not get a confirmed diagnosis of endometriosis until 2019, which meant nearly three decades without one. The average time to diagnosis for someone with endometriosis is ten years. In this time, the effects of the disease do not pause, and as Gillberg points out, "During the years in which [disabled scholars] are ill without a diagnosis, they risk being misunderstood, stigmatised and maligned, and losing their jobs and family support. The absence of a legitimate diagnosis can mean loss of status, loss of identity and loss of life, be that through suicide or premature death."[11] As much as I "powered through" the chronic pain and illness I was experiencing, something in me knew my trajectory was not sustainable. During my PhD, I could hide my suffering when I wasn't in physical spaces with others. While I sometimes taught five classes per week and delivered module-wide lectures alongside my research and coursework, on days I didn't teach, I barely left my bed. I needed time for my writing, but I needed recovery time more. When I returned to full-time work requiring my bodily presence in the office every day, there was little I could do to prevent my chronic conditions from impacting my attendance.

II. "You Don't Look Disabled"

I have often been able to "pass" as fully-abled in my student and working lives. I knew I was expected to succeed, so I developed coping mechanisms to adapt. The consequences of failure were not viable (especially when living on my own), so "soldiering through" seemed my only option. But over the course of the last several years, my pain became too unbearable to live with silently.

As the severity of my endometriosis progressed, almost no one knew except those closest to me and eventually my line managers. Thankfully, I had compassionate managers in the years around my first surgery in 2019 (which was unsuccessful but finally granted me a diagnosis) and my second, more in-depth surgery in 2023, requiring an eight-week medical leave period and phased return. When I returned to work, several surprised colleagues mentioned they had no idea of the pain I was in. I always did my best not to show it, conditioned to never make my pain someone else's problem.

Elisabeth Griffiths considers how her own experience "coming out" as someone with a chronic illness has altered her sense of academic and professional identity as well as the uncomfortable ambiguity of considering oneself "disabled."[12] Griffiths cites the neoliberal citizen's core identity of a worker who is willing, capable, and able, considering the slipperiness of "ability" with its contextual and temporal limitations.[13] The current academic environment, steeped in standards of "excellence," makes

---

[11] Claudia, Gillberg, "The Significance of Crashing Past Gatekeepers of Knowledge: Towards Full Participation of Disabled Scholars in Ableist Academic Structures," *Ableism in Academia*, eds. Nicole Brown and Jennifer Leigh (University College London Press, 2020), 13–14.
[12] Ibid.
[13] Griffiths, "But You Don't Look Disabled," 125–126.

living with chronic illness and disability increasingly difficult. As Griffiths points out, the expectation that "the 'willing, capable and able' worker can perform to an excellent standard in everything *all of the time*" creates a "highly pressurised working environment and this frenetic pace of activity has somehow become normalised."[14] While this makes life difficult enough for the able-bodied and neurotypical individual, for those with an invisible chronic illness, the difficulty is amplified because while we are both "*willing* and *capable*, we cannot always perform to those intense standards."[15] In my lived experience, I have found that chronic illness is also not straightforward, particularly chronic pain. Some days you're able to function with minimal disruption, other days every part of your body is agony, and you can't get out of bed. This fluctuation causes you to fear you won't be believed (and you may not be) and doubt the validity of your experience. Also, when you have chronic pain every day of your life to varying degrees, you get used to it and it becomes normalized. To be clear: the pain is there, you feel it, and *it hurts*, but you don't always externally exhibit an expected pain response. Pain's constant presence is exhausting; it consumes your resources for living, taking away energy and time you could certainly use elsewhere.

III. The Poetics of The Body

In her piece "Preparing the Body for a Reopened World: The Challenges of Emerging from Lockdown," American Poet Laureate Ada Limón meditates on the poetics of the body, but also a body in pain: "It wasn't until recently that I realized that I am in pain more than others . . . For a long time I thought pain levels, for most people, hovered around 5. That is apparently not true."[16] I relate to this immensely. I cannot remember a time without some kind of pain in my body, but I thought everyone must be experiencing this, too. While mercifully my daily pain is less now than before surgery, I am still not without pain, as other conditions persist. When, briefly, I may feel vital and without pain, I realize how used to pain I am, comprehending Limón's words with new meaning: "The other day, I realized my body was not in pain, and it made me worry. I thought, I cannot feel my body! I do not have a body! Pain is how I have always experienced my body and suddenly there was no pain."[17] Limón also recalls the freedom of not being perceived by others, or being present to others as just a head and face. When speaking to Krista Tippett as part of the *OnBeing* podcast, Limón reflects on the return to in-person interactions, as someone who "[has] pain, so I've moved through the body in pain . . . there was an ease . . . living in the head-only

---

[14]Ibid., 125–126.
[15]Ibid., 126.
[16]Ada Limón, "Ada Limón on Preparing the Body for a Reopened World: The Challenges of Emerging from Lockdown," *LitHub,* April 19, 2021, https://lithub.com/ada-limon-on-preparing-the-body-for-a-reopened-world/
[17]Limón, "Preparing the Body."

world . . . a kind of a poet's dream on some level."[18] Limón's head-only existence is as much to do with negotiating with the body on your own terms as it is with the tangled issue of being perceived. Solitude allows you to tend to your body's needs without judgment. Space for the mind in solitude allows for less distraction, too, as much as it allows for a more permeable membrane between bodiless and embodied existence. But this experience is disrupted when the body is placed into the frenetic and expectant context of others, whether it is an academic department, a literary festival, or an in-person workshop.

Similar to Limón's "head-only" existence, Finesilver, Leigh, and Brown recall Leder's 1990 concept of the "absent body," a phenomenon where most people are not actively aware of their bodies when they are working well, unless injured, sick, or in pain, or to a lesser extent, experiencing something like hunger.[19] While active embodiment is essential for a writer, the embodied experience of chronic pain is fundamentally different. Finesilver et al. address the experience of the academy more generally, pointing out that "if a person is in chronic pain, or disabled by their body not working as it 'should', such awareness . . . is no longer a choice but instead a constant, chronic, unavoidable reality. For those of us who live with chronic pain or disability, our bodies are continually present and reminding us of their presence."[20] And as Griffiths reminds us, "The academy values the mind, the intellect and the work of its inhabitants, in all but a few disciplines to the exclusion of their bodies," while the very structure of academic work makes "our bodies invisible and unimportant."[21] When the body asserts itself, this becomes an embarrassing requirement, betraying the Cartesian divide academia clings to, rewarding one and disposing of the other, wherever possible.

Teasing apart how we base our identity in our minds or hearts until "our bodies betray us," Limón confesses that though "body and mind are absolutely connected" she sometimes wishes she "could only think about the inner self."[22] The freedom of poetry's creative process is an audience with our inner self—solitude with an idea, moving us closer into communion with that self. Perhaps, for those of us with chronic pain and illness, it can also become a truce: an opportunity for reconciliation between the body and the mind, a place for them to converse honestly and without expectation.

I track mentions of "body" through Limón's words in "Preparing the Body for a Reopened World" and find forty-six instances, the orange highlight in my web browser illuminating each bright "body" as it moves down the page. Sometimes, through

---

[18] Ada Limón, "To Be Made Whole," *OnBeing with Krista Tippett* (podcast), Feburary 16, 2023, https://onbeing.org/programs/ada-Limón-to-be-made-whole/#transcript
[19] Carla Finesilver, Jennifer Leigh, and Nicole Brown, "Invisible Disability, Unacknowledged Diversity." *Ableism in Academia*, eds. Nicole Brown and Jennifer Leigh (University College London Press, 2020), 143.
[20] Ibid., 144.
[21] Griffiths, "But You Don't Look Disabled," 144.
[22] Limón, Ada. "A Conversation with Ada Limón," interview by Polly Buckingham et al. *Willow Springs Magazine* 89 (2021), https://inside.ewu.edu/willowspringsmagazine/a-conversation-with-ada-Limón/

repetition, a word will tend to lose meaning. Instead, with each mention, there is a new context, a new image, a new meaning. Limón realizes at the close of the piece that she does not have to disclose and share her body out of obligation, but can choose to share her words instead, "the remnants of the body." Words as representation of embodiment, on her own terms.

I ask my body what it needs, and it replies: understanding, tenderness, rest, and care. Space for healing, space to be safe, space to just be. To pass permeably between the boundaries of Sontag's "kingdom of the well and in the kingdom of the sick,"[23] without arbitrary constrictions, the embarrassment of the body within the world. Freedom, and permission, to choose only what is healthy and right for myself. Disclosing my condition only when I feel able and willing.

I ask myself what I need to write, to think, and find my words. All of the above, and lack of judgment. Even if the only one who can provide this is me. If the academic and creative writing worlds value the presence and input of those with chronic illness and disability, a sea change must take place, as well. The capitalist, neoliberal, market-driven model is a machine eating the lot of us, not just the divergent "outlier." The sooner we all acknowledge this the better, and make a collective change, for equality's sake, for the sake of knowledge, for the sake of poetry, for the sake of everything.

Bibliography

Brown, Nicole. "Introduction: Theorising Ableism in Academia." *Ableism in Academia*. Edited by Nicole Brown and Jennifer Leigh. University College London Press, 2020.

Finesilver, Carla, Jennifer Leigh, and Nicole Brown. "Invisible Disability, Unacknowledged Diversity." *Ableism in Academia*. Edited by Nicole Brown and Jennifer Leigh. University College London Press, 2020.

Gillberg, Claudia. "The Significance of Crashing Past Gatekeepers of Knowledge: Towards Full Participation of Disabled Scholars in Ableist Academic Structures." *Ableism in Academia*. Edited by Nicole Brown and Jennifer Leigh. University College London Press, 2020.

Griffiths, Elisabeth. "'But You Don't Look Disabled': Non-Visible Disabilities, Disclosure and Being an 'Insider' in Disability Research and 'Other' in the Disability Movement and Academia." *Ableism in Academia*. Edited by Nicole Brown and Jennifer Leigh. University College London Press, 2020.

Kale, Ahmet, et al. "Comparison of Isolated Sciatic Nerve and Sacral Nerve Root Endometriosis: A Review of the Literature." *Journal of Minimally Invasive Gynecology* 29, no. 8 (2022): 943–951. https://doi.org/10.1016/j.jmig.2022.05.017

Knights, Karl. "No Disabled People Wanted Here: Accessing The Estate of Poetry," *Poetry London* 102 (2022). https://poetrylondon.co.uk/no-disabled-people-wanted-here-accessing-the-estate-of-poetry/

---

[23] Susan Sontag, "Illness as Metaphor," *The New York Review*, January 26, 1978, https://www.nybooks.com/articles/1978/01/26/illness-as-metaphor/

Limón, Ada. "A Conversation with Ada Limón." Interview by Polly Buckingham et al. *Willow Springs Magazine* 89 (2021). https://inside.ewu.edu/willowspringsmagazine/a-conversation-with-ada-Limón/

Limón, Ada. "Ada Limón on Preparing the Body for a Reopened World: The Challenges of Emerging from Lockdown." *LitHub*, April 19, 2021. https://lithub.com/ada-limon-on-preparing-the-body-for-a-reopened-world/

Limón, Ada. "To Be Made Whole." *OnBeing with Krista Tippett* (podcast), February 16, 2023. https://onbeing.org/programs/ada-Limón-to-be-made-whole/#transcript

Nezhat, Camran et al. "Thoracic Endometriosis Syndrome: A Review of Diagnosis and Management," *JSLS: Journal of the Society of Laparoendoscopic Surgeons* 23, no. 3 (2019): 943–951. https://doi.org/10.4293/JSLS.2019.00029

Sontag, Susan. "Illness as Metaphor." *The New York Review*, January 26, 1978. https://www.nybooks.com/articles/1978/01/26/illness-as-metaphor/

19 Barriers to Inclusion in Creative Writing: Questioning Practice in and Beyond the Writing Classroom

AUDREY T. HEFFERS

The myth of the writer is a romanticization of suffering. This myth is founded in the link between suffering and creativity without acknowledging any of the challenges of needing accommodations or accessibility considerations. The suffering is the point, and as such accommodations would get in the way of the creative process—or such is the implicit messaging of the myth. So, what might these often unexamined, invisibilized barriers for success of neurodivergent and disabled writers in creative writing look like? To answer this question, this essay will largely use a question-and-answer (Q&A) format, providing insight and guidance for creative writing educators and others in the field of creative writing, including editors and publishers.

I. How Does Homogeneity—Both in the Academy and in Publishing—Exclude Marginalized Writers?

In creative writing pedagogy groups, it is not uncommon for educators to ask each other for recommendations for assigned readings for upcoming classes and workshops. At times, these requests can be incredibly specific, with a direct intention of diversifying a syllabus—for example, "Can you recommend your favorite short stories by African writers?" or "Can you recommend spoken word poetry by queer poets?" Shmulsky, Gobbo, and Vitt stress the value of this in terms of neurodiversity, saying that "instructors may review curriculum to include perspectives and intellectual work of people of color, LGBTQIA+ people, and other cultural groups, they can include neurodivergent voices where applicable. Openly neurodivergent individuals have contributed to diverse fields, and instructors can seek out their work."[1] As bell hooks writes, "Progressive professors working to transform the curriculum so that it does not reflect biases or reinforce systems of domination are most often the individuals willing to take the risks that engaged pedagogy requires and to make their teaching practices a site of resistance."[2]

---

[1]Solvegi Shmulsky et al. "Culturally Relevant Pedagogy for Neurodiversity." *Community College Journal of Research and Practice* 46, no. 9 (2022): 681–685. https://doi.org/10.1080/10668926.2021.1972362

[2]bell hooks, *Teaching to Transgress: Education as the Practice of Freedom* (Routledge, 1994), 21.

However, when this search for work to assign to students is left more open-ended, such as "looking for recommendations for intro to fiction stories," the responses reflect a very particular pattern. Many of the same stories are recommended again and again, such as Ernest Hemingway's "Hills Like White Elephants," Tobias Wolff's "The Bullet in the Brain," and Kate Chopin's "The Story of an Hour." It often, though certainly not always, reflects a kind of canon, one that is overwhelmingly white, straight, cisgender, abled, neurotypical, male, etc. Kazim Ali writes that "The cultural and racial homogeneity of creative writing programs is self-perpetuating,"[3] and certainly some of the predominant modes of this perpetuation are assigned readings and the ways in which writing is addressed in workshop. These assigned stories are often not contemporary; they are the stories that have been taught for decades, even generations. We must ask: where are the openly neurodivergent writers? How much neurodiversity is authentically[4] and directly represented in these stories? Is neurodiversity represented with dignity, nuance, and complexity? Or is it solely a source of humor, pity, and/or trauma?

These markers can certainly be incorporated in efforts to diversify curricula so that they are more representative of the general population. Hui Niu Wilcox suggests that "through integrating and rethinking embodied ways of knowing, we can empower ourselves and our students to critique Eurocentric, male-dominated modes of knowledge production and, ultimately, to envision alternatives."[5] Incorporating neurodivergent and disabled writers and their texts into curricula works toward implicitly welcoming neurodivergent writers, including those who may be in our classrooms. Additionally, if an instructor chooses, it is possible to directly incorporate discussions of neurodivergence/neurodiversity into the classroom. Paratextual work, such as interviews or craft essays, may help to supplement such discussions. Belongingness is not only a key tenet of inclusive pedagogy; it also gives writers a greater sense that they belong in the writing world beyond the confines of the classroom.

---

[3] Kazim Ali, "Addressing Structural Racism in Creative Writing Programs." *The Writer's Chronicle* (2016), quoted in Janelle Adsit, *Toward an Inclusive Creative Writing: Threshold Concepts to Guide the Literary Writing Curriculum* (Bloomsbury Academic, 2017), 137.
[4] I pose this question while also acknowledging that "authenticity" is a fraught term when thinking about representation in creative writing. Authenticity is going to look differently to different people, but it should be a consideration when marginalized people are represented. Here, "authentically" is being used in an effort to avoid forms of representation that may be tokenizing or stereotypical.
[5] Hui Niu Wilcox, "Embodied Ways of Knowing, Pedagogies, and Social Justice: Inclusive Science and Beyond," *NWSA Journal* 21, no. 2 (2009): 104–120. http://www.jstor.org/stable/20628176

II. How Do Ableist Attitudes in Writing Workshops Contribute to Writing Beliefs and Practices, or Vice Versa? How Do Participation Requirements, Attendance Requirements, and Overall Workshop Structures Exclude Those with Disabilities and Forms of Mental Illnesses, Like Anxiety and Depression?

Workshop structures and participation requirements often go hand in hand. Much has been critiqued about "The Iowa Model" writing workshop in recent years, particularly the traditional belief that writers need to be in the "cone of silence" and the ways in which critiques are given, often with racist, sexist, homophobic, transphobic, etc. under/overtones. However, should students in writing workshops even be required to participate orally? Wilcox writes that,

> If we take embodied knowledges seriously, it is not enough to simply add new tricks to our teaching, research, or activism oeuvre; we must reexamine our old tricks as well as our institutions . . . our ultimate goal is not to add embodiment and stir; it is to invite conversations concerning embodied knowledges and their radical implications. For such conversations to take place, we must first commit to embodied practices.[6]

With this in mind, we need to remember that some students may communicate better in writing. Some students may communicate better in smaller groups than larger ones. Some may not feel comfortable speaking much or at all. There are benefits to oral feedback just as there are benefits to written feedback. Furthermore, the workshop space may be difficult for students to participate in for any number of reasons, including forms of neurodivergence, such as autism, and forms of mental illness, such as social anxiety. Why is oral participation *required*? Is it to fill up class time? To reiterate the traditional workshop values that have been passed down to us? Even if we have more meaningful rationales—such as the potential for talking through stories/poems/essays as a way to come to different understandings—is there truly no room for adjustment?

Attendance policies are all too often another symptom of an ableist academy, even in the practices of those who claim to be inclusive. The oft-cited text *The Anti-Racist Writing Workshop* by Felicia Rose Chavez has been praised for working to create more inclusive writing workshops, particularly involving race and giving voice to marginalized writers. However, we must question if Chavez's teaching strategies have their own set of harmful prejudices (or at least gaps in understanding) regarding disability. In chapter 2 of her book, Chavez lists her strategies for student "Engagement," which she sums up as follows: "How do you make them care? Start

---

[6]Wilcox, "Embodied Ways," 118.

by making them accountable."[7] Under her proposed "Attendance Accountability" method, students have no opportunity to miss classes; each missed class deducts half a letter grade from the final course grade, and missing a workshop is to "risk failure."[8] Chavez even admits that "Well-meaning colleagues have criticized [her] mandatory attendance policy as unnecessarily harsh and unrealistic,"[9] though she is seemingly unwilling to relent to the informed, well-meaning advice of her colleagues where attendance is concerned. When Chavez informs students via email of her attendance policy, she says she receives "polite requests that [she] pardon students' 'special' circumstances," explaining the nature of those requests as follows:

> At the predominantly white liberal arts college where I work, this means an athlete's away games,[10] a family vacation abroad, a great aunt's birthday celebration, a camping trip, a concert. Sometimes it's acute anxiety or depression. I make it clear to these students that my attendance policy is firm.[11]

Certainly, some parts of Chavez's list seem more trivial than others, and it's alarming that these reasons for missing class would be lumped together. The connection Chavez makes between these excuses for missing class and the whiteness of her institution also seems to make the unfortunate implication that students of color don't experience conditions like acute anxiety and depression when in fact mental illness and other forms of disability are experienced by students of all races and backgrounds.

I want to begin my critique of Chavez's attendance policy by stressing that it is not the instructor's place to judge students' choices or to "make them care," but rather, it's the students' responsibility to keep up with class work and attendance; it's their prerogative to choose what they care about. Students have rich lives outside of the academy and cannot reasonably be expected to sacrifice all else for being a student—or even a writer. This, too, feels like an unhelpful continuation of the myth of the writer—that the writer must be so committed to writing that little (or nothing) else matters. Furthermore, it is ableist and flippant to add "acute anxiety or depression"[12] at the end of a list of attendance excuses that includes "camping trips" and "concerts." Is it fair for faculty to expect a student to, for example, attend workshop in the middle

---

[7] Felicia Rose Chavez. *The Anti-Racist Writing Workshop: How to Decolonize the Creative Classroom* (Haymarket Books, 2020), 52.
[8] Ibid., 54.
[9] Ibid., 53.
[10] In my personal experiences, there are university-level excused absences that must be honored, such as for student athletes or bereavement.
[11] Ibid., 54.
[12] It's highly important to note that the Americans with Disabilities Act (ADA) covers and protects those with diagnosed forms of mental illness from discriminatory practices. Mental illnesses, including anxiety and depression, are not character flaws or "excuses." They are *real* medical conditions and are protected forms of disability, deserving of—and guaranteed—reasonable accommodations.

of a panic attack?[13] What of students who may develop PTSD from, for instance, rape or sexual assault? Will a student whose depression makes it difficult to perform even basic bodily necessities be able to make it into a classroom, and should they be expected to? How about a physically disabled or chronically ill student who cannot *physically* make it to class one day? Does that student *want it* less? Chavez equates her students' final grades—which are heavily impacted by their attendance, their ability to merely show up to class—with their "commitment to [their] creative power."[14] Is this not reiterating the ableist idea that disabled, neurodivergent, and chronically ill writers are simply 'lazy' and/or not trying hard enough? How does forcing students to come to class at all costs and in all situations add value to learning, writing, and workshopping?

Elsewhere in her chapter, Chavez writes about how she values engagement, mindfulness, and generosity. If we are going to treat students as embodied humans in an inclusive approach, then it is vital that we are just as generous and compassionate toward neurodivergent, disabled, and chronically ill students as we are toward their neurotypical, abled, and healthy counterparts. These writers have just as much right to our patience and understanding, to our expertise and guidance, and to our classroom community, as anyone else does; importantly, they also have legal rights to accommodations. To imply otherwise is not only an exclusionary pedagogy and praxis; it is also the whispered implication that those whose minds and/or bodies are not the abled, neurotypical, cultural ideal do not belong in the writing classroom or in the writing world. Perhaps Chavez makes attendance-related allowances for students with some forms of disability, though she notably does not mention it in this section. Rather she reiterates, and thus reinforces, the toxic, ableist writing belief we hear over and over again: "To be a writer is to choose to write, to show up every day and do the work. There's always an excuse not to."[15]

In her introduction, Chavez makes the claim that "Silencing writers is central to the traditional writing workshop model,"[16] and her work aims to combat this for writers of color, which is an incredibly powerful—and empowering—endeavor. But, perhaps without realizing it, her policies silence other marginalized student-writers. And because disability, neurodivergence, and mental health impact writers of all races, she may even be silencing some of the very writers she aims to support. In *Craft in the Real World*, Matthew Salesses makes a strong argument that "It is instructors' responsibility to remake things—and that starts with burning the old models down."[17]

---

[13]During my first semester of college, I began to have symptoms of C-PTSD (Complex PTSD). When I emailed a professor about missing a class meeting for an Intro to College course because of a panic attack, he insisted this would not be excused without documentation, something that I did not yet have as someone who was still in a dangerous and trauma-inducing situation. But the policy was the policy, plain and simple.
[14]Ibid., 54.
[15]Ibid., 53.
[16]Ibid., 2.
[17]Salesses, Matthew. *Craft in the Real World: Rethinking Fiction Writing and Workshopping* (Catapult, 2021), 129.

But, this can't just involve *some* areas of "the old models." Faculty must reconsider all approaches, accommodate all reasonable student needs, and consider all forms of inclusivity.

III. How Can the Workshop Be a Space in Which Neurodivergent Minds Can Thrive?

Shmulsky, Gobbo, and Vitt provide options for how neurodivergence can become more accepted in the classroom:

> Faculty can expand the window of what is acceptable by self-disclosing their own neurodivergence or identifying as an ally. Faculty may prefer to signal acceptance more subtly by displaying stickers, posters, or posting a diversity statement in the syllabus that includes neurodiversity. Students recognize subtle cues about whether they belong in a setting, and faculty can use this as an opportunity to show acceptance.[18]

These suggestions align with bell hooks' liberatory framework of education. In *Teaching to Transgress*, hooks writes that "When professors bring narratives of their experiences into classroom discussions it eliminates the possibility that we can function as all-knowing, silent interrogators . . . . But most professors must practice being vulnerable in the classroom, being wholly present in mind, body, and spirit."[19] Certainly, these strategies to welcome neurodiversity in our classrooms—whether a more overt self-disclosure of neurodivergence or a more subtle display—would signal acceptance of neurodivergent bodyminds in the classroom. Salesses argues that a "workshop should not participate in the binding but in freeing the writer from the culturally regulated boundaries of what is possible to say and how it is possible to say it."[20] But how can this be pushed further in the field of creative writing—in the workshop, but also beyond the academy? What are the *practical* strategies that we can experiment with to help these students not only survive through masking or covering[21] but *thrive* as learners and beyond? These important questions need careful consideration and research.

---

[18]Shmulsky et al., "Culturally Relevant," 681–685.
[19]hooks, "Teaching to Transgress," 21.
[20]Ibid., xxiii.
[21]In *Covering: The Hidden Assault on Our Civil Rights* (2007), Kenji Yoshino discusses "covering" in terms of how queer people "feel increasing pressure . . . to fade gracefully into the mainstream" (78). It could be argued that this happens with other marginalized identities as well, such as those with neurodivergence or disability.

IV. If We Reject Notions of One-Size-Fits-All Writing Instruction, How Can We Give All Student-Writers the Tools to Write to Their Own Potential and Desire? In Educational Programs and in Publishing, Where Can We Build in Flexibility, Adaptability, and the Space for True Inclusion?

One source that provides an answer to these questions is Toller and Farrimond, who write that "we [educators] can find ways to help [chronically ill] students to 'prepare for the worst-case scenario' and to support them when it happens."[22] In this article, Toller and Farrimond discuss chronic illness and what Brianne Benness calls "dynamic disability,"[23] though their suggestions apply to working with students with all forms of disability, illness, and/or neurodivergence. In truth, the bodymind's potential is variable, ever changing, and extremely individual. It is impossible to account for each bodymind in advance, but listening to students' (or, more generally, writers') experiences and particular needs can help to guide us toward more inclusivity in our classrooms. As Toller and Farrimond write,

> Perhaps most importantly, students need to be listened to and believed when discussing what adjustments would help them; after all, they are the only people who truly know their unpredictable bodies. Just as individual students find they have to be creative in developing effective ways to work within and around their limitations, so universities may need to be willing to step outside the box of what they usually provide and offer a wider range of personalised options in order to better support students who do not neatly map onto conventional images of disability.[24]

Similar to Toller and Farrimond, I have found in my own experience as an instructor that students who advocate for their accessibility needs (in a classroom environment that encourages such advocacy rather than treating it with suspicion) help not only themselves but their peers and future students. If, for example, a student has accommodations because they benefit from access to lecture notes after class, it may actually help all students—those who are neurodivergent as well as those who are neurotypical—to make these materials accessible. Informed, productive changes help everyone.

Shmulsky, Gobbo, and Vitt also give voice to the reality that many "qualifying students will not have a diagnosis due to issues of access and cost."[25] They also argue that this is one of the benefits of the Universal Design for Learning (UDL), an approach to the classroom that,

---

[22]Louise Toller and Hannah Farrimond, "The Unpredictable Body, Identity, and Disclosure: Identifying the Strategies of Chronically Ill Students at University," *Disability Studies Quarterly* 41, no. 2 (2021): https://dsq-sds.org/index.php/dsq/article/view/7049/5941øp
[23]Brianne Benness, "My Disability Is Dynamic," *Age of Awareness* (Medium.com), December 8, 2019, https://medium.com/age-ofawareness/my-disability-is-dynamic-bc2a619fcc1
[24]Toller and Farrimond, "The Unpredictable Body."
[25]Shmulsky et al., "Culturally Relevant," 681–685.

aims to make education maximally accessible thereby removing barriers for undiagnosed and diagnosed students. In a UDL classroom, the instructor provides different ways for students to gain knowledge and formulate what they know. Content can be offered in variety of formats, including video recorded lectures, audio recordings, and texts at different levels of complexity. Where appropriate, faculty may consider a menu of assignment options.[26]

With this in mind, one step that would be valuable in this quest toward inclusivity and access—via the routes of adaptability and flexibility—is to assess what types of power each of us holds in the creative writing world. This could be in the academic world, such as an instructor/professor, for example, or a program director, an academic advisor, a department chair, or a committee member. This could be outside of the academic world, such as those who are readers, editors, or managers for publishing houses or for literary magazines. What if, for instance, a writer doesn't find a particular style of submission accessible? How might offering alternatives to all who need it democratize access to publishing so that we can more genuinely welcome talented writers who have been traditionally excluded because of their neurodivergence or disability, even if it may be an extra step or minor inconvenience for the publisher/editor/magazine?

Our power can be individual or collective—often, we have some iteration of at least one, if not both. When we have assessed the places and ways we have power, we can then ask ourselves, honestly:

- What do we do with our power?
- How can we help neurodivergent and disabled writers thrive?

Below, I will list some generative questions. I encourage writers in positions of relative power to consider, experiment with, remix, and rethink the following.

Pedagogy-Related Questions

- What are our attendance policies and why? How can we build in more flexibility?
- What are our participation policies and why? How do we measure participation? What are some alternatives that we might offer for disabled or neurodivergent, and/or chronically ill students: written? Oral? Multimodal?
- What might be productive ways for instructors to be vulnerable in the workshop?
- Are there professional development opportunities to learn more about different kinds of neurodivergences and how we can build that knowledge into the classroom? Could that information be crowdsourced, either locally within a university/department/program, or in a more accessible environment such as a digital space?

---

[26] Ibid.

- What readings do we assign? How does neurodiversity play into our choices—or not? How does neurodiversity and/or disability get discussed (or ignored) in the classroom?
- How do we respond to criticism that could potentially improve our engagement with neurodivergent writers?

Publishing-Related Questions

- How might we change the notion that a story/poem/essay lacks "relatability" because of some disability or neurodivergence-related factor (e.g. a poem's speaker is bipolar, thus unrelatable; an essay about ADHD is written non-linearly, etc.)? How do we bypass our own biases/preferences and think of readers who may want to read more non-traditional experiences?
- In what ways is there a demand for neurodiversity to be palatable to neurotypical readers? How can this demand be challenged, both on the individual level and the systemic one?
- What in our mission statement, catalog, and/or submission guidelines might be exclusionary or inaccessible? How can we make inclusive changes?
- How can we communicate with writers in a way that is clearer, more precise, and more inclusive of all cognitive processing types (as possible)?
- How do we respond to criticism that could potentially improve our engagement with neurodivergent writers and readers?

Each of us can add to this list, based on our own experiences and the experiences that have been shared with us. The more open and engaged we are with neurodiversity and disability, the more radically potent this list can become.

Conclusion

Ultimately, "the myth of the writer" is designed to force writers into a particular mold. That mold is necessarily exclusionary, even if some "exceptions" are made. In actuality, making space for all kinds of minds and experiences increases not only the potential for representation but also the potential for more talent to be introduced into the playing field. It's time to face the reality that we live in a world where the following is true:

- "Anxiety disorders will affect nearly 1 in 3 adults."[27]
- "More than 1 in 6 say they are depressed or receiving treatment for depression."[28]

---

[27] Lisa Howard. "Anxiety Disorders Will Affect Nearly 1 in 3 Adults: Here's What You Need To Know," *UC Davis Health News*, May 10, 2023, https://health.ucdavis.edu/news/headlines/anxiety-disorders-will-affect-nearly-1-in-3-adults-heres-what-you-need-to-know/2023/05
[28] Deidre McPhillips, "More Than 1 in 6 Adults Have Depression as Rates Rise to Record Levels in the US, Survey Finds," *CNN Health*, May 17, 2023, https://www.cnn.com/2023/05/17/health/depression-rates-gallup/index.html.

- "More than 366 million adults worldwide have ADHD."[29]
- "Over 5.4 million adults in the United States have autism spectrum disorder."[30]

Writers within these demographics, and others, are often marginalized and/or invisibilized. As such, educators need to be more aware of and more inclusive to disabled and neurodivergent students. In terms of publishing, the best it feels like we can hope for, at present, is that a literary magazine will clearly state in a submission's call that they are open to neurodivergent writers. More accommodations and opportunities need to be considered and implemented.

The creative writing field at large is set up against those who think, write, engage, and connect differently; it is set up toward a norm that it is likely no one *actually* fits. Diversity doesn't happen of its own accord in systems that marginalize. Instead, the systems must be changed, dismantled, reconfigured, or reconstructed altogether, and this change is only possible through many people using their power to make many choices toward that change. This may look like neurodivergent and disabled people relying on our own particular skills to self-advocate and advocate in solidarity, but the possibility for change will be stronger when neurotypical writers, editors, and educators ally themselves with neurodivergent and disabled writers to make the writing world a more radically inclusive and supportive space. And, ultimately, the writing that can thrive in the wake of such a movement makes all of literature more interesting and more authentic to the vast variety of human experience.

Bibliography

Ali, Kazim. "Addressing Structural Racism in Creative Writing Programs." *The Writer's Chronicle* (2016). Quoted in Janelle Adsit. *Toward an Inclusive Creative Writing: Threshold Concepts to Guide the Literary Writing Curriculum*. Bloomsbury Academic, 2017.

Benness, Brianne. "My Disability Is Dynamic." *Age of Awareness (Medium.com)*. December 8, 2019. https://medium.com/age-ofawareness/my-disability-is-dynamic-bc2a619fcc1

Chavez, Felicia Rose. *The Anti-Racist Writing Workshop: How to Decolonize the Creative Classroom*. Haymarket Books, 2020.

hooks, bell. *Teaching to Transgress: Education as the Practice of Freedom*. Routledge, 1994.

Howard, Lisa. "Anxiety Disorders Will Affect Nearly 1 in 3 Adults: Here's What You Need to Know." *UC Davis Health News*. May 10, 2023. https://health.ucdavis.edu/news/headlines/anxiety-disorders-will-affect-nearly-1-in-3-adults-heres-what-you-need-to-know/2023/05

---

[29] Jennifer Wirth. "ADHD Statistics and Facts In 2025," *Forbes.com*, August 24, 2023, https://www.forbes.com/health/mind/adhd-statistics/

[30] "The Facts About Autism in American Adults," *University of Maryland Medical System*, effective July 3, 2025, https://health.umms.org/2022/03/25/adults-and-autism/

McPhillips, Deidre. "More Than 1 in 6 Adults Have Depression as Rates Rise to Record Levels in the US, Survey Finds." *CNN Health*, May 17, 2023. https://www.cnn.com/2023/05/17/health/depression-rates-gallup/index.html

Salesses, Matthew. *Craft in the Real World: Rethinking Fiction Writing and Workshopping*. Catapult, 2021.

Shmulsky, Solvegi, Ken Gobbo, and Steven Vitt. "Culturally Relevant Pedagogy for Neurodiversity." *Community College Journal of Research and Practice* 46, no. 9 (2022): 681–685. https://doi.org/10.1080/10668926.2021.1972362

Toller, Louise and Hannah Farrimond. "The Unpredictable Body, Identity, and Disclosure: Identifying the Strategies of Chronically Ill Students at University." *Disability Studies Quarterly* 41, no. 2 (2021). https://dsq-sds.org/index.php/dsq/article/view/7049/5941øp

Wilcox, Hui Niu. "Embodied Ways of Knowing, Pedagogies, and Social Justice: Inclusive Science and Beyond." *NWSA Journal*, 21, no. 2 (2009): 104–120. http://www.jstor.org/stable/20628176.

Wirth, Jennifer. "ADHD Statistics and Facts In 2025." *Forbes.com*, August 24, 2023. https://www.forbes.com/health/mind/adhd-statistics/

Yoshino, Kenji. *Covering: The Hidden Assault on Our Civil Rights*. Random House, 2007.

Index

ableism
    accidental ableism, 3
    awareness of, 6
    challenging of, 83, 149
    communal ableism, 192
    creative writing as microcosm of wider world, 3
    by disabled/neurodivergent persons, 9
    dismantling of, 6
    embodiment of, 83
    experience of, 7
    and inclusiveness, 201
    institutional ableism, 158, 192
    internalized ableism, 64, 119
    mental ableism, 15
    within professional expectations upon disabled/neurodivergent persons, 192
    systemic ableism, 167
    within writing programs, 155–156, 163
academia. *see* higher education
ADHD, 1, 7, 8, 51, 58, 104–107, 109, 114, 117, 156, 166–167, 170, 176, 207–208
anti-ableism. *see* ableism
aphasia
    avant-garde aphasia, 18
    creative possibilities from, 21
    and creative writing, 22–25
    disjunction and, 21
    "errors" of, 17
    motor aphasia, 18
    personal responses to, 16–17
    and Poem Brut, 129
    poetry of, 17, 21
    possible benefits of, for writers, 17
    post-stroke experience of, 13, 16
    and process of writing, 19
    silence and, 16
    as style, 18
authenticity
    appreciation of, 107
    autism and, 188
    celebration of, 131, 188
    within connection, 180
    criticism and, 104, 108
    direction of, 109
    identity and, 125
    within literature, 208
    and mainstream media, 7
    need for, 85
    nurturing of, 109, 189
    originality and, 131
    self and, 180, 188
    voice of, 105, 106, 110, 170, 180, 200
autism
    with ADHD, 105, 107
    authenticity and, 188
    Autism Network International, 64
    "autistexts", 70, 72
    autistic burnout, 72
    autistic inertia, 72
    autistic "languaging", 67–68
    autistic masking, 72
    autistic meltdown, 114, 117
    autistic mindblindness theory, 63
    autistic poetics, 141–148
    autistic shutdown, 114, 117
    and bipolar disorder, 44
    broader autism phenotype (BAP), 1
    confident characters with, 29
    and connection, 71–72
    creative and imaginative (non-literal) thought, 45
    definition of, 64, 188
    depression and, 44
    diagnosis, 29–30
    dyspraxia and, 185
    echolalia, 142–143

engagement with objects, 145–146
hyperfocus, 144–145
ICD-10 classification system, 144
"inside the box", structure-based thinking, 107, 167
intersectionalities of, 149
late diagnosis, 68, 182, 186–187
linguistic insufficiency theory, 149
markers of, 28
movement and, 148–149
and other conditions, 44
and perceptiveness, 47, 68
and personality disorder, 58
poetic expressions, 149–150
poetry and, 136–138
and poetry writing, 30–35
population of people with, 208
public speaking, and public reading, ability, 162
repetitive interests, 144–145
and space/time perception, 47–48
stims, 141–142
suicide and, 28–29
synaesthesia, 143–144
teaching and, 35–38
and theory of mind, 61–62
tropes of, 29
verbal autism (silence), 114
visuality, 146–148
women with, 28–29
"word spinning" poetry, 138–141

Baggs, Amanda Melissa, 136–137, 145–146
Baron-Cohen, Simon, 61, 63
belongingness, 5, 44, 130, 139, 155, 191, 200, 203, 204. see also inclusiveness
Berryman, John, 54
Biggs, Victoria, 187
bipolar disorder
autism and, 44
late diagnosis, 95
legal recognition of, 94
manifestation of, 7
medication, 96
population of people with, 94
stigma of, 97
blindness, 155, 159, 168. see also visual impairment
Block, Laurie, 5
bodily pain. see chronic pain

Bowman Jr., Daniel, 186–188
Brillantes-Evangelista, Grace, 44–45
Brown, Nicole, 155–157, 191

Carozza, Linda, 22
Carvalho, Ana Candida, 147
Chavez, Felicia Rose, 163, 201–203
chronic disease, 170
chronic fatigue, 1, 30
chronic illness, 2, 3, 6–7, 9, 77, 78–79, 84, 113, 119, 125, 155, 156, 158, 167, 168, 191–195, 197, 203, 205, 206
chronic pain, 8, 82, 192, 194, 195, 196
Correa, Josiane, 148
Cosgrove, Patrick, 132
creative writing
ableism and, 3, 6, 7
essential conditions for, 17
negative experience of, 2
neurotypical emphasis of, 3
originality as key value of, 6
teaching of, 2
creative writing programs, 109, 155, 156, 158, 169, 200. see also writing workshops
Culler, Jonathan, 141

Dahoul, Safwan, 53
De Jaegher, Hanne, 47
Deleuze, Gilles, 66
disabled people
ableism shown by, 9
ableist professional expectations upon, 192
population of, 4
WHO report on health inequities against, 5
"world's largest minority group" (UN), 5
discrimination, 5, 29, 182
Doidge, Norman, 14
Doyle, Nancy, 5–6
dyslexia
and chronic fatigue, 1
dyspraxia and, 185
late diagnosis, 91–92
memory and, 130
and Poem Brut, 129
shame of, 1
structural exclusion within creative writing, 90, 163
and typographical errors, 164–165

undiagnosed dyslexia, 1, 87
variety of manifestations, 90
dyspraxia, 129, 178, 184–185

embodiment
of ableism, 83
boundary between bodiless and embodied existence, 196
embodied knowledge, 201
empowerment via, 200
essentiality of active embodiment, 196
of experience, 47
of experience of chronic pain, 196
of fact of being a disability expert, 73
of "good man speaking well", 15
inclusiveness and, 203
inclusivity and, 203
of "inner realities", 48
words as representation of, 197
empowerment, 127, 180, 182, 184, 187, 200, 203
exploitation, 7

Farrimond, Hannah, 205
Fowler, S. J., 8, 129–135
Francis, Vievee, 56
Freitas, Ana, 144
Fuerholzer, Katharina, 18

Gobbo, Ken, 199, 204–205
Goodall, Gemma, 157–158
graduate creative writing programs. *see* creative writing programs
Grandin, Temple, 81, 146–147
Griffiths, Elisabeth, 194–195
Grobstein, Paul, 133–134
Guattari, Felix, 66
Guthrie, Laura, 29–30

Hawkins, Paul, 132
Henrique, Luiz, 142
higher education
ableism within, 8, 157
autism within, 139
creative writing programs, 3
creativity within, 107–108
prescriptive approach to neurodivergence, 109
"right fit" within, 107
time pressure within, 168
undiagnosed people within, 182

illness. *see* chronic illness
inclusion, 5, 134, 157, 163, 188–189
inclusiveness. *see also* belongingness
and ableist practices within writing workshops, 201
autism and, 8
and belongingness, 200
of creative writing teaching, 188
embodiment and, 203
inclusive lesson plans and workshop strategies, 164
of learning environments, 183
and MFA workshops, 8, 121, 125–127, 156–159, 163–164, 166, 169
of neurodiversity terminology, 185
and Poem Brut, 129–133
practical provisions to promote, 207–208
teaching and, 2
of writing, 7
within writing communities, 192
and writing workshops, 8, 201
inclusivity, 123, 125, 133, 156, 203, 204, 205, 206
Ireland, Chris, 17

Jakobson, Roman, 18

Kalenjuk, Elvira, 171
Kalsched, Donald, 56
Kasirer, Anat, 45
Kiljunen, Juho, 164
Knights, Karl, 191–192
Kuusisto, Stephen, 155

language disorder. *see* aphasia
Limón, Ada, 195–197
Luck, Jessica Lewis, 22–23

Manning, Erin, 66–67, 70
Mashal, Nira, 45
Meyer, Anne, 183
Miserandino, Christine, 123n5
Moura, Milena Martins, 140
Mukhopadhyay, Tito, 137–138
Murray, Dinah, 43

neurodiversity, definition of, 185
Neves, Flavia, 141

Paterson, Don, 45
Pennebaker, James W., 54–55

physical pain. *see* chronic pain
Piepzna-Samarasinha, Leah Lakshmi, 72–73
Plath, Sylvia, 54
Poem Brut
    as applied neurobiology, 134
    avant-gardism, 133
    balance between culture and science, 133–134
    belongingness and, 130
    creative language processing within, 133
    definition of, 132
    diagnoses as neurodiversity learning opportunities, 130
    dynamic growth of, 131–132
    experimental form, and practices, of, 8, 129, 133
    exploration of cognitive difference, 129
    impact on participants, 134–135
    inclusiveness of, 130
    involvement within, 134
    neurodiversity as starting point, 129
    neurotypical world, 129
    originator of, 8
    as performance series rather than reading series, 129
    project series, 132
    and self-insight, 133
    website, 134
    writing as sensual process, 129–130
    YouTube channel, 134
poems (titles and authors)
    "Anima" (Ribeiro), 146
    Asymmetry (collection) (Coleman), 17, 19–21
    "The Choice" (Yeats), 127–128
    "Epitaph as My Mother's Daughter" (Rizzo), 58
    "The Female Alien's Dictionary" (Readman), 31
    "The Figure a Poem Makes" (Frost), 52
    "First Lines" (Pierce), 53
    "Glossolalia (speaking in tongues)" (Nichols), 34–35
    "I'm Stone" (Vieira), 146
    "I've Been Thinking About Love Again" (Francis), 56
    "Lady Lazarus" (Plath), 82
    "Late Diagnosis: *superbus digitalis* (arrogant foxglove)" (Nichols), 33–34
    "The Love Song of J. Alfred Prufrock" (Eliot), 63
    "A Martian Sends a Postcard Home" (Raine), 31
    "The Moon and the Yew Tree" (Plath), 55, 57
    "Not from Round Here (Foreign)" (Nichols), 32–33
    "Note about Alice" (Eugenio), 145
    "Poem Beginning with a Retweet" (Smith), 179–180
    "Poetry and the Moon" (Ruelle), 52
    "Something Is Missing" (Moura), 140–141
    "Sometimes I don't stop" (Neves), 141–142
    "what the neighbourhoods tell" (Magnani), 142–143
    "Why Didn't You Know" (Nichols), 30
    "Word To Your Mama" (stage text) (Barclay), 66–67
    "The World Is Too Much with Us" (Wordsworth), 52
    "[you]" (Callazans), 144
Porter, Gill, 182
post-traumatic stress disorder (PTSD), 7, 51, 203
prejudice, 138, 140, 141, 186, 188, 201
Price, Margaret, 15

Raine, Craig, 31
Readman, Angela, 31
Rees-Jones, Deryn, 181–182
rejection sensitive dysphoria (RSD)
    accommodations for students with, 108–109
    ADHD and, 8
    authenticity and, 107
    and constructive criticism, 107, 108
    effect of, 105
    lies of, 106
    motivations for writers with, 106, 109–110
    reframing of "successful" outcomes, 107–108
Rodas, Julia M., 137–138
Rose, David H., 183

Savarese, Ralph, 137–138
Shafi, Noel, 22
Shankey, Jennifer, 142
Shmulsky, Solvegi, 199, 204–205
Silberman, Steve, 62, 64

Simpson, Kate, 183–184
Singer, Judy, 139, 185
Smith, Maggie, 178–181, 188
speech disorder. see aphasia
Sterponi, Laura, 142
stigma
    within academia, 160
    de-stigmatization, 30, 163
    upon disclosure of disability, 157
    dismantling of, 6, 97, 157, 158, 186
    experience of, 3, 94, 96–97, 126, 172, 176
    freedom from, 182, 186
    labelling and, 184
    persistence of, 5
    risk of, 194
    segregation and, 182
Stirman, Shannon Wiltsey, 54–55
student writing programs. see creative writing programs

theory of mind, 61–62, 136
Toller, Louise, 205

United Kingdom
    definition of dyspraxia, 184–185
    definition of neurodiversity, 184–185
    National Health Service (NHS) autism assessment, 29
    neurodivergent population, 4, 180
    Poem Brut, 131
    population with autism, 28
United States
    Americans with Disabilities Act (ADA), 94, 173
    disabled population, 4
    population with bipolar disorder, 94
    undergraduate population with disability, 156–157

visual impairment, 158, 168. see also blindness
Vitt, Steven, 199, 204–205

Walker, Nick, 184
Wilcox, Hui Niu, 201
Williams, Donna, 64
World Health Organization
    estimate of global disabled population, 4
    on health inequities against disabled population, 5

Yergeau, M. Remi, 68